"*The Whole Life Adoption Book* is a comprehensive guide for adoptive parents, from the point of considering adoption through raising strong, well-adjusted children to adulthood. The wealth of experience and wisdom within these pages will be of immeasurable value to adoptive parents. This book should be in the library of every adoptive family."

> —BETSY KEEFER SMALLEY, manager of adoption and foster care training, Institute for Human Services; coauthor of *Telling the Truth to Your Adopted or Foster Child: Making Sense of the Past*

"Full of wisdom and honesty about the joys and challenges adoptive families face, *The Whole Life Adoption Book* is a wonderful resource for families, both before and after they decide to build their families through adoption. Informative and encouraging, it is a valuable book to have and refer back to time and time again."

> —KRIS FAASSE, ACSW, LMSW, director of adoption services, Bethany Christian Services

REVISED AND UPDATED

the WHOLE LIFE

ADOPTION
BOOK

REALISTIC ADVICE FOR BUILDING A HEALTHY ADOPTIVE FAMILY

JAYNE E. SCHOOLER
& THOMAS C. ATWOOD

NAVPRESS ®

For a free catalog
of NavPress books & Bible studies call
1-800-366-7788 (USA) or 1-800-839-4769 (Canada).

www.NavPress.com

The Navigators is an international Christian organization. Our mission is to advance the gospel of Jesus and His kingdom into the nations through spiritual generations of laborers living and discipling among the lost. We see a vital movement of the gospel, fueled by prevailing prayer, flowing freely through relational networks and out into the nations where workers for the kingdom are next door to everywhere.

NavPress is the publishing ministry of The Navigators. The mission of NavPress is to reach, disciple, and equip people to know Christ and make Him known by publishing life-related materials that are biblically rooted and culturally relevant. Our vision is to stimulate spiritual transformation through every product we publish.

ISBN-13: 978-1-60006-165-3
ISBN-10: 1-60006-165-6

Cover design by The DesignWorks Group, Nate Salciccioli, www.thedesignworksgroup.com
Creative Team: Kris Wallen, Traci Mullins, Kathy Mosier, Darla Hightower, Arvid Wallen, Kathy Guist

Some of the anecdotal illustrations in this book are true to life and are included with the permission of the persons involved. All other illustrations are composites of real situations, and any resemblance to people living or dead is coincidental.

All Scripture quotations in this publication are taken from the New American Standard Bible (nasb), © The Lockman Foundation 1960, 1962, 1963, 1968, 1971, 1972, 1973, 1975, 1977, 1995; and the New King James Version (nkjv). Copyright © 1982 by Thomas Nelson, Inc. Used by permission. All rights reserved.

Library of Congress Cataloging-in-Publication Data

Schooler, Jayne E.
  The whole life adoption book : realistic advice for building a healthy
adoptive family / Jayne E. Schooler and Thomas Atwood. -- Rev. and
updated.
      p. cm.
  Includes bibliographical references.
  ISBN 978-1-60006-165-3
  1. Adoption. 2. Adoptive parents. I. Atwood, Thomas. II. Title.
HV875.S365 2008
362.734--dc22

                              2007049391

Printed in the United States of America

1 2 3 4 5 6 7 8 / 12 11 10 09 08

Dedication

From Jayne
To David,
My best friend and delight of my life

From Tom
To Eileen and Chris,
My precious and loving family

CONTENTS

ACKNOWLEDGMENTS
page 9

INTRODUCTION: A RELATIONSHIP OF PROMISE
page 13

PART ONE
ADOPTION: A LABOR OF THE HEART

1. MAKING ROOM IN THE FAMILY:
Unique Challenges Adoptive Parents Must Face
page 19

2. CREATING A FAMILY:
Understanding the Adoption Process
page 33

3. NAVIGATING INTERCOUNTRY ADOPTION:
Preparing for the Journey
page 49

4. TRANSCULTURAL ADOPTION:
Blending Different Worlds
page 63

5. WHAT BUILDS HEALTHY ADOPTIVE FAMILIES?
Six Critical Success Factors
page 77

6. DEVELOPING A SUPPORTIVE ADOPTION ENVIRONMENT:
How to Prepare Biological Children, Family, and Friends
page 97

PART TWO
WHEN A CHILD COMES HOME

7. BARRIERS TO ADJUSTMENT:
Strategies to Ease the Transition
page 121

8. ATTACHMENT, DEVELOPMENT, AND THE IMPACT OF TRAUMA:
What Adoptive Parents Need to Know
page 137

9. LIVING WITH CHILDREN WITH ATTACHMENT TRAUMA:
Understanding the Terminology, Diagnosis, and Parenting Strategies
page 151

PART THREE
COMMUNICATING ABOUT ADOPTION
10. HOW DO WE FEEL ABOUT ADOPTION?
Understanding the Different Perspectives of Parents and Children
page 167

11. TALKING TO CHILDREN ABOUT ADOPTION:
When and How
page 181

PART FOUR
GROWING UP ADOPTED
12. WHAT'S INSIDE AN ADOPTED ADOLESCENT?
Helping Teens Resolve Five Crucial Issues
page 201

13. SEARCHING FOR A PAST:
Why Adopted Children Seek Their Roots and How Parents Can Respond
page 219

14. CREATING A NURTURING FAMILY:
Giving Our Children What They Need
page 235

APPENDIX 1:
Attachment Theories
page 245

APPENDIX 2:
Tools and Resources for Talking to Children About Adoption
page 247

NOTES
page 253

ABOUT THE AUTHORS
page 265

ACKNOWLEDGMENTS

In the years since the first edition of *The Whole Life Adoption Book* was published, not only has the American culture grown in its understanding of the beauties and challenges of adoption, but also I, as an adoption professional committed to the training and education of adoptive and foster families and professionals, have truly grown. That growth has come through the encouragement and support of colleagues for over twenty years.

I first began my work in adoption at Warren County Children Services, Lebanon, Ohio, in 1986, coming to that position as a former educator and foster parent. I experienced incredible support then as the first edition of *The Whole Life Adoption Book* was being written. It was the executive director, Mr. R. D. Burchwell; my supervisor, Mr. Steve Kelhoffer; and many other colleagues who encouraged me in that very first effort.

Since becoming a full-time national and international adoption educator, I have had the privilege of working with many individuals from the Institute of Human Services in Columbus, Ohio, and being part of the Ohio Child Welfare Training Program. I would like to express my deep appreciation to the following colleagues at IHS:

- Dr. Ronald Hughes and Dr. Judith Rycus, founders and directors of IHS, who gave me a place to serve and a rich environment in which to learn
- Betsy Keefer Smalley, a dear friend and cowriter of numerous curricula, articles, and a book, who continually challenges me to observe, study, and learn
- Norma Ginther, Lois Tyler, Pam Severs, and Dr. Denise Goodman, who mentored and encouraged me and from whom I have learned much and continue to do so

I am indebted to many other colleagues from IHS and other adoption professionals from around the country whose paths I only briefly crossed but who influenced and changed my career nonetheless. I am also indebted to all the regional coordinators for the Ohio Child Welfare training program, who gave me a place to improve my training skills and to serve.

One of the most enjoyable experiences of working on the updated version of this book has been to work alongside a coauthor and two other contributing authors for the first time and to team up again with the original editor of *The Whole Life Adoption Book*. I would like to thank Thomas Atwood, president of National Council For Adoption, for joining me as coauthor. Thanks also to Chuck Johnson, NCFA vice president of Training and Agency Services, and Nicole Ficere Callahan for their willingness to assist with this project and for all the expert additions to the book. Because of their support, *The Whole Life Adoption Book* was updated to meet the needs of adopting families in the twenty-first century.

Two contributors, Dr. Timothy Callahan and Elizabeth Tracy, have brought incredible knowledge and life experience to this project, which has added depth and understanding. Because of their time and effort, I know families and children will be helped.

A huge thank you goes to my editor, Traci Mullins, who captured the vision for this book over fifteen years ago. It was my incredible privilege to work with Traci on the first edition, and it was once again my privilege to work with her on this updated version.

I want to thank my husband, David, my most treasured source of friendship, encouragement, and support, for continuing to believe in me and for carrying additional responsibilities so the revised addition of this book could be written. I thank my son, Ray, who joined our family by adoption at age sixteen, for sharing his life with us. I have learned much about adoption and the needs of children from him. Now forty-one, he has matured into a remarkable young man and awesome father to beautiful Lacey.

Fifteen years ago, I commented in the acknowledgments that my then sixteen-year-old daughter hoped to pursue a degree in social work. Kristy Schooler Matheson is now a social worker as well as a wife to Rick and mom to two awesome children, Micah and Annalise. It is a great joy to share our common passion for foster care and adoption as Kristy serves as an adoption professional in Ohio. We often trade adoption stories and could talk for hours about our shared vision.

I truly believe that each connection I have had the privilege of making along the way has been orchestrated by God. He has brought incredible people into my life. They have taught me and challenged me and allowed me to live out my passion. God has given me an incredible love for children and families touched by the issues of foster care and adoption, which continues today. I thank Him for directing my path beyond anything I could have imagined.

Jayne E. Schooler

Shortly after my wife, Eileen, and I adopted our son Christopher eighteen years ago, I said to our adoption counselor, "I hope some day I'll have the opportunity to write about adoption. I have some thoughts." Little could I imagine that the Lord would eventually call me to lead the National Council For Adoption (NCFA) and to coauthor this book. So I, too, like Jayne, humbly acknowledge and thank God for how He has directed my path to learn about and serve this wonderful mission of finding families for children through adoption.

Many thanks also to Jayne Schooler for inviting me to coauthor this edition of *The Whole Life Adoption Book*: It is an honor to help her build upon her previous fine work of advising and assisting adoptive parents in providing the best possible families for their children. I thank the board of directors of the National Council For Adoption whose confidence in me has enabled me to fulfill my fond desire to serve adoption and share those thoughts I sensed eighteen years ago. From the NCFA staff, Nicole Ficere Callahan and Chuck Johnson also have my deep respect and appreciation for their assistance with drafting and editing. Nicole's expert research and writing and Chuck's insightful editing were invaluable.

Finally, I cannot begin to thank enough my cherished partners in the promise and miracle of adoption, Eileen and Chris. They are the joys of my life. Our life together inspires my courage, passion, and whatever wisdom I may be blessed to share in this book.

Tom Atwood

A RELATIONSHIP OF PROMISE

There are two kinds of relationships in life. One type of relationship is genetic, which we share with our relatives through birth: biological children, parents, brothers, sisters, grandparents, aunts, and uncles. No matter what happens, that genetic relationship remains. Nothing can erase the permanency of the biological connection.

The other kind is a union that begins with a promise. Marriage is such a union. Adoption is another. The adoption tie, established by a promise and recognized in law, provides loving parents and family for the child whose biological parents are not both willing and able to parent. Like marriage, adoption is a legal act. It is the legal transfer of parental rights and responsibilities from one parent or set of parents to another parent or set of parents.

Adoption is a miracle in much the same way as birth: Each one is unique and beautiful in its own way. We believe that God makes families through adoption, just as He makes families through procreation, and this is a cornerstone of what we teach in our own adoptive families. Talk to any adoptive parent, even one who does not have a religious perspective, and he or she will tell you, "This child belongs in our family." People who were adopted will tell you, "My true family is the one I grew up in." Birthparents will tell you, "Adoption was the most right and loving thing I could do for my child." The adoptive family is the adopted child's true and permanent family.

The adoptive family mirrors the biological family in almost every way. The power of the love between adoptive parent and adopted child is tremendous, and the challenges and differences of adoption can be overstated. However, while adoption is healthy and normal, there are times in the lives of many adoptive families and their children when any one of a number of adoption-related matters presented in this book may surface. Excited adoptive parents may enter this relationship of promise with limited perception of or inadequate preparation for the unique challenges that can occur in adoption. Some of these issues may follow parents and children throughout life. When issues that normally occur within the framework of adoption arise unexpectedly, parents can experience a wide range of unsettling reactions: guilt, failure, inadequacy, fear, or helplessness. But with wisdom, understanding, patience, and love—and commitment to the promise—the family can handle the challenges. Without sensitive handling, these fragile concerns can become painful, possibly even threatening the foundation of the adoption promise.

Since the publication of the first edition of *The Whole Life Adoption Book* in 1993, the number of adoptive families in the United States, adopting both domestically and internationally, has grown immensely. For example, in 1993 there were approximately 38,000[1] children adopted from the foster care system. According to the most recent statistics available from the government accounting office (2005), that number rose to 51,323. In 1993, there were 7,377 intercountry adoptions, according to the government accounting office. That number has risen to over 19,000 intercountry adoptions a year.[2] A total of approximately 150,000 children are adopted every year.[3] This figure includes domestic infant adoptions, domestic older child adoptions, relative and kinship adoptions, and intercountry adoptions.

The past fifteen years have been a time of incredible growth and understanding within our culture of the beauty of adoption. Adopted children and adoptive families find themselves embraced in a world of love and support, no longer feeling that the adoption must be a secret kept at all costs as it was by some, decades ago. Through research, observation, and experience, a deepening understanding of what adopted children and their families need has emerged within the adoption community, especially in regard to the effects of neglect and abuse that children may have experienced prior to being adopted and methods for dealing with those effects. In response to this deeper understanding, there have been a number of changes to the original book authored by Jayne Schooler.

The new edition includes an up-to-date look at the process of intercountry adoption, as well as insightful information on the lifelong journey of families touched by transcultural adoption. Dr. Timothy Callahan's contribution to this book, which addresses the issues of attachment and trauma from the most current and up-to-date research, will prove invaluable in helping parents and children. Adoption affects not only the parents but also the biological children in the home. Elizabeth Tracy, who grew up as a birth child in a home with foster children, lends her life experience and academic research to a subject that has not been covered in this format in any earlier adoption literature.

The purpose of the revised edition of this book is fourfold:

1. To acquaint prospective and new adoptive parents with the options and issues surrounding the early steps of the adoption journey.
2. To provide awareness and knowledge to these parents regarding the needs of the children who enter their homes through adoption. Those needs include an understanding of the developmental stages of adoption, the impact of growing up in a transracial and/or trans-cultural family, the impact of trauma on the developing child, and the need many adopted children have to know their past.
3. To validate the concerns of adoptive families in the middle of the child-rearing years who find themselves wondering if what they are experiencing is normal and how best to solve unexpected pressures and problems.
4. To offer direction to parents facing the crucial transitional years of adolescence and young adulthood.

This book has been written not only from the perspective gained through working with many adoptive families but also from the hearts of two adoptive parents. We hope that our effort will encourage families to take the journey into adoption with excitement and anticipation, bolstered by the knowledge and understanding that will create a happy, nurturing family.

PART ONE

ADOPTION:
A LABOR OF
THE HEART

MAKING ROOM IN THE FAMILY
Unique Challenges Adoptive Parents Must Face

"Is she your real daughter?" they asked me. "Real?" I questioned.
"What do you mean by real? She is a child not born of my flesh,
that's true. But she is a child truly born within my heart . . .
within my soul. Yes, she is real."
— *an adoptive mother*

In the spring of 2006, five-year-old Jeffrey and his two-year-old sister, Janelle, joined their new family. The arrival of these beautiful children brought indescribable joy to Rob and Angie Cordova. Parents by birth of one-year-old Alise, they longed for a larger family. Now it was happening. A phone call changed their lives. They are adoptive parents.

Kimberly was a severely neglected, malnourished three-month-old when she was placed into the foster home of Bob and Debbie Jackson. For two and a half years the Jacksons' desire to become Kimberly's permanent family grew with each passing month. Their hope teetered back and forth from court decision to court decision. After waiting twelve months for the decision of an appeals court, the word finally came. It was over. Kimberly could now be adopted. She would stay with them forever. Bob and Debbie are adoptive parents.

Years of humiliating medical exams, endless questions, and emotional pain brought no hope to Catherine and Michael Johnston. "You have unexplained infertility," doctors told them. "There is nothing else we can do for you medically." They made a decision to pursue adoption. That was four years ago. Their son, Michael, born in Central America, steals the heart of everyone who meets him. Catherine and Michael are also adoptive parents.

These families, along with thousands across this country, all have in common the choice they made to love, nurture, and embrace a child for a lifetime. It was a promise made to a genetically unrelated human being: "We want you to become one of us. We will be your family forever."

The events that brought these families to this common decision, however, are as diverse as the families themselves. For many of these couples, dreams of a household filled with the noisy, delightful confusion of children lay crushed by the distressing reality of infertility. For them, adoption was the very last hope for ever having a family. For others, involvement in the temporary supervision of a child through a foster care program encouraged them to make a permanent home for the one they had grown to love. Still others, already biological parents, felt called to assume parenthood of an older, emotionally fragile child with a traumatic history of abuse, neglect, or abandonment.

In most ways, parenthood for adoptive couples is just like parenting a biological child; the required skills overlap. However, from the inception of the adoption relationship, adoptive parenting presents additional responsibilities that biological parents do not face. Without laying the proper groundwork in knowledge of these issues, parents who adopt can walk into their responsibilities without adequate understanding.

There are unique perspectives to be aware of in this relationship of promise. For example, families considering adoption must often prepare differently for this distinctive parent-child relationship, especially when the child has special needs or has suffered neglect or abuse. These preparations present challenges not faced within the usual biological parenting experience. Before the family takes the first step into the process, they must decide that the journey into the adoption experience is a viable option for them. And then throughout the adopted child's life, adoptive parents need to be sensitive to her evolving interest in and understanding of adoption and help her with the questions that will naturally arise. Parenting is always a labor of the heart, and adoptive parenting is even more so because of these potentially tender issues.

MAKING THE DECISION TO ADOPT

Most couples or single parents ponder the decision to take the first step toward adopting a child for a long time. They know that the decision to adopt, just like the decision to have a biological child, is a decision that will alter the course of their life. The idea emerges first as a hope. It grows and gathers energy, and finally a family is born.

Before families involve themselves in the adoption process, it is important that they engage in a thorough assessment of attitudes about themselves, their current situation, their current family life, and their support system. The following questions are written for prospective adoptive parents who are married couples since these are the most common adopters. It is understood that single adopters would need to address these questions as well.

1. What are the reasons we want to adopt?
2. How do we see adoption as a positive way to build our family?
3. In what ways do we have the kind of lifestyle that will be enhanced by the addition of a new family member?
4. How will our extended family respond to our adopted child?
5. Do we have personal problems that we think may improve if a child enters our family?
6. Is our motivation for adopting to "save a child"?
7. What is our perspective on the potential relationship: Do we want a child for ourselves, or are we a family for a child? In other words, what are our expectations for the child in this relationship?
8. Are we adopting to acquire a playmate for our biological child?
9. Can we love and nurture this child without knowledge of his or her history, no matter what may arise because of that history? Are we prepared for any special needs our child may have?
10. Adoption is a team effort involving parents, agencies, attorneys, and other individuals. How capable do we see ourselves of working through the system?
11. When we think of a child, do we envision a child who comes with a history or a child who comes with a blank slate?
12. If infertility is an issue, what point of resolution have we reached regarding our inability to conceive? How has infertility affected our marriage?
13. If singleness is the reason I don't have children, what point of resolution have I reached regarding the possibility that I may never marry and have biological children with a spouse?
14. How has childlessness affected our relationships with relatives, friends, and their children?
15. Have we asked ourselves, "Who in our extended family or circle

of friends would best understand the unique needs of our adopted child?"

These questions may prove helpful in assessing a family's readiness for the adoption experience. After potential adoptive parents explore their own outlook on adoption, the preparation can begin.

PREPARATION: CHARTING AN UNKNOWN COURSE

When Sam and Cynthia first contacted an agency because of their interest in adoption, they had no knowledge of how to prepare for the process. As they attended a training course, they became familiar with six sensitive areas that set apart readiness for adoption from readiness for parenting biological children. Their new understanding enhanced their own attitudes toward adoption and helped prepare them for the uncertainties ahead. What did they learn?

INFERTILITY: THE STEALER OF DREAMS

When most young adults approach marriage, they assume that at some point they will start a family. In their childhoods they likely filled hours of playtime rehearsing mother and father roles, projecting that someday in the future they would be just like Mom or Dad. They instinctively and naturally desire to parent.

For some, the assumption of this natural course of events disappointingly proves false. Infertility steals the dream. Forced to face the reality of their situation, couples find themselves coping with feelings and fears totally foreign to peers loaded down with babies and diaper bags. In a survey conducted several years ago but still relevant to the infertile couples of today, men and women provided emotionally penetrating responses to the following question: "There was once a time in your life when you wanted children but could not have them. What word or words describe your feelings at that time?"[1]

Women, with a profound sense of hopelessness, responded that they felt "forlorn, unfulfilled, useless, absolutely heartsick, bitter, utterly desolate." Men, projecting feelings similar to those of their wives, replied that they felt "disappointed, concerned for their wife's reaction, frustrated and inadequate."[2]

Catherine and Michael lived under the shadow of unexplained infertility through four years of painful tests and procedures that shed no light on their circumstance. Chained to a calendar and thermometer that dictated the timing of their physical relationship, they felt trapped in a pursuit that had no end. Those circumstances nearly destroyed the joy and beauty God intended for them to experience in this dimension of their marriage.

"I can take you back to the hospital room where I made a decision," Michael commented. "As I stood beside Catherine while she endured the pain of her sixth artificial insemination procedure, I knew right then and there — this was the last time. Four years on the roller coaster, hoping from month to month for a positive word, were enough. No more attempts at anything. We would have to change directions. We would have to struggle now with being childless or deciding what steps to take next in relation to adoption."

As the biological clock ticked away in the lives of Doug and Dorothy Hammon, their hope for a family diminished with each passing year. "I came from a family of seven children," Dorothy said. "Doug came from a family of five children. We loved large families and planned to follow the same course. I couldn't imagine anyone not being able to have a baby. It was beyond my belief that God would require that heartbreak of anyone."

Involuntary childlessness produces what adoption expert David Kirk calls a role handicap. Couples moving toward adoption as a result of infertility enter parenthood from a different direction than they had expected. They have to alter their plans. Their disappointed hopes and dreams of having children may overwhelm them emotionally. Most couples who move on to adoption from this disappointment do so maturely and soundly, after grieving their loss. Some, however, turn to adoption in desperation, on the rebound, not fully prepared for the additional responsibilities of adoptive parenting.

Couples who view adoption as their last and desperate hope for a family face potentially major losses, especially in their expectations of themselves and what they perceive to be the expectations of others. These include "the loss of oneself or one's partner as capable of conceiving a child, and the loss of the status of a biological parent and the presentation of a child to grandparents." In addition, they face the loss of "the hoped-for birthchild to carry on the family line."[3]

A primary challenge in preparing for the adoptive parent role is to mourn the loss of the dream. Couples should also realize that if they do not resolve this loss, it may quietly follow them all their lives, subtly affecting their responses to their children.

Prospective adoptive parents may perceive they have other challenges to deal with as well, and we'll explore all the issues mentioned below more deeply in later chapters.

NO MODEL TO FOLLOW

Forced to change course, couples find themselves facing still other challenges and role handicaps in preparing for adoptive parenthood. John and Marilyn Martin had finally decided that children would never be a part of their future unless they adopted. But they were troubled by the fact that they didn't know anyone who had taken this route. There was no one they could turn to for guidance. They needed answers for their questions but hesitated to keep calling the social worker, figuring that what was important to them would probably seem insignificant to her. So they didn't call.

Unlike biological parents, who are likely to have seen this type of parenting modeled in their own family of origin, "adoptive parents have little or no intimate contact with other adopters as adoptive parents."[4] They might not even know an adopted child. David Kirk noted that this may present a second major challenge in the preparation process: *Adoptive parents may feel that they have no role models to steer them through the process.*

While this may have been the reality for adoptive parents in decades gone by, role models and mentors abound in our culture today. According to a national adoption survey, over two-thirds of the American population has been touched by adoption in some way. Many people have known someone who was adopted, know a family who has adopted, or are related to a person who was adopted.

OUR BUSINESS IS NOT OUR OWN

In addition to the emotionally charged motivation to have a family, complicated by the perceived lack of role models, couples entering the adoption journey lack a sense of privacy and control.

Biological parents are rarely subject to the personal scrutiny, decisions, and influences of others in the process of building a family. Adoptive parents have no choice. Each step of the way they must seek direction from professionals in the field. They must walk through a network of intrusive examinations by outsiders, ranging from social workers to court officials. They feel that they must monitor what they say and how they say it out of fear that a trivial comment may disrupt the procedure.

These factors create a third concern during the preparation stage: *Adoptive parents soon begin to feel that their future is out of their control. Their hopes and dreams are in the hands of strangers.*

THE WAIT CAN BE SO LONG

A fourth difficulty for adoptive applicants is the time factor. When anticipating the arrival of their baby, pregnant couples have a pretty good idea (usually within a few days or weeks) of when to plan for the event. Adoptive parents must wait indefinitely just to get on an agency list for a homestudy. The homestudy is that process which enables agencies and families to assess if adoption is right for them. This is fully explained in chapter 2. Then they must wade through a maze of paperwork and interviews during this process. Finally, once the homestudy and training has been completed, the suspense really begins. Each ring of the phone may be the agency informing them of a child in need of a family.

When should couples tell their family and friends that they are adopting—when they first decide? Or during the homestudy? Or should they wait until they get the phone call? How can couples gather support around themselves when all they can answer to the when and who questions is "I don't know"?

Therefore, the fourth frustrating challenge in making the transition into adoptive parenthood is that *these expectant adults have no sense of a reliable timetable. They have very limited knowledge of what to expect regarding when their new family member will join them.*

OTHER PEOPLE DON'T ALWAYS UNDERSTAND

"Why would you want to adopt?" "Why would you want to take on other people's problems?" "Can't you have any children of your own?" These are questions encountered by prospective adoptive parents every day. Questions like these can come from inside the family as well as from friends and acquaintances, and such comments can feel very invalidating to adoptive parents.

A fifth challenge for adoptive parents is *to understand that people in their life may not validate their role in their child's life to the extent they hoped they would.* "With my family and my husband's family, they view it as different from biological parenting. In fact, they were quite negative about it before we adopted," said one adoptive mother. "They actually said that the children would not really be 'their' grandchildren. However, as soon as our parents met our children, all those feelings were gone. I think they just didn't know how they would fit into the lives of these children who came to us at six and nine."

Shared Parenting for a Season

A sixth obstacle in preparing for adoptive parenthood crops up immediately after the child arrives: the question of parental rights over the newest child in the home. When are adoptive parents really the parents? On the day the child enters the home? Physically, yes. In many states, legally, no. The child may still remain in the legal custody of a birthparent, an agency, the public, or the court. A social worker and/or a court worker will regularly visit the home for a period of six months prior to finalization.

These visits can be a reminder of how parenting by adoption is different in those early months from parenting by birth. For the child's best interest, parental status is not fully granted in most states until that trial period expires and the court processes the finalization paperwork. And so a sixth and final test for adoptive parents as they enter their new role is that *they must cope with the lack of full entitlement as parents while functioning in the position as if they were.*

Preadoptive families who realize that they must prepare for their role differently than birthparents do will be more successful in managing the uncertainties that are a natural course of events. They will be better prepared for encountering adoption's four unique tasks, which will be introduced in this first chapter. The rest of this book will explore the adoptive family relationship in depth and give practical guidelines for dealing with the additional responsibilities.

It is most important that during the preadoptive stage parents begin to understand the unique tasks and realities of the relationship they are entering. It is equally important that mothers and fathers in the midst of parenting stand back and evaluate how they have approached the unique tasks of adoptive parenting.

TASK NUMBER ONE:
HOW DO WE SEE OUR FAMILY?

Joe and Gayle Smith and Robert and Joyce Bennett had something in common. They had waited five years for that all-important phone call from the private adoption agency serving them. Within two months of each other, the calls finally came. For both couples, the waiting was over.

Three-week-old John joined the Smith family immediately. Within two years, Alicia, a month-old infant, completed the family circle. That was over twenty-one years ago. To this day, both children (now, of course, young adults) have no idea that they were adopted. Gayle and Joe decided that their family was "just like anyone else's." They decided to pretend the children were theirs by birth and to build the relationship from that perspective.

The Bennett family approached the adoption relationship very differently. Almost from the moment that two-week-old June captured the hearts of her waiting parents, the Bennetts communicated her special position in the family. Now an adult, June says of her parents' conversation about adoption, "They told me that even from the time I was in the cradle, they would talk to me about adoption. They would say things like, "We wanted a baby so badly; we are so fortunate to have you." They would always say how much they loved me. There was never a time that my parents had to sit me down and tell me I was adopted. I always knew it. It was just built in as part of our relationship."

Note the dissimilarity between these two approaches. The Smiths chose to cover up the role of adoption in building their family, even to their children and themselves, as if it were something abnormal and unnatural. This plan might have helped them meet their need to lessen the sting of infertility and be just like everyone else. The strategy likely worked — for a while. The consequences of such a decision would not be felt for years to come.

The Bennetts, on the other hand, acknowledged adoption and its additional responsibilities and challenges and embraced its role in their daughter's life. They had reconciled their struggle with infertility and arrived at a healthy understanding of their role as adoptive parents. They were able to say, "Yes, our daughter came to us in a different way from the usual; nevertheless, we are a family and she is where she belongs." By talking to their child about adoption from an early age, in age-appropriate ways, the whole family understood adoption better and was comfortable with it.

Adoptive parents must learn the delicate balance between denying the difference in the nurturing process and acknowledging it by communicating to the child about his or her past. (This balance is more fully examined in chapter 10.) By keeping adoption a secret or, more commonly, by generally avoiding the topic of adoption and feeling uncomfortable with it, parents can subtly communicate to their children that there is something wrong with them and their family. Thankfully, almost no adoption professional today recommends keeping adoption a secret from the child, nor do many parents seek to do so.

TASK NUMBER TWO:
HOW DO WE DEVELOP AN ENVIRONMENT
THAT COMMUNICATES BELONGING?

Just like adopted children, when children are born into a family, they are "strangers" who seek to be accepted for who they are. However, because of their biological connection and the birth experience itself, it is easier for parents—physically, emotionally, and psychologically—to incorporate biological children into the family than it is children who join the family through adoption. The same needs for blending the family exist for adopted children, but a heavier assignment is added to the parents' responsibilities.

Goal one of adoptive parenting is to accept, know, and honor each child for the unique characteristics, temperament, and genetic gifts he or she brings to the family. These, of course, come from the child's birthfamily. Chuck Johnson, an adoptive father, mentioned that Christian, his eight-year-old son, is a naturally gifted athlete. "He is the first Johnson to hit a grand slam or score a three-pointer in basketball, and I am talking from a long line of non-sportsmen. I know this gift comes from his birthfather and I honor that."

Goal two is to incorporate or integrate children into the family. Creating an environment in which children feel secure, loved, and that they belong provides them a foundation they can build on.

Parents then begin the third goal of adoptive parenting: developing secure, autonomous children. They must help their children differentiate from their family of origin and fully join and attach to the adoptive family. Newborns and toddlers are completely dependent upon their parents for survival, and trust and interdependence are developed during this stage. Thus for them, bonding occurs quite readily in the beginning, and differentiation occurs later as they develop and mature. The first test starts as children move out into their neighborhood and then into preschool and beyond. Their ability to function well outside the home is determined largely by the quality of attachment and sense of belonging they experienced early on in their home. For children who have existing and ongoing relationships with birthparents, attachment and differentiation can be more complicated, but it is still almost always achievable.

The adoptive parents' role with their new child is like the biological parents': to integrate the new child into the family. But from the beginning of the adoptive relationship, parents should be communicating the reality of adoption to their child.

Tom and Eileen began speaking lovingly about his adoption to their son, Chris, when he was an infant, well before he could understand what it meant. But in so doing, he got used to the word, and Tom and Eileen became comfortable with talking about it. When Chris got older and his understanding increased, he felt natural and at ease about the role of adoption in his life. It was part of his identity, and he was comfortable with it because it was never hidden from him and did not suddenly appear in his life as a surprise. This honesty and openness in communication about adoption is crucial to bonding within the family and to the child's long-term psychological well-being. We'll talk more about it in chapters 7 and 11.

TASK NUMBER THREE:
WHAT DO WE NEED TO KNOW ABOUT OUR CHILD, AND WHAT SHOULD WE DO WITH WHAT WE KNOW?

When an infant joins her new family, most agencies make sincere efforts to obtain social and medical history about the family of origin. Although this is often nonidentifying information, it gives parents something of a handle on anticipating future talents and strengths as well as behavioral, educational, or medical problems that might be related to genetics.

When an older child with a history of his own enters an adoptive family, parents are given information not only about the birthfamily but also about the social, medical, psychological, and educational history of their child. This material allows potential adoptive parents to make realistic decisions concerning the child. Some parents fail to realize that it is in everyone's best interest and is their right as parents to gather as much information about their child as possible.

David and Jennifer Dotson were determined to adopt. As far as they were concerned, they could handle any problems a child might have. They believed that love would conquer all. They just wanted a child—any child.

When they went into the agency for an interview concerning a possible child for their family, they went in with blinders on. They asked no questions. They explored no possible problems. They failed to hold the agency accountable to give them all the information it had available. In fact, they declined to read some very important medical information about their child. In the following years, it proved almost impossible to retrace steps to get the information they had earlier avoided.

Biological parents question a doctor from the first moment of a child's life. But adoptive parents often hesitate to assert themselves when presented with a child in need of adoption. They feel inadequate. They don't know what to ask. They are not sure they are entitled to any information. They may be influenced by others to assume that they should simply be grateful for the opportunity and should avoid rocking the boat.

However, parents have a right to know about their child's genetic potential and history. It is the parents' job to be proactive in asking questions. The child, in turn, will someday need to have that information passed on to him or her. Chapter 11 will explore this task in fuller detail.

TASK NUMBER FOUR: HOW DO WE FEEL ABOUT OUR CHILD'S BIRTHFAMILY?

For years, statistics have told us of increasing cultural problems, such as alcohol or drug addiction and sexually transmitted diseases. The tragedy is that some children are born to unwed mothers who are trapped in such a lifestyle. Child abuse and the subsequent termination of parental rights among these parents are also increasing dramatically. Both situations plunge innocent youngsters into the adoption arena.

Parents who adopt confront a fourth task. They must face their feelings about their child's history, racial and cultural ties, and birthfamily. They must acknowledge the possibility of genetic liabilities, prenatal substance exposure, or problems caused by a lack of prenatal care. They must reconcile their attitudes toward these realities in light of their own value structure. Finally, they must recognize that such a negative beginning can have far-reaching consequences for the child (through behavior and/or disabilities) and for themselves (in their parenting workload and ultimate ability to accept the child fully). Adoptive parents must decide how, when, and how much of the truth of those circumstances they will communicate to the child, knowing that an adopted child's self-esteem can be affected by his or her perceptions of genetic origins.

Adoption is truly a labor of the heart—and head! It begins with a time of difficult preparation. It is filtered through months, even years, of process. By its very nature, adoption carries with it evolving responsibilities that if approached with love, sensitivity, wisdom, and hope can lead to a healthy adoptive relationship for a lifetime.

SUMMARY

Adoptive parents enter adoption with six major challenges unique to preparing for the adoptive parenting experience:

1. They may have to mourn the loss of their dream: their ability to conceive children, their status as biological parents, and their biological child.
2. They may feel they have no role models to guide them through the process.
3. They must realize that their hope for a family will be dictated by the input of strangers.
4. Preadoptive parents have no clear timetable by which to plan their future.
5. Adoptive parents must filter through the comments and opinions of others and manage experiences of invalidation.
6. Permanent parental rights are generally not granted until at least six months into the relationship. Adoptive parents must manage shared parenting authority for a season.

Parents will journey through a lifetime of tasks that are unique to the adoptive family relationship. Adoptive parents' journeys involve four tasks, answering these questions:

1. How do we see family? Do we deny the fact of our child's adoption, or do we acknowledge adoption as a healthy act and the process by which our child joined our family? How do we think others see us?
2. How do we develop an environment that communicates belonging? When and how do we begin to communicate with our child about adoption?
3. What do we need to know about our child, and what should we do with what we know? How can we get important facts about our child's past? When should we communicate those facts?
4. How do we feel about our child's birthfamily? How do we reconcile our child's beginnings with our own value system, and how do we relate this to our child in positive ways?

QUESTIONS FOR SMALL GROUPS

1. What particular challenges have you had in preparing to become an adoptive family?
2. If infertility has been an issue, what problems has it created in you, in your marriage, and in your relationships with couples who have children?
3. How have you handled infertility or singleness in relation to your hopes and your personal faith? In what ways have you worked through bitterness, anger at God, feelings of inadequacy, and so forth?
4. What messages are you receiving from extended family members and friends about your desire to adopt? How do those messages make you feel?
5. What are your needs and expectations of yourself, of your spouse, and of the agency with which you are working?

CHAPTER TWO

CREATING A FAMILY
Understanding the Adoption Process

When Catherine first came, it seemed impossible to me that any child
wouldn't respond to a warm and nurturing home. As I learned to watch
her and understand her pain, I knew beneath that hardened shell was a
child trying desperately to feel and to love again.

— *Cynthia, an adoptive parent*

Jeff and Gwen Stewart had planned a week together at the beach. One phone
call from their attorney changed everything. "Mr. and Mrs. Stewart, this
is Mr. Barrett. We have just received word that your baby's arrival will come
sooner than expected. Instead of three more weeks, it could happen any day. I
suggest that you not leave town." They canceled their vacation plans.

The Stewarts joined hundreds of families waiting each day for a phone call
or home visit to bring their deepest desire to reality. Like many prospective
adoptive parents, Jeff and Gwen went through a preparation period, not only
formally through classes, but also emotionally, psychologically, and spiritually.
They emerged ready to walk through the process of adoption best suited for
them.

When a family decides to pursue adoption, there are several avenues they
can explore: domestic infant adoption through an agency or attorney, adoption
out of foster care, or international adoption. Each option, however, requires a
homestudy, which is a thorough examination of the prospective parents' home,
quality of relationships, financial security, motivation, and lifestyle. Details of
the process can vary from agency to agency. The homestudy is and should be a
deliberate and substantial process. After all, we are talking about the transfer
of parental rights and responsibilities for a child. Life does not get much more
meaningful than this. But the homestudy is not something to be feared.

THE HOMESTUDY JOURNEY

For some adopting families, the homestudy process can be a time of uncertainty and anxiety. Families often fear that agencies are looking only for perfect families. That isn't the case since there are no perfect families. What agencies are looking for are realistic families who feel they can prepare to parent children, some with unique needs and challenges.

Knowing about the homestudy journey can help prospective parents enter the process with confidence. There are no standardized national homestudy requirements, which means that the process varies greatly from state to state, even from agency to agency in many states. Also, most countries have their own requirements for homestudies that U.S. agencies must follow. However, here are some general guidelines prospective adoptive parents can expect to encounter during the homestudy process.[1]

- Training. Many agencies require prospective adoptive parents to attend a certain number of classes before they can be approved. These courses help parents better understand the process, the types of children available for adoption, the needs of the children, and much more. A valuable training resource for intercountry adopters is "The Intercountry Adoption Journey: Hague Compliant Training," written and published by the National Council For Adoption.
- Documentation. Many agencies will require the prospective adoptive parents to write an autobiography. In this document, parents are asked to describe their family of origin, growing-up experiences, attitudes and beliefs about adoption, relationships, daily life, parenting attitudes, and more. In an era of increased intercountry adoption, agency accreditation, and interagency agreements, homestudies are getting much more complex. They may include personality and temperament testing. Parents who look at this requirement as a time of self-discovery will enjoy the process, for it is truly that. Other documentation includes health statements, income statements, criminal background checks, and references.
- Interviews and home visits. This is the time to meet the social worker face-to-face. Many adoption professionals approach this requirement not from the perspective of investigator, looking for something to screen the family out, but as a time of mutual assessment and education. Both parties involved need to ask and answer this question: "Is adoption right for

this family?" The purpose of this time is to explore with the family what type of child would best fit into their family—an infant, an older child, a sibling group, or a child adopted from another country. The number of interviews and home visits vary from agency to agency. During this time the social worker and family will discuss relevant attitudes and lifestyle issues as well as other topics, such as motivation and expectations, interpersonal stability, openness of the family system, and more. In a two-parent family, some of the interviews will be together and others will be separate. Most agencies are required to interview everyone living in the household, including children and extended family relatives, such as a grandparent.

- Time frame for the process. The time frame for the completion of the homestudy varies. Many states now have time frame requirements, which means that once a prospective family has submitted an application, the agency has a certain amount of time to schedule their training and to complete the written documentation. Families can generally count on this process to take three to six months.
- Counting the cost. The cost of the homestudy process depends on the type of adoption the family is considering. Families who adopt a child from the foster care system generally do not have a fee other than lawyers' expenses, and these expenses are usually reimbursed after the adoption is finalized. Families adopting domestically through an infant placing agency, internationally through an intercountry adoption agency, or independently adopting through an attorney will be charged varying amounts. For a full accounting of the costs related to adoption, visit the following website: http://www.childwelfare.gov/pubs/s_cost/index.cfm.

CHOOSING THE ADOPTION OPTION THAT IS RIGHT FOR YOU

PUBLIC AGENCY ADOPTION

Public agencies are run by either state or county governments. Children are legally freed for adoption prior to placement. Many public agencies do not charge a fee. When an older child or sibling group adoption is arranged, state and federal financial subsidies often are available to the family to help with ongoing expenses for medical or psychological care. Even legal expenses are reimbursable in most states.

Public agency waiting lists for very young children can be long. Families who are interested in adopting children over the age of three may be given a higher priority in homestudy completion. Many states have initiated a foster-to-adopt program since it's in the child's best interest to avoid multiple moves. There are generally two routes into adoption with public agencies: direct agency adoption and foster care adoption.

Direct Agency Adoption

One Sunday morning, Angie Cordova walked by the church nursery and glanced in at the children. She caught sight of a little fellow sitting with a delicate little girl whose sad eyes cried out for someone to notice her.

Angie asked the care provider about the children and was told that little Jeffrey and his younger sister, Janelle, were living in a foster home. Her heart went out to the children, whose family was visiting her church that day. She wanted to gather them in her arms. Little did she know that in a very short time, they would be walking into her home, on the way to becoming her son and daughter.

The Cordovas began their adoption journey as a result of infertility. With little chance for a birthchild, Angie and Rob decided to adopt. They contacted the local public children services agency and began the homestudy process. After finishing the requirements, they sat back anxiously to wait.

While they were waiting, something happened that put their adoption plans on hold. Their "miracle" daughter, Elise, was conceived, and they decided to postpone adoption. A year later, their desire to adopt resurfaced, and they contacted the local public agency to let them know of their renewed interest. It turned out to be perfect timing.

One cold, snowy February morning in 2005, just a few weeks after the Cordovas had reinitiated the procedure, they received a phone call. "Would you be interested in discussing the adoptive placement of a sibling group of two?" Upon hearing a brief description of the children, Angie realized they were the same youngsters who had tugged at her heart in the church nursery just weeks before. Her new family was right under her nose.

Jeffrey and Janelle came for a number of preplacement visits to get to know their new family. They moved into their new home on Easter weekend 2005. Following a six-month waiting period, the family filed for adoption in court to make the children a permanent part of the family.

In the summer of 2006, the family jointly made the decision to adopt again. All three children, Elise, Jeffrey, and Janelle, were excited about opening their hearts and home to four-year-old Stephanie.

Foster Care Adoption

Bob and Debbie Jackson had no intention of becoming adoptive parents when they entered the foster care program of the local children's services agency. The Jacksons, parents of two daughters who were heading into the teen years, wanted only to open their home to an abused child for a little while. What they had not counted on was falling in love with Kimberly.

Kimberly, who is now five years old, came to live with them at the age of three months. When she was brought to their door by the agency social worker, she was severely malnourished, desperately dirty, and lethargic. Weeks of tender care and nurture brought color and life back to the child. The Jacksons' job was to work as members of the agency team in helping Kimberly's mother do a better job of caring for her.

Debbie commented,

As we cared for this little girl, our lives and futures were on hold. Each week, we would take her to visit her birthmother. Sometimes she would stay overnight. Kimberly would always cry when we left her there. She didn't understand who this person was. When she would return home, we had to deal with tantrums, sleeplessness, and eating problems for several days. Just as she settled back down, it was time for a visit again.

We were advised not to become too attached. But how could a small child feel secure if we withheld affection from her? If we kept our distance, it would be easier for us but devastating to her. So we loved.

As the months passed, we began to feel that she was one of us — but, of course, she wasn't. We wanted to map out a design to enlarge our home if she stayed, but there were no assurances of that. We wanted to plan a family vacation but were uncertain where to go. If Kimberly was with us in the summer, we wouldn't plan a hiking vacation.

There were times I would become so angry! We were doing so

much for this little girl, and it seemed that her neglectful mother ran the program. I had to believe that God had Kimberly's best interests in mind far more than even we did.

Over an eighteen-month period, the weekly visits with Kimberly's mother failed to bring improvement. The emotional ups and downs for this family seemed to end with a court order terminating her parental rights. However, the birthmother appealed the lower court decision, and the final outcome was postponed for another fourteen months.

After caring for this child for over two and a half years, the Jacksons received the word. It was finally over. What began as a temporary desire on the part of a family to make a difference in their world had turned into a permanent commitment. Following the termination of parental rights, the Jackson family applied to the public agency to be approved as adoptive parents. Kimberly's future was secure.

Domestic public agency adoption is one option. Intercountry adoption is another.

INTERCOUNTRY ADOPTION

The next chapter will provide a wealth of information for families considering the option of intercountry adoption. Briefly, parents choosing to adopt a child from another country should know that they will be involved with adoption service providers in both the U.S. and the country of origin. First, the couple is required to work with an agency in this country to complete an initial homestudy and paperwork. Following that, the agency works with the adoption service providers in the country of origin, including the government authority responsible for adoptions, and sometimes directly with an orphanage, attorney, or caretaker who has legal custody of children needing families to secure the referral of a child to the prospective adoptive parents.

Depending upon the country, the wait can be from six months to well over a year. As soon as a child is matched with a family, paperwork including visas, passports, immigration applications, and other essential documents must be gathered. Laws and regulations within both the U.S. and the country of origin are in place to ensure that the child is legally eligible to be adopted and that the prospective adopters are suitable parents.

Just when Catherine and Michael Johnston had laid aside their dream of having a family, a dramatic series of events reignited their hope. "When we made the decision to adopt," Michael recalled, "we really didn't know how to go about it. We went to see a pastor we knew who had helped other families. We figured he would direct us toward adoption in this country. Instead, he encouraged us to meet with another couple who had recently arrived home from Guatemala with their adopted infant son." Interestingly, Michael had just returned from a church-sponsored trip to that same country. While there, his assignment was to work in an orphanage. He quickly fell in love with the Guatemalan youngsters.

When Michael and Catherine drove to another part of their state to consult with the adoptive couple, they had a growing sense that perhaps this was the first step toward starting a family. The O'Briens informed the Johnstons of the procedure for adopting a child from Guatemala, suggesting that they contact the same agency with whom they had worked. Michael immediately contacted the local adoption agency when they returned home. The journey began for this excited couple.

During the following months Michael and Catherine spent hours writing extensive autobiographies and gathering thorough references and other complicated documents. All their paperwork had to be funneled through the Guatemalan consulate in the U.S.

Finally, anticipation turned into reality when the Johnstons were informed that they were matched with a baby boy. They were given instructions to prepare to leave for Guatemala. They were to spend two weeks in the country with their new son before he would be eligible to leave. On a Thursday evening in January 2003, thirteen months after they had started the process, the phone rang. It was their agency representative. He told them to make plans to leave the following Wednesday. Their son was waiting for them.

Bright, spirited Michael Justin had been born in October 2002. He was placed into the Johnstons' arms in January 2003. Catherine reflected on the events that brought their son to them:

> When we went to see the O'Briens, it was almost to the day that Michael was conceived. There were periods of great apprehension. Would this fall through? We knew we were involved in an incredible risk. Anything could happen. The country could turn us down when we got there. The mother could change her mind. Our son might be too ill to leave. It

was one of the most dramatic periods in our lives in which we had to place our faith totally in God, day by day.

INDEPENDENT ADOPTION

Dear Doug and Dorothy,

I wanted to keep you informed on how I am doing. I went to the clinic last week. The doctor said that I had gained weight, but that was to be expected at this point in the pregnancy. He listened to the baby's heartbeat, and everything sounds just fine. He thinks that the baby is due October 21. That means we only have two more months. My parents will call you as agreed so that you can be with us in the delivery room. Thank you for being willing to love my baby.

I'll write again soon,
Patti

For Doug and Dorothy Hammon, that letter and earlier contacts represented their only prospect for a family. Each short note from the birthmother of their prospective child brought them closer to the fulfillment of their deepest desire—to have a family.

The Hammons spent eight years and thousands of dollars looking for an answer to their infertility problem. When Dorothy turned thirty-five, they decided that adoption was their only option for a family.

Dorothy commented,

I began making calls to public and private agencies. They wouldn't even put our names on the waiting list. The prospects for a healthy white infant were bleak.

One afternoon Doug's boss walked into his office and shut the door. He related that the fifteen-year-old daughter of a friend of his was pregnant and the family wanted to have the child adopted by a good family. He asked if we would be interested. When Doug called me at home, for the first time in a very long time, I felt that we had a chance to add a child to our family.

During the next several months, the Hammons and the teenage birth-mother and her family spent time together in their respective homes. Patti kept the family regularly informed through letters or phone calls. Both families obtained lawyers, and the Hammons agreed to pay all legal expenses. Patti's medical expenses were covered on her parents' health insurance policy.

Finally, the Hammons received the long-awaited call. Patti was on the way to the hospital. Because of the openness of the adoption that both families had accepted, Doug and Dorothy were in the delivery room at the time of their son's birth. Within one hour after his arrival, Dorothy held him in her arms. "In that moment," Dorothy recalled, "I felt overwhelmed with thanksgiving. I was totally awed."

The next few days were difficult for this waiting family. They left the hospital the evening after the birth so that Patti and her family could spend time with the baby. They knew that at any moment, Patti could change her mind, right up until she signed the permanent surrender document. Fortunately for Doug and Dorothy, she did not. Carter is now three years old. The Hammons send yearly updates to his birthmother and talk with her, usually at Christmastime. A deep desire of the heart has been fulfilled.

There are generally two kinds of independent adoptions: those arranged by an attorney and those arranged by an adoption facilitator. An attorney retained by a prospective adoptive family will typically work with the family to help match them to a prospective birthmother and handle the legal side of the adoption. The adoptive family will still have to work through a licensed adoption agency (or approved agent) to complete the required homestudy and to ensure that the birthparents receive counseling and other adoption-related support. For this reason, many families and birthparents prefer the ongoing support usually offered by a licensed adoption agency. Like an adoption agency, an adoption attorney is licensed and required to adhere to a code of ethical and professional responsibilities.

Considered the most risky and one of the most expensive options is an independent adoption arranged by an adoption facilitator. Illegal in many states, adoption facilitators are unlicensed agents that advertise for birthparents and will match birthparents with adoptive families for a fee. They avoid licensure by stopping short of providing social or legal services. Some adoption facilitators may be in business with the best of intentions and may even have a long list of satisfied clients, but many recent adoption scandals have involved adoption facilitators who lacked the necessary experience to provide adoption services.

Many families have found pursuing grievances against adoption facilitators difficult, if not impossible. The National Council For Adoption recommends caution in using the services of an unlicensed adoption facilitator without a thorough background check.

OPENNESS IN ADOPTION

According to adoption expert David Brodzinsky,

> Openness in adoption is best understood as a communicative continuum. . . . At one end of the continuum are those individuals characterized by a greater willingness to explore adoption-related issues in their lives, to share their thoughts and feelings with others, and to be empathically attuned to those around them; at the other end of the continuum are those individuals who are reticent to acknowledge and discuss adoption-related issues and are cut off from their own feelings and the feelings of others regarding these issues.[2]

The popular media in America are fascinated with openness in adoption placements, but as expressed in the preceding quote, when it comes to a healthy adoptive family and adopted person, it's openness *about* adoption that counts. As we will discuss in later chapters, the adoptive family who acknowledges and accepts the role of adoption in the family's life together and is able to communicate about it freely when questions arise is most likely to be able to walk gracefully through any challenges that present themselves, whether these challenges are common to all families or particular to adoptive families.

Most domestic infant adoptions today do involve some degree of openness toward the birthfamily, especially the birthmother. The most common placement allows the birthmother's involvement in the selection of the parents, a meeting or two between the birthmother and the adoptive parents before or at placement, and letters and photographs from the adoptive family to the birthmother throughout childhood. Some placements go further and include the exchange of identifying information and birthmother visitations with the family for several years or throughout childhood. Studies show that the most important variable to the birthmother's future well-being is her involvement in the selection of the parents. It is also usual procedure for the adoptive parents to receive as complete a record as possible regarding the medical history of the birthparents and biological grandparents, as well as a social history, though perhaps not as complete.

After many years of research and debate, leading researchers of openness in the adoptive placements of infants have found that "the development of adoptive identity . . . does not appear to be significantly dependent on level of openness." The feelings and desires of adopted persons, adoptive families, and birthparents regarding placement openness and contact between family and birthfamily could not be more diverse and personal. The research shows that "a 'one-size-fits-all' approach is not warranted" in considering the "desirability and undesirability of fully disclosed or confidential adoptions."[3] It is important to note that the meaning of openness in this context refers to openness in placement.

Most agencies allow prospective parents to indicate the level of openness they feel they can accept. Because most birthmothers today expect at least to be involved in parent selection, to meet the parents, and to receive updates on the child, prospective parents who are not willing to consent to any of these may find themselves waiting longer to adopt. However, this does not mean they should accept an arrangement they do not feel right about.

It has become fairly common for birthparents and adoptive parents to make agreements regarding post-placement contacts. The degree to which these agreements are legally binding varies from state to state. In our view, a law that makes these agreements court-enforceable undermines the adoptive family. But in any case adoptive parents should exercise good faith in keeping these agreements and only make agreements they intend, and realistically expect to be able, to keep.

Openness in adoptions out of foster care is becoming more common, especially for older children who desire to maintain some contact with their biological families. This arrangement can be positive for the child, but prospective adoptive parents are also advised to be sure that this openness does not compromise the child's safety, considering that the child had to be removed from the family due to abuse or neglect.

At this time, there is not a great deal of openness in international adoption. Countries of origin keep records of the children, birthparents, and adoptive parents. But it would take a great deal of effort and good fortune on a birthparent's part to be able to search for and find the adoptive family. Most countries of origin maintain the adoptive family's privacy, primarily because the countries have not yet received many requests for this information. Perhaps they will in the future.

Betsy and Kenneth are three-year-old twins. They entered their adoptive home at four days old. Prior to their birth, their birthmother and birthfather selected an adoptive family and met them on several occasions. Kathy, the birthmother, now lives in a different city but feels very free to contact the children's parents two or three times a year to check on the children. So does Matt, the birthfather. Once a year, Susan, the adoptive mother, sends pictures to both Kathy and Matt, which they in turn share with their parents. This arrangement has worked beautifully for this family.

Most agencies today are committed to promoting varying levels of openness. It is important to realize that openness in adoption does not mean coparenting. It often means that birthparents play an active role in choosing the adoptive parents and are able to follow the child's progress through updates, pictures, and in some cases varying degrees of visitation in the years ahead.

ADOPTION AGENCY CONSIDERATIONS[4]

The process of adoption can be difficult and confusing. There are many options and directions a family can take. It is important to enter the adoption journey well equipped with information. The following are some basic guidelines adoptive parents can follow when selecting a private agency with which to work:

1. Contact your state licensing authority for a list of all adoption agencies that are licensed and in good standing. If you have a particular adoption agency in mind, confirm its license status, complaint history, and compliance history. The state licensing specialist[5] should have all licensing information.

2. The Internet can be a rich source of information in exploring options, but it is wise to use caution and validate resources. It can be full of misinformation and even corruption.

3. Contact your community's Better Business Bureau or other consumer complaint agency to determine if the adoption agency has a complaint history in regard to its general business practices. Ask for a copy of the adoption agency's most recent annual report and most recent independent audited financial statements.

4. Read adoption literature, both about adoption generally and about any adoption agencies you are considering. The Internet and public

libraries are good sources. Speak with friends or others who have used adoption agency services. Ask the adoption agency if it can put you in contact with any current or former clients to ask about their experience.

5. Require the adoption agency to provide you a written agreement that includes all fees and costs in an itemized fashion. The agreement should also specify the services the adoption agency will provide. At a minimum, the adoption agency should confirm in writing whether its services will include adoptive parent counseling, education, and training; identification of a child needing a permanent home; completion of the homestudy; any necessary coordination with adoption regulatory entities (for example, as part of completing an adoption assistance agreement when adopting a special-needs child); services with respect to the adoption court approval; provision and/or coordination of post-adoption services; and refund policy, particularly should there be an adoption disruption due to a circumstance beyond your control, as is the case when a birthmother decides not to place her child for adoption.

6. Contact your state licensing specialist with any questions about applicable adoption laws and processes, as they may vary from state to state.

7. Find out if the adoption agency is a member in good standing of any national child welfare organizations, such as the National Council For Adoption.

8. Determine whether the adoption agency is accredited by an independent oversight body, such as the Council on Accreditation, keeping in mind that accreditation is not a requirement for adoption agencies to provide services but is an indication that an agency has allowed an external review body to evaluate its service quality.

9. Assess whether the adoption agency professionals have a work style that makes you feel comfortable. Take into consideration how the adoption agency responds to questions about its service history and requests for documentation, including the request for a written fee agreement that itemizes fees and describes all services to be provided.

SUMMARY

As parents prepare for adoption they have several tasks to accomplish and options from which to choose.

1. The homestudy journey includes training, documentation, interviews, and home visits. The process may take from three to six months. Cost for adoption varies according to the type of adoption the family is pursuing.
2. The adoption options include public agency adoption (direct adoption or foster to adopt), private agency adoption, independent or attorney adoption, and intercountry adoption.
3. Openness in placements refers to a continuum of possible degrees of openness between the birthparents and the adoptive family and child. Adoption practice has shifted from a paradigm of totally closed to varying degrees of openness and contact before and after placement.
4. Choosing an adoption agency with which to work requires prospective adoptive parents to be educated about the process so they can investigate and assess whether or not an agency is right for them.

QUESTIONS FOR SMALL GROUPS

1. What questions do you need to have answered regarding the homestudy process? How do you feel about it?
2. What are your thoughts and feelings related to openness in adoption?
3. Do you feel that you have ready access to your agency and are received in a respectful and helpful manner? What questions have been left unanswered for you?
4. What difficulties have you encountered as you have begun to explore your adoption options?
5. What types of children, coming to you through what avenues, do you feel you could best parent? How did you arrive at that decision?
6. What level of openness toward birthparents do you feel would be right for your family?

7. How open will you be in your communication regarding adoption with your child?

8. What messages are you receiving from extended family members and friends about your desire to adopt? How do those messages make you feel?

CHAPTER THREE

NAVIGATING INTERCOUNTRY ADOPTION
Preparing for the Journey

> We adopted our daughter Julia from Ukraine in May 2004. She was six years old at the time. We just celebrated her third "Adoption Day" with a picnic. We have done this every year since we brought her home, and she loves inviting more and more people as her circle of family and friends increases each year. She loves looking at the photos of our trip to Ukraine to bring her home and showing the photos to everyone who comes to the picnic. What a blessing this adoption has been for our family!
>
> — *Corrie Cook, adoptive mother*

Four-year-old Isaac was adopted from Guatemala as an infant. After traveling with his parents to Guatemala to adopt their second son, Samuel, Isaac became convinced that the sole purpose of boarding a plane was to bring home another baby. When he joined his parents and brother on a family vacation to California, he was devastated to learn that there would be no new baby adopted at the end of the trip.

"Isaac is aware that not every kid is adopted," his mother, Annie, explained. "To keep things simple, we refer to adopted children as 'airplane babies,' as opposed to 'belly babies.' Isaac is always far more impressed when he meets other airplane babies."

In the past few decades especially, intercountry adoption has become an increasingly popular choice in adoption, and American families are the most likely to adopt children from other nations and cultures. Their reasons are as diverse as the children they adopt. Some parents choose to pursue intercountry adoption due in part to the tremendous need, considering there are hundreds of thousands of children currently living in foreign orphanages or other forms of institutional care who need loving families of their own. Some families choose intercountry adoption because they may perceive it to be easier, faster, or legally safer than domestic infant or foster care adoption, particularly given the impression they may have (which may be inaccurate) regarding the risk of birthparents later challenging the adoption or intruding on the family. Others may feel themselves drawn to a particular country or culture, and so they wish to adopt a child from that country and blend that culture with their own family heritage.

While the majority of people who adopt from another country view their experiences and outcomes in a positive light, some families and their internationally adopted children have faced considerable challenges. Parents who plan to adopt children from other countries must understand that they are making a permanent, legal, and moral commitment to become a child's permanent family. Any potential concerns about their ability to unconditionally love and accept the child and to meet any struggles, whether expected or unexpected, must be addressed prior to completing the adoption and returning home with the child.

Whatever the reasons for wanting to adopt internationally, it is essential for parents to educate themselves about the benefits, risks, and potential complications associated with intercountry adoption.

UNDERSTANDING INTERNATIONAL LEGISLATION

According to the U.S. Department of State, the Hague Convention on Intercountry Adoption, which entered into force for the U.S. in 2008, establishes "internationally agreed-upon rules and procedures for adoptions between countries that have a treaty relationship under the Convention."

The Convention was established to help protect children from exploitation or child trafficking, while enabling intercountry adoptions. Under the Convention, a central authority in each Hague-compliant country provides one authoritative source of information for prospective adoptive parents throughout the intercountry adoption process. All American adoption agencies that coordinate intercountry adoptions between the United States and a fellow Hague Convention nation must be accredited and approved.

The Hague Convention and America's implementing legislation, the Intercountry Adoption Act of 2000, outline precise requirements for accredited intercountry adoption agencies, as well as investigations into any adoption agency suspected of fraudulent activity. Hague agency standards and regulations provide an additional level of security and protection for adopted children, as well as for families wishing to adopt internationally.[1] While U.S. adoptions from non-Hague countries will still be permitted, adoption professionals expect that over time, the Convention will help to streamline and regulate more effectively the intercountry adoption process, even in countries that are not Hague-compliant.

To date, the majority of children adopted by American parents have come from China, Guatemala, Russia, and South Korea. These four sending countries have been consistently ranked among the top nations from which Americans choose to adopt. Other countries that have been in the top sending countries in recent years include Vietnam, Ethiopia, Kazakhstan, Ukraine, India, and Columbia. Romania was once a substantial country of origin but, sadly for the children, is currently shut down for political reasons. To see a breakdown by country, visit the Department of State website at http://travel.state.gov/family/adoption/stats/stats_451.html. To view more specific information about international adoption by country, see http://travel.state.gov/family/adoption/country/country_369.html.

Under the Hague Convention, prospective adoptive parents are required to complete ten hours of preadoption training in order to prepare themselves for the intercountry adoption process. The adoption agency a family chooses will work with them to make sure they complete the appropriate training. The National Council For Adoption offers a flexible Web-based training curriculum for adoptive parents, which satisfies eight out of the ten required hours. For more information, call 1-866-21-ADOPT or visit www.hagueadoption.com.

PROCEDURES AND DOCUMENTATION

The successful completion of an intercountry adoption relies on submitting proper documentation and following established procedures. Prospective adoptive parents must work closely with their agency, following each step outlined to complete their adoption. Documented proof of the child's identity and his or her legal status as an orphan, as well as proof of the parents' identity and their moral, financial, and physical ability to raise a child, is required by numerous authorities both in the United States and abroad.

Here are the steps that parents can expect in the intercountry adoption process:

1. Applying to an intercountry adoption agency
2. Submitting forms to the agency as well as Citizenship and Immigration Services (CIS) in the Department of Homeland Security
3. Receiving criminal and child abuse clearance from their state
4. Receiving homestudy approval
5. Obtaining clearance from CIS
6. Collecting and authenticating forms and information for the dossier
7. Receiving a referral for a child; accepting placement; choosing a child in-country if there is no referral prior to travel
8. Obtaining documents for finalization and the child's visa
9. Finalizing adoption
10. Receiving post-placement visits and providing information for post-placement reports

When a family adopts through a U.S.-based intercountry adoption agency and a Hague Convention country, basic information about the child must be made available before the referral and adoption can take place. Child welfare officials in the sending country will attempt to gather documentation regarding the child's identity and social and medical background, as well as the reason for the child's institutionalization. The basic information contained in the child's record may include his or her birth certificate, social and medical history, and information about the termination of parental rights.

Parents must understand that receiving a child's referral information does not give them a legal right to the child. Legal custody of the child still belongs with child welfare authorities abroad. Referrals do occasionally unravel during the early stages of the adoption, although this is very rare. For example, individuals in the child's homeland may decide to adopt the child, or the adoptive parents may decide that the child is not right for their family. In these cases, the adoption agency can help parents identify another child available for adoption.

Wherever adoptive parents live and wherever they travel to adopt, they will find that several sending and receiving countries have developed regulations for the accreditation of adoption agencies. These agencies work in compliance with the country's laws and assist state welfare workers in finding permanent homes for children. The agencies employ individuals to act as liaisons between welfare workers, orphanage directors, courts, clerks, local guides and drivers, and prospective adoptive parents. While the Hague Convention requires an adoption agency to provide adequate management of their in-country staff, and agencies work hard to encourage collaborative working relationships within each country, it is important to note that they have limited or no legal authority over child referrals, court decisions, laws, delays, or the procedures of the particular country.

Some parents make it a goal to adopt from another country, and they choose an adoption agency based on its availability of intercountry adoption programs. Other couples find an agency they feel comfortable working with and choose from among its offered programs. Whether you choose the country or the agency first, make sure that you and your family feel at ease with your agency professionals. The intercountry adoption process can be long and complex, and it is important for you to trust in the counsel and advice of your agency before, during, and after the adoption.

SPECIAL CHALLENGES WITH INTERCOUNTRY ADOPTION

Although major glitches in the adoption process do not often occur, some problems or delays in processing paperwork are inevitable, and prospective adoptive parents must remain as patient and flexible as possible.

The following are some possible delays prospective parents must be prepared for:

1. Records relating to the child's history may be incomplete, misplaced, or lost, and this is information that must be collected before an adoption can be approved.
2. A search for the relatives of an abandoned child, if their consent or more information is needed, may cause further delays.
3. The sending country may lose a document, require a duplicate copy or additional document, or change the process midstream.
4. From time to time, a sending nation may impose a temporary (or sometimes permanent) moratorium on adoptions. If the delay is significant enough, homestudies or other paperwork may need to be redone or updated and then resubmitted.

Agencies are required to comply with the requests made by a sending country, and the cooperation of prospective adoptive parents is essential in order to keep the adoption process moving forward. Only in the most rare or extreme cases will delays be significant enough to require prospective adoptive families to abandon their plans to adopt a specific child from a particular country.

Parents adopting abroad must also understand that children living in orphanages are at risk for many medical, developmental, and emotional difficulties that must be screened for and treated upon adoption. Adoptive parents should have their child evaluated by an international adoption specialist in order to best identify these problems and deal with them as quickly as possible. Problems can be minimized by timely diagnosis and treatment.

The following are some potential health risks among children adopted internationally:

1. Developmental delays (speech, motor skills, and so forth)
2. Malnutrition
3. Premature birth/low birth weight/small head size
4. Infectious diseases
5. Problems resulting from maternal substance abuse
6. Autism
7. Health issues related to environmental toxins
8. Attention deficit hyperactivity disorder (ADHD)
9. Issues resulting from abuse/neglect
10. Trouble with parental or family bonding

Although the majority of institutionalized children over six months of age are somewhat delayed in age/stage development skills, most adopted children catch up over time. In a few cases, however, children may not improve or their problems may worsen. While the orphanage, adoption agency, or foster home will most likely make available some information about the child's health status, this information may very well overestimate or underestimate certain health problems.

Parents should have their adopted child examined by a pediatrician as soon as possible after returning to the United States, preferably by a doctor with knowledge of health risks and diseases common among foreign-born children. Never be afraid to ask questions or request follow-up testing. If a child's delays seem more pronounced or the parents sense something is wrong, these concerns should be addressed with a physician immediately.

Despite every precaution taken to ensure that parents adopt a child with the most optimistic prognosis, it is not possible to reduce all risks, and families considering adopting a child from another country must accept this reality. After the intercountry adoption is finalized, the child is the new parents' legal and moral responsibility. Parents must understand that they are making a permanent and unconditional commitment to nurture, love, and be responsible for a child, regardless of that child's health or special needs.

"The best decision you can hope to make is one that is well-reasoned, based on the information that is available, accompanied by a 'leap of faith' that is a mandatory part of all conscious decisions to parent," noted Dr. Dana Johnson, international pediatric specialist and founder and director of the International Adoption Clinic at the University of Minnesota. "If you cannot knowledgeably assume this risk, international adoption—particularly of an institutionalized child—may not be for you."[2]

ADOPTION FRAUD

The Hague Convention on Intercountry Adoption is designed to promote transparency in the intercountry adoption process, protecting both adoptive parents and children. But not all countries with intercountry adoption programs will choose to adopt the Hague Convention. Various nations have different parental guidelines and requirements. In many places, there is still a serious lack of oversight and regulation in the adoption process.

Some families wishing to adopt internationally simply expect a certain level of corruption; perhaps they even expect to be asked for large sums of money that may not be part of the standard adoption fee. It is important for prospective parents to *question* apparent corruption and not feel pressured to merely accept it as the status quo. Adoptive families should endeavor not to cooperate with or perpetuate any pattern of fraud or abuse in any intercountry adoption program. This may be more difficult in some countries than others, but the Hague Convention represents a serious and important attempt on the part of many nations to regulate the intercountry adoption process and prevent fraud, and such efforts deserve our respect and cooperation. There will always be risks involved in attempting intercountry adoption. But the more transparent the intercountry adoption process, the better for children and families.

Here are some ways prospective parents can help to ensure that they do not become victims of adoption fraud, bribery, or corruption:

1. Do your homework. Read as much as possible, consult with adoption agency staff and those families who have adopted internationally, and do your best to fully understand the process.
2. Become an expert on the country and culture from which you want to adopt.
3. Check the credentials of all the people you talk and work with rather than simply accepting them and all they say at face value. No wishful thinking!
4. While a certain degree of flexibility is necessary in order to pursue intercountry adoption, prospective parents must do all they can not to be taken by surprise.
5. Read and follow every formal procedure to the letter. Follow through on all agreements made. Foreign governments expect adoption agencies and adoptive parents to honor the agreements made prior to and during the adoption, and if these requirements are later ignored, it perpetuates abuses within the intercountry adoption system and can lead to adoption delays and shutdowns, preventing other children from finding families of their own.

WHAT TO EXPECT WHEN TRAVELING TO ANOTHER COUNTRY TO ADOPT A CHILD

"We felt like we were pretty prepared when we adopted Julia," said Corrie Cook. She and her husband, Darren, adopted their daughter from Ukraine.

We educated ourselves by reading books and by being involved in various adoption forums online before we left. We had taken a community college course in Russian before we left, and that was very helpful. We got many compliments on our attempts to speak a few words in Russian and to pronounce them well. The adoption judge even told us that we didn't sound like Americans (that was a compliment!). We even took the time to research what clothing styles would be like in Ukraine and planned our wardrobe accordingly. We found a link online to a webcam in Kiev to watch people walk by in real time and note what they were wearing.

Like Darren and Corrie, prospective adoptive parents should do all they can to prepare for international travel. Here are some suggestions:

1. Take a language class before traveling to the child's country.
2. Buy a pocket dictionary and guidebook. Learning to read and speak a few key words and phrases will make communication possible during those times when an interpreter is not available.
3. Consult with the adoption agency and read the information pages at the U.S. Department of State website to prepare for any potential problems or delays.
4. Learn as much as possible about travel security, passports, visas, customs, and any required medical checkups or immunizations. (Several months prior to travel, vaccinations may be needed.) International adoption health clinics may prove especially helpful because the physicians there are experts in intercountry adoption and are aware of potential health risks associated with a particular country. These clinics are available in many major cities; to find one, ask your adoption agency, look online, or check your local phone directory.

When prospective parents arrive in the sending country, whether the purpose of the trip is to formally adopt or just visit the child or receive a referral, they should request a consultation with the foster parents or orphanage and arrange for a translator to interpret the child's medical and social history reports.

"The orphanage was wonderful," Corrie Cook recalled, "and we could tell that they truly cared for all the children there. Through our translator, we were able to ask Julia if she would like us for parents and if she would like to come to America. It melted our hearts when she said, 'Yes! But I have to get my hair clips first.' That was our first clue that she was going to be a fashion queen."

First impressions are extremely important to children. It is important for parents to avoid having preconceived ideas about how the first meeting will go. The first meeting may go very well, or the child may be terrified and cry inconsolably. It may take hours or even days for the child to calm down and trust his or her new parents.

"On the emotional side, it was a roller coaster to be sure," Corrie related.

We didn't realize how quickly our daughter would attach to our translator because she knew the language. On the day our translator said good-bye to us, Julia cried and cried. She would say in Russian that she wanted our translator or that she wanted the orphanage. It was then that the fear set in our own hearts about our ability to parent this child well and to get home in one piece! But, thankfully, we came prepared with some stickers and other toys in a bag that we had not shown her yet. That managed to distract her and we were able to make the trip home pretty easily. But it took time for the wounds to heal. Now, looking back, Julia doesn't believe that she cried like that and wonders what we would have done had she not said she wanted to come to America with us.

Adoptive parents may want to travel with a little bag of age-appropriate toys that are small enough to fit in a purse or backpack but too big to be swallowed. These toys can be a pleasant diversion, a source of comfort, and a bridge to bonding.

Every country has its own procedures that dictate when custody is transferred from the government or orphanage to the adoptive family. In Asian countries, parents are usually given custody right away. This is also true in Latin American nations. At times an effort is made to ease the transition for an older child by having the child spend his or her nights at the orphanage until the day of departure. In Eastern Europe, parents usually are not given custody until the adoption is finalized.

A child's departure differs from country to country and sometimes within orphanages or foster homes as well. The child may be too young to understand what is going on and may be uncertain about what is going to happen. Some orphanages throw a party for the child on the day of discharge, especially if the child is old enough to remember caregivers and friends. Parents may wish to ask the orphanage director if their child can keep an item of clothing or a toy from the orphanage as a keepsake.

Further delays may occur in-country as the adoption is being finalized. Prior to assisting with the United States orphan visa, the attorney or agency representative must obtain the child's passport and meet other immigration requirements particular to that country. The documentation requirements of

American consulates abroad vary among countries. However, nearly all require identifying documents for the adoptive parents and child, as well as adoption and immigration documents. Photos and a medical evaluation of the child are usually required in order to obtain the orphan visa, and this process generally takes one to three days. The orphan visa will not be issued until all the consulate's requirements are met and requested documents are received.

WHAT TO EXPECT ONCE A CHILD IS HOME

Many countries require that parents register the child with the country's embassy. Adoptive parents will need to examine their child's passport stamp to determine the type of visa that was issued. The type of visa issued determines when the child qualifies for U.S. citizenship. Registration of the adoption or readoption is the only way to officially rename a child, if this is desired. After registration or readoption, the child will be issued a new birth certificate, citing the birthplace but listing the adoptive couple as the parents. Your adoption agency should know lawyers with international adoption experience who can assist in this process.

In most cases, children adopted in other countries become automatic U.S. citizens at the time of the adoption, but other documentation may be required. Some countries require that adopted children keep their original nationality until age 18; the United States recognizes dual citizenship in all of these cases. Proof of U.S. citizenship is needed for a foreign-born child's participation in various state and federal programs, school enrollment, Social Security, and traveling abroad. Parents will need to provide a document such as a U.S. passport or a U.S. certificate of citizenship for the child.

Adoptive parents should not hesitate to rely on the expertise of their adoption agency and their international adoption specialist. Adoption agencies have typically built up referral networks of medical and psychological professionals as well as organizations that provide support services to families and children. These agencies can be an invaluable resource of information and help to adoptive families. Couples should also be sure to address any medical concerns, lifestyle struggles, or difficulties they or their child may be experiencing.

Understanding what their child's life, customs, and culture were like prior to the adoption may help adoptive parents understand the child's behavior and equip them to assist him or her in adjusting to a new way of life. Depending on the country of birth, the child may look very different from his or her parents and others in the community, and adoptive parents must be sensitive to the impact this can have on a child. Helping the child recognize his or her intrinsic worth and embrace these differences is a very important step in maintaining a healthy identity and self-esteem. (See the next chapter on transcultural adoption for more information about understanding and exploring a child's cultural heritage.)

Although the child will become a United States citizen and adopt the traditions of the adoptive family, many intercountry adoption experts recommend that parents work to ensure that their child remains connected to his or her birth culture and heritage. While the degree to which children may want to engage in cultural discovery varies individually, many children adopted from other countries are very interested in their culture of origin and should be given ample opportunity and encouragement to explore it. Here are some ways families might explore the child's cultural heritage together:

1. Preparing ethnic meals
2. Listening to native music and playing games from that culture
3. Celebrating traditional holidays
4. Developing and maintaining relationships with people who are part of or familiar with the child's culture
5. Reading books and watching movies centered on the child's culture
6. Visiting the child's birth country as a family

The adoption agency should also be able to help connect adoptive families to other children, families, and organizations familiar with intercountry and transcultural adoption.

SUMMARY

The decision to pursue an intercountry adoption can be reached only after significant care and planning on behalf of prospective parents. Families wishing to adopt internationally must be prepared for not only the cost, travel, and requirements involved but also the unique risks and rewards of intercountry adoption. While not all intercountry adoptions are transracial, all are transcultural, and parents must consider whether they are fully committed to parenting a child of another culture and helping the child to feel some connection to his or her country of birth while he or she grows and thrives within the new family.

QUESTIONS FOR SMALL GROUPS

1. What are your reasons for wanting to pursue an intercountry adoption?
2. How much do you know about the country or culture from which you are hoping to adopt a child?
3. Why do you feel drawn to that particular country?
4. List some ways that your family can explore and learn about the adopted child's country of origin before his or her arrival.
5. Do you know other parents who have walked through an intercountry adoption? How can they be of support and guidance to you?
6. How can you best prepare for the delays or challenges that may arise during the intercountry adoption process?

CHAPTER FOUR

TRANSCULTURAL ADOPTION
Blending Different Worlds

Transracial adoption: Adopting a child of another race
Intercountry adoption: Adopting a child from
one country by a family of another
Transcultural adoption: Adopting across national, ethnic,
and/or racial lines.

"I used to feel, shortly after we brought our first son home from Guatemala, that our little family stuck out in public," said Annie, an adoptive mother. She and her husband, Michael, are both Caucasian and have two adopted sons from Guatemala.

"I used to feel that everyone was staring at us," Annie continued. "But now, three and a half years and another transracial adoption later, it simply doesn't occur to me that our family looks different. I do seem to notice more and more transcultural families, parents who have children who were clearly adopted, and I think they notice us too. We enjoy giving each other that meaningful smile and nod of approval as we pass in the mall, the grocery store, at the park. Adoption is an instant common bond and conversation starter, and I've had the pleasure of meeting wonderful parents and families in the most random places."

Today, many families are like Michael and Annie's, multicultural or multiracial by adoption. Increasing numbers of parents are making the decision to adopt across cultural or ethnic lines, in our own country and abroad. Why are transracial and transcultural adoptions becoming more and more common? What is behind this growing phenomenon?

There are a number of contributing factors, and the great diversity within American society may be the most significant factor. Many families are no longer of a single race or culture. People are far more likely to date and marry across ethnic and racial lines and to have children who possess a blended heritage. Additionally, in recent decades intercountry adoption has become easier and far more widespread, and adoption agencies with well-run international adoption programs offer hope to prospective parents who want to have a child within a given time frame.

Adopting a child of another race or culture, here in America or from another country, is now a highly visible phenomenon. As prospective adoptive parents witness more and more families opting for transracial and transcultural adoption, they are able, in increasing numbers, to consider it as a means of expanding their own families.

Many adoptive parents feel that in addition to providing a family for a child in need, they are giving a powerful witness by adopting a child of another race and culture. Transcultural adoption helps parents, family, and friends of the adopted child to learn about that child's culture or country of origin and may also encourage an appreciation for transcultural adoption and diversity within the community.

One adoptive couple, Caucasian parents who adopted a Korean baby, wondered how their families would react. "No one in our family had adopted before — most of them had probably never even thought about it," the mother explained. "I was a little worried about my own mother, who like many older people has a few leftover racial prejudices that were part of her own upbringing. But from the moment I put her new granddaughter in her arms, my mother thought that she was 'perfect, just perfect.' She made such a fuss over her and said she was beautiful. And from that day on, I never heard a single negative word from anyone in our family about adopting an Asian baby."

Another adoptive mother said, "My kids are Latino and clearly look different from my husband and me. Sometimes strangers I meet in public get that look in their eye, like they want to ask questions about it but don't want to appear rude. I have no problem talking with anyone about adoption, so sometimes I will casually mention something about our adoption experience and then take the time to educate people I meet about adoption. When your children don't look like you, people will notice, and it can open the door to helping them understand and appreciate the gift of adoption."

Whether a parent adopts a child of another race or culture through domestic infant adoption, adoption from foster care, or intercountry adoption, there are questions and challenges unique to welcoming that child into the family and raising him or her as a minority in the United States. These issues require careful consideration by prospective parents.

HOW DO TRANSRACIALLY ADOPTED CHILDREN FARE?

Many studies mentioned elsewhere in this book clearly illustrate the positive outcomes experienced by adopted children, who tend to fare as well as their nonadopted counterparts, particularly if adopted at a younger age. Children adopted transracially share the same positive outcomes.

While there has been and will continue to be much discussion about the merit and meaning of transracial adoption, particularly as it becomes more and more common, studies of children adopted by parents of another race have not revealed any significant differences in terms of adjustment or development when compared to the patterns and outcomes of children adopted by parents of the same race. This has led many such studies to conclude that transracial adoption does not harm the adjustment, family bonding, or normative development of children.[1] In the study "Growing Up Adopted," a massive Search Institute survey of 715 adoptive families that included 881 adopted adolescents, children adopted transracially fared as well as adopted Caucasian children in same-race families. The study authors went on to note, "Transracially adopted youth are no more at-risk in terms of identity, attachment, and mental health than are their counterparts in same-race families."[2]

While some child welfare professionals and cultural organizations still maintain that in-racial adoption is always preferable to transracial or transcultural adoption and that it may be more difficult for Caucasian parents to help a child of another race grow up with genuine appreciation for and attachment to his or her cultural identity, numerous studies have shown that adoption is clearly in the best interests of children in need of families. Children who are adopted into a permanent family, including those adopted across racial lines, fare better and experience far more positive outcomes than children who remain in foster, state, or institutionalized care. Many transracially adopted individuals report feeling a deep connection and trust within their adoptive families, as well as a strong appreciation for their own ethnicity and culture.[3] Like their Caucasian and American-born counterparts, children of varying races enjoy all the benefits and rewards of belonging to a family through adoption.

HOW CAN PARENTS PREPARE TO ADOPT TRANSRACIALLY OR TRANSCULTURALLY?

First, examine your motivation for wishing to adopt across racial or cultural lines. Is it something you are sure about? Are you doing it simply because it is more difficult to find "a child who looks like you" and you will see your child as second best? Are you doing it to make some kind of statement or to prove some personally held belief about love and family — for instance, that love is color-blind, that race doesn't matter, or that culturally blended families can in some way alleviate racial misunderstandings between people or cultures?

While compassion is a valuable motivation for parents wishing to adopt transculturally, whether internationally, domestically, or from foster care, the best and most important reason to adopt is to love a child and give that child a family forever. Adoption should always be focused on the child. An adoption is successful when parents enter into a loving, nurturing, and honest relationship with their child.

In addition to examining their motives to adopt transculturally, parents can prepare by learning as much as possible about their child and the child's culture before the adoption is finalized. Parents should also consider how their families, friends, neighbors, coworkers, and others may react to a child of another race or culture joining their family.

Here are some important questions to consider if you are thinking of adopting across racial or cultural lines:

1. How do you expect your family members will react to a child of another race?
2. Will children of another race or culture be easily accepted in your community and among your peers?
3. Can you find opportunities for your child to be with other children and families who share his or her culture?
4. What will it be like when the child goes to school? Are the schools in your area filled with children from a variety of cultures and backgrounds?
5. What are your neighborhood, church, and social circle like? Will your child be the only ethnic minority in the room at various events?

The decision to adopt transculturally need not be made on the basis of reactions from others. But it is important for parents to consider and be aware of what their family may experience following a transracial or transcultural adoption. Putting yourself in your future child's shoes and recognizing that there may be specific challenges within your family, social network, or community are both important steps when you are considering an adoption across racial or cultural lines.

WHAT ARE SOME OF THE SPECIFIC CHALLENGES UNIQUE TO TRANSCULTURAL ADOPTION?

Not all transcultural adoptions are also transracial, of course. For those that are, it will be obvious that the child is adopted because he or she will look different from the parents. Questions may be asked about the child's adoption that might not be asked in a same-race adoption since people will notice immediately that the child is not genetically related to his or her parents.

The authors of the Search Institute study found that most adopted adolescents were quite comfortable with their adoption, regardless of race: 84 percent of youth adopted transracially and 81 percent adopted by parents of the same race agreed with the statement, "I am glad my parents adopted me," and transracially adopted children were no more likely than their same-race adopted peers to claim that "adoption is a big part of how I think about myself." The vast majority of the youth surveyed maintained that "adoption has always been easy for me," independent of racial factors.[4]

But as the Search Institute survey and many others studying transracial adoption have pointed out, children adopted across racial lines must contend not just with adoption but with being people of color and minority members of American society.

"I looked different from my parents, so I got questions about adoption from a much younger age than I might have if I were Caucasian," explained Nicole Ficere Callahan, who was born to Korean birthparents and adopted as an infant in Seattle before moving to a small town in southern Oregon. "The questions people asked ranged from 'Where did they get you?' to 'Do you remember your birthparents?' I was adopted from the hospital when I was two months old; of course I didn't remember my birthparents. I realized at a very young age that there is a lot of curiosity about adoption, as well as a lot of ignorance."

For some minority children, the entrance into elementary school throws them into a world that may not be as friendly or warm as the safe, happy home environment they have enjoyed. In some areas of the country, racial prejudice still lingers, and this can filter down into the school-age population, particularly among younger children who may not yet have learned how to deal with differences honestly and sensitively.

"I never felt terribly out of place in my adoptive family because I was Korean," Nicole said. "But growing up Korean in a town with a very low Asian population was a whole different matter. That was very difficult at times, particularly when I was younger. My parochial elementary school was quite small, and I was one of maybe two or three Asian students in the entire school."

Although encounters with genuine racism were few during her childhood, Nicole remembers being teased on the playground when she was eleven or twelve years old. "A boy I knew used his fingers to pull his eyes into slits, and then he made fun of me in this high-pitched, fake Asian accent," she recalled. "I was incredibly hurt and angry, but I didn't know what to do. I had never really encountered that kind of teasing before and wasn't sure how to respond."

Helping a child develop coping strategies for racial or cultural insults is a critical task for parents. Most parents readily feel their child's emotional pain when injuring remarks are made, but their parental instinct may be to minimize the problem in an attempt to defuse the situation. This approach does not deal adequately with the child's painful experience.

Following are some important points to remember when talking with a child who has encountered racial or cultural prejudice among his or her peers:

1. *Don't overreact or rush out to confront the offender.* You cannot act without the facts, and if you are busy leaping to your child's immediate defense or fighting his battles for him, then you are not listening to his story or sharing in his pain.

2. *Ask the child to explain to you exactly what happened without leaving anything out.* While an insult may have been clearly intended, it may also have been accidental. Either way, the child's feelings are legitimate, but it's important for her to be able to tell you the entire story so you know exactly what happened and she knows you are there to listen.

3. *Encourage the child to tell you how he felt.* Ask him to use descriptive terms and be specific: "I felt angry; I felt scared; I felt sad; I felt embarrassed; I felt lonely."

4. *Ask what the child said in reply.* She may not have responded, but if she did and the situation was handled well, you can praise her for her maturity and quick thinking.

5. *Ask the child to consider how he might handle it differently in the future.* Your child may have doubts about how he handled the situation. Explain to him that he does have choices in how he fields questions or rude remarks about his race, culture, or adoption. If he has trouble coming up with possible options for future encounters, help him identify some alternatives.

Parents should also ask their child whether or not he or she wants you to do anything about the situation. While most children will not want direct parental involvement, it will help them know that the possibility exists and that their parents are on their side.

Children also need to know that parents are on their side if insensitive or insulting comments come not from other children but from adults, even adults within their own extended families. While some family members may possess certain reservations about transcultural adoption and its real and perceived challenges, often this uneasiness or fear melts away as soon as the adopted child is introduced to the family. However, in some cases extended family members or close friends may never come to fully understand or accept the adoption.

A former agency director recalled one Caucasian family who adopted a biracial child. Prior to the adoption, the parents had consulted with family members, who gave their blessing, and even moved to a more diverse neighborhood and joined a racially integrated church. For the first several years after the adoption, they encountered very few negative comments, until one day when their son got into a toddler scuffle with his cousin at a family reunion. The adopted child's uncle became extremely upset with his nephew and made a racial slur about the boy. The adoptive mother, of course, leapt to her son's defense. Over a year later, the mother still had not seen or spoken to her brother because she and her husband were both deeply concerned about the wounding effect future insensitive or prejudiced remarks could have on their son. The adoptive family was shocked that an uncle who had formerly seemed supportive and accepting of his nephew in fact harbored serious racial prejudice, but they had to put their son's needs ahead of family harmony.

In most cases, transracially adopted children will encounter simple curiosity about their adoption as opposed to outright prejudice or racism. They are likely to hear probing questions at a young age because in transracial and transcultural adoption, the physical differences between child and parent will be obvious to others. Many people will ask questions because they are supportive of adoption and want to show that they care; the majority will ask simply because they are curious.

Some children may be perfectly comfortable with the extra questioning and attention they receive as adopted children, but others may become upset, angry, or embarrassed, particularly if they are made to feel different. No matter how a child reacts to such comments or questions, it is up to the parents to be aware of how the child feels and respond to questions in such a way that will help both curious outsiders and the child to better understand what adoption is.

Parents can give their children ways to cope with invading questions by discussing what can or should be shared with strangers. Children are not obligated to tell anyone their life story; they have personal boundaries that others must learn to respect. But they can identify, with their parents' help, which facts they feel comfortable sharing with others and can have a confident and assertive reply ready when questions are posed. To help develop your child's answers, the following suggestions may be helpful:

1. *Determine the possible questions that may be asked in situations the child will encounter.* For example, imagine your child's introduction to neighborhood children, questions her teacher or classmates may ask on the first day of school, or what could happen if your family joined a new church or community organization.

2. *Establish what information should be shared.* Children often have difficulty determining what information can be shared and what should be kept private. To help your child resolve this dilemma, ask him to think of basic and polite responses to common questions, such as his name, his country or culture of origin, and the circumstances of his adoption.

3. *Make sure the child knows how to respond to questions that make her uncomfortable.* If a person is probing into some matter your child is uncomfortable addressing, whether it is a question about race, culture, adoption, or your family, the child should understand that she does not have to answer. She can ask questions of her own, or she can simply state, "That's our family's business" or "You'll have to ask my parents" or "We only talk about it at home."

Parents cannot shield their minority children from possible racial prejudice or the curious prying of others. They may consider joining a school system, church, or neighborhood community that is diverse, but this may not prevent possible uncomfortable or wounding situations.

Parents should always make it clear that they are on the child's side. As children are given the opportunity to express offenses, deal with their corresponding feelings, and recognize the choices they have for responding appropriately, they will develop a clearer understanding of how to handle insensitive people or comments.

HOW CAN PARENTS HELP PREPARE THEIR TRANSCULTURALLY ADOPTED CHILDREN TO EXPLORE THEIR IDENTITIES?

Families of transracially or transculturally adopted children can help to equip those children with a healthy sense of belonging, personal and racial identity, and cultural connections. If children understand and feel secure in their own family history and cultural identity, they will be more comfortable answering questions posed by others about their adoption or background.

One adoptive mother shared this story: "Last year, my then-three-year-old son was playing quietly behind the couch where my father-in-law was sitting, unaware of his presence. Isaac snuck up on his grandfather, who was surprised by his stealth and exclaimed, 'Isaac, where'd you come from?' Isaac happily and proudly answered, 'I come from Guatemala!'"

It is important for adoptive parents to nurture a family environment that recognizes, accepts, and celebrates differences in race, heritage, and culture. Children such as Isaac who know their background, including where they came from and how and when they joined their families, are more likely to grow in their understanding of and appreciation for adoption than children whose families do not speak openly about adoption or cultural differences.

In a 2006 research article on the cultural socialization of internationally adopted children, researchers pointed out that many adoptive parents were once instructed to approach transracial adoption as "color-blind." Some of these parents then taught their children that race or culture do not matter. But in recent years, there has been a growing focus in transracial adoption on the cultural and ethnic differences between adopted children and their parents, and many adoption professionals now stress to adoptive families that it is important to both embrace and incorporate these differences into the adopted child's identity and sense of self. Many adoptive families have found that this approach works well and gives their children the benefit of strong cultural appreciation and identification.[5]

Children are always curious about their own individual stories, their lives, and their families, and transculturally adopted children are no different. Parents can share with the child their thoughts and feelings as they prepared for his adoption and brought him home. If parents traveled to another country to adopt him, they can share what they remember of their time there and their thoughts and impressions as they experienced and learned about another culture and society.

An adopted child of another race or nationality can benefit from maintaining some ties to her cultural heritage. Parents are encouraged to do their best to learn about their child's cultural heritage and introduce her to it from a young age. If she wants more information as she grows, then you can research it together. Parents can attend cultural education classes with their child, learn how to speak the child's native language, and celebrate the child's heritage by learning about the history, art, literature, music, food, and traditions of her country or culture of origin. Age-appropriate opportunities for cultural exploration should be taken together as a family, but this should never be presented as more important than the child's place in your family.

In addition to cultural exploration, it can also be very helpful for adoptive parents and adopted children to find and access an understanding, supportive transcultural adoption community. Many parents of transculturally adopted children have found support, friendship, and helpful advice from individuals from the child's country or culture of origin, as well as from social networks or communities centered around that heritage. Support groups of families affected by transcultural adoption are often formed among adoptive parents through adoption agencies, churches, schools, or other community organizations. "There are challenges and joys associated with raising a child of another race or culture that only families who are experiencing the same thing could understand," an adoptive father claimed.

One adoptive mother of two African American children expressed gratitude for the support she has found in other parents of transracially adopted children: "Our children see other children who not only look like them but have Caucasian parents just like they do, and they feel proud of their culture and proud of being adopted," she reported. "And it's important for me to be able to talk to the other mothers as well. We get together every so often, offer support and suggestions, and ask questions of the rest of the group. We can be honest about our struggles and learn from each other's experiences."

The support of friends who understand transcultural adoption is especially important in helping adopted children accept or celebrate their differences. "Our daughter was never that interested in her culture when she was small. Then when she was about nine years old, she decided she was tired of looking different from all her friends, and all she wanted was blonde hair and blue eyes," recalled an adoptive mother of three children, a girl and two boys from China. "For years, our family had been in contact with several other adoptive parents and adopted kids from China. My husband and I talked with some of the other parents, and they gave us so many helpful suggestions. We had always told our daughter she was beautiful, but we began to show her how her specifically Asian features were especially beautiful to us. We showed her pictures and movies featuring Chinese celebrities. We also got her involved in more play dates with adopted Chinese kids and celebrated the Chinese New Year together. She began to understand and appreciate her heritage, and she also realized that even though she didn't know many Chinese children at school, she was not alone—here were all these other kids who were adopted from China, just like her. Within a couple of years she was expressing great pride in being Chinese and a sincere appreciation for her heritage."

It must be noted that there is a sharp difference between recognizing and celebrating the differences between child and parents and focusing on these differences too closely. Children may begin to feel isolated or alienated if racial and cultural differences are constantly stressed at the expense of their belonging to the family. Parents should realize that while some children will be very interested in learning more about their heritage from an early age, others may not have any interest at all.

For example, it could be that a ten-year-old girl adopted from Guatemala has little interest in doing a school project on Guatemala, taking Spanish language classes, or learning about Latin American art or history. Try to take whatever cues the child gives you and respect her wishes; when she is twelve or fifteen, she may feel differently. It's important to help her foster a connection with her heritage and encourage her if she shows real interest, but she shouldn't be pressured if she isn't ready or truly engaged.

Any loving, healthy parent-child relationship requires sensitivity, awareness, and communication. In this sense, a child adopted from another race or culture is no different from any other child. He wants to know that he is loved. He wants to know with whom and where he belongs. No two children are alike, and every child will understand, learn about, and come to terms with his adoption and cultural identity in his own way, with the help of his parents. Just do your best to listen to your child, know how he is feeling, be aware of his responses and reactions even when he may not be, and above all constantly show him that he can always feel safe and secure with the family who loves him.

SUMMARY

Transracial and transcultural adoptions can be beautiful things, providing loving permanent families for children who need them and promoting greater tolerance and acceptance in American society. It has already contributed to the great increase in transcultural families. Transcultural adoption can help ease the interaction among races as well as between America and other nations.

Families who choose to adopt a child across racial or cultural lines are making the decision to become a transcultural family forever. Parents can prepare for this step by evaluating their motivation for adopting and assessing their readiness for the unique challenges and rewards it will present. With the great increase in transracial and transcultural families, parents may also be able to seek out and gather information and advice from individuals and communities in order to prepare for their transcultural adoption and help children of another race or culture explore and appreciate their heritage.

Transcultural and transracial adoption may seem especially intriguing, particularly to those experiencing it for the first time. Some transcultural adoption stories are indeed thrilling and exciting, involving long distances traveled and new cultures explored. But an adoptive family of blended cultures is a family because of their love for and commitment to one another, just like any other family.

QUESTIONS FOR SMALL GROUPS

1. Are you most interested in pursuing an intercountry transcultural adoption (see chapter 3 for more information) or a transcultural adoption from foster care? What are your motivations for this choice?

2. How would you describe your own ethnic or cultural background? When did you become aware of your own cultural identity? What does it mean to you?

3. Many transcultural/transracial adoptions involve parents adopting children from American foster care or from foreign orphanages. While most children adopted from state or institutional care do very well, there are special issues and challenges associated with adopting a child who may have been abused or neglected. Are you prepared to meet these challenges if you are considering intercountry adoption or adoption from foster care?

4. Do you think a family who is unwilling or unable to help foster a child's cultural identity should consider an adoption of this type? Why or why not?

5. What kind of statement do you think it makes about adoption and family when parents love and welcome a child who does not look like them?

6. Do you think a parent who may have some doubts about his or her ability to raise a transculturally adopted child can still rise to the challenge? Why or why not?

CHAPTER FIVE

WHAT BUILDS HEALTHY ADOPTIVE FAMILIES?
Six Critical Success Factors

All children who need to be looked after outside their own homes, for whatever reason, are children at risk. . . . The people who adopt them are in a unique position to prevent life crises from becoming pathogenic, to prevent separation experiences from developing into deprivation, to provide the kind of upbringing for each child that will make good his past deficiencies.

— *Sula Wolff,* Children Under Stress

Jon and Cheryl made a wise decision. Before the arrival of their newly adopted toddler twins, they sought the wisdom of experienced adoptive couples. Katherine, a single adoptive mom, did the same before her daughter arrived home from Guatemala. All three adults knew that building an adoptive family was, in most ways, just like parenting birth children. However, they also knew that they would need to gain knowledge and understanding to navigate the unique issues found in the adoption relationship.

At an adoptive parent support-group meeting, Jon and Cheryl asked an important question: What goes into creating a healthy adoptive family? This chapter will explore what they learned that night. By incorporating these six critical factors for success into the parenting process, adoptive families will be well on the way to a positive experience for them and their children. Ignoring these factors can rip away at the beauty and foundation of this unique relationship of promise.

FACTOR ONE: HEALTHY ADOPTIVE PARENTS HAVE EXPLORED THEIR MOTIVATIONS AND EXPECTATIONS FOR ADOPTION IN AN OPEN AND HEALTHY MANNER AND ARE IN AGREEMENT

As a family moves into the process of adoption, understanding the motivation for adoption and expectations for everyone is a vital and healthy step. Motivation was discussed briefly in chapter 1. Research has been done to explore the motivation for pursing adoption—either infant adoption or older child adoption. Many parents have reported in assessment instruments the following:

- I want to make a difference in a child's life.
- I want to give back.
- My children are gone, and I have room in my heart for more.
- I cannot have a child or any more children.
- I want a larger family.
- I want a companion for my biological child.
- I want a child to love me.
- I think a child will help our marriage.[1]

Real motivations? Yes. Will they all lead to success? That depends on how the adoptive family makes adjustments when expectations and reality do not match.

Another important issue in regard to motivation has to do with the level of agreement between parents as the adoption moves forward. In a two-parent family, it is of utmost importance that the husband and wife are in agreement regarding the adoption. The following descriptions depict the various interactive roles often seen during the homestudy process. Only one of them will lead to a healthy, successful adoption experience for everyone. The three roles are dynamic-dormant, active-antagonistic, and energetic-energetic. Either partner can play either role.

DYNAMIC-DORMANT PARENT ROLES

Kathy waited for Robert to meet her at the adoptive training session. Although quiet by nature, Robert was abnormally uncommunicative about this adoption idea. Usually assertive with him, Kathy didn't want to push this issue. She just wanted to know where he stood. Whenever she asked him, his only response was, "If that's what you want." Kathy knew Robert wasn't against it. But she wondered, *Is he for it?*

Robert and Kathy Cook's dynamic-dormant parent style can be damaging to an adoptive placement. Nationally known adoption specialist Barbara Tremtiere calls this the "dragger and the draggee." The dynamic person in this family wholeheartedly pursues adoption. The dormant one hesitantly follows along, rarely expressing his or her thoughts.

A problem arising in this adoption triad (mom, dad, and child) is that once the child comes, the dormant partner tends to retreat from developing a parenting relationship with the newest family member. When conflicts arise, the dormant partner offers little consolation and marginal support, quietly reminding the dynamic one that the problems belong totally to him or her.

ACTIVE-ANTAGONISTIC PARENT ROLES

Patty nervously twisted a loose string on her jacket. She just wasn't sure how her husband, John, would behave. He wasn't exactly enthusiastic about this whole adoption thing.

As they sat waiting in their car for the training room to open, the atmosphere was silent and tense. Patty, a warm and nurturing mother of two teenagers, missed caring for young children. She had long carried a dream to adopt.

John was an all-business type of father. He let Patty know that he wasn't very interested in doing this "child thing" all over again.

"I hope this doesn't last long," he complained.

"Don't worry," assured Patty. "I promise this will be my responsibility. You won't have to do a thing."

John and Patty Wyman definitely fit the active-antagonistic parent style. Adoptive parents within this disposition follow a basic line of thinking. One is for it; the other is against it. But they try to keep the tension a secret from others outside the family.

From the very beginning, the antagonistic partner generally avoids contact with the agency. Nonessential issues become major. After the child arrives, the resistant partner avoids all situations that would allow him or her to develop a relationship with the child and often finds more excuses to be away from home. As the adoptive placement continues, the active spouse must learn to juggle the relationships of each person in the family in order to keep peace. Often that person becomes the dumping ground for frustrations from all sides and soon grows weary of the role. If this particular scenario describes a family in the preadoptive stage, they will need to defer the process until a mutual decision is made regarding what is best for the family.

ENERGETIC-ENERGETIC PARENT ROLES

Paul and Judy Walker arrived early and waited in the hall outside the training room. Adoption had originally been Paul's idea, but Judy enthusiastically agreed. This energetic-energetic parent style promises a strong foundation for beginning adoptive parenting. Both Paul and Judy are excited about it and have committed themselves to share equally in the parenting tasks.

Building a family through adoption can promote dynamic growth and understanding within the family. This has the best chance of happening in an environment of mutual support, common goals, and equal energy for the task.

ADJUSTING FOR ADOPTIVE PARENT ROLES

When confronted with the assignment of assessing their adoptive parent styles, all three couples learned several concepts that helped them discern their individual roles and make adjustments accordingly.

1. *Explore the motivation for adoption.* Discuss if one partner seems passive or resistant to becoming an adoptive parent. Explore the reasons why. Those reasons may range from fear of the experience to questioning one's abilities to take on the task. It may not be the right time. This evaluation may require that the family reconsider and wait to begin.

2. *Keep in mind that attitudes toward adoption may fluctuate.* Circumstances can affect anyone's outlook on any given day. The long-term perception of the experience is what's crucial to the long-term commitment.

3. *Adjust expectations of each other.* One adoptive mom said, "I expected my husband to plan regular activities with our new son. When he didn't, I became frustrated with him. Expecting him to jump right in when he didn't know

where he stood with Jimmy was unfair."

4. *Keep communication open and honest as the responsibilities increase.* Linda, a struggling first-time adoptive mother of two active toddlers, commented,

> I dreaded getting up in the morning and facing the tasks of the day. The honeymoon period with Katie and Callie had dimmed. I was exhausted and overwhelmed, and I gradually grew resentful of them. But I kept my fatigue, depression, and anxieties hidden. I kept asking myself, *What have we done?* Of course, it wasn't the girls. I had neglected to communicate my own needs. That was the wrong approach. I just didn't want to appear to be a failure.

In the 1995 Spring issue of *Roots and Wings* magazine, June Bond first coined a term that is still applicable for some families today. That term is post-adoption depression syndrome.[2] Similar to six of the seven symptoms of post-partum depression, the causes can be many, ranging from unmet expectations to a sense of loss of control of one's life.[3]

It is important for adoptive parents to know that "these feelings are normal and common. Expert upon expert agrees that stress, depression, ambivalence and anger are emotions they frequently see, and part of the assistance they offer to parents is to help them realize these feelings are normal."[4]

These feelings can occur in healthy adoptive families, as they can occur in healthy biological families, alongside the many joys and satisfactions of parenting. Appropriate motivation and expectations and an agreement between parents are foundational in moving into the adoptive relationship. Another key factor is that adoptive parents demonstrate healthy interpersonal relationships.

FACTOR TWO: HEALTHY ADOPTIVE PARENTS DEMONSTRATE STABILITY AND QUALITY IN THEIR INTERPERSONAL RELATIONSHIPS[5]

Successful adoptive families have demonstrated stability in their relationships within and outside of the family. What do some of those characteristics look like? Healthy family characteristics can be categorized in the following areas:

1. *In a two-parent home, parents model a strong marital relationship.* In a two-parent family, as the marriage goes, so goes the rest of the family. In his

book *How's Your Family?* Dr. Jerry Lewis discussed areas that determine family competence. "Although many things go into the making of a healthy family," he said, "none is more important than the nature of the parents' relationship."[6]

Answers to a number of questions shed light on the health of the marriage: Who carries the power in the relationship? Is it equally shared with mutual respect? What are the levels of communication achieved in the family? Is there a sense of intimacy in the marriage? What is the quality and intensity of the marital alliance? How well do the individual personalities fit together?[7]

2. *Family members demonstrate the ability to resolve conflicts and problems.* Perhaps the most important function of the healthy home is the ability of family members to resolve conflicts. Healthy adoptive families, like all healthy families, have the ability to disagree and to negotiate differences without feeling personally threatened.[8] Individuals within a family develop their own style of conflict resolution. Some will yield to the other simply to avoid conflict. Some withdraw. Others deny there is a problem or dominate the weaker partner.

To the extent that parents rely on the process of negotiation, families confront and resolve problems in a positive way. Children joining an adoptive family at an older age probably have not seen or experienced a healthy approach to solving problems in the home. This type of healthy home environment may be foreign or strange to them.

3. *Family members evidence the ability to deal with feelings.* Adoptive parents who allow each other to express a range of feelings and respond empathically will create an atmosphere in which a child can do likewise. Families who block feelings or deny their existence will block the healing of wounds that are deeply rooted in a child.

4. *Both couples and single parents have a strong support system.* That support system consists of family members and community connections such as church affiliation. They regularly tap into this network for emotional support, guidance, and direct assistance when needed.[9]

FACTOR THREE: HEALTHY ADOPTIVE PARENTS DEMONSTRATE FLEXIBILITY AND OPENNESS IN THE FAMILY SYSTEM

Flexibility within an adoptive family system is another key factor of success. What does openness and flexibility in the adoptive family system look like?

1. *Family members demonstrate the ability to accept and deal with change.* When a new child enters the family, whether as an infant or an older child, the entire family system shifts. New patterns of interaction and everyday living evolve. New relationships form. Stresses unique to this experience arise, and occasionally the adopted child bears the brunt of blame.

A healthy adoptive family understands that this kind of change is temporary; the family shifting will eventually lessen and give way to a new normalcy. The family members persevere through the unsettled environment, all taking responsibility for working through the change.

2. *Family members manage flexible boundaries, allowing people in and out of their lives.* When a family chooses to adopt, by the very nature of the process, people will be coming in and out of the family system. It starts first with the homestudy process. Once a child is identified for the family, other social workers will be involved with the family from the moment of placement to two to three years beyond legalization of the adoption, in some international situations.

3. *Family members value differences.* We often hear biological parents say, "All my children are different." The same is true with adopted children, only in that case there are genetic differences that can manifest themselves on a larger scale. Each child who is adopted arrives with a bushel full of differences from his or her adoptive family. The most obvious, of course, may be physical appearance. As the child grows, differences will emerge in mannerisms, interests, habits, and performance ability.

Successful adoptive families value these differences rather than rejecting them. They highlight the positive distinctions that create the child's individuality. They put in respectful focus the various dissimilarities that set the child apart from his or her adoptive family. And they balance that with the understanding that as one human race, all people are genetically far more similar than dissimilar.

4. *Within the structure of a healthy and open family system, parents readily seek support and resources when help is needed.* A family's success with an emotionally needy child is often determined by their openness to disclose weakness and struggle within their own household.

The adoptive family, especially with an older child who has suffered abuse or neglect prior to adoption, may require a larger framework of assistance than does the family parenting children born into the family. This network of service may include school teachers, social workers, counselors, and therapists. Families who willingly acknowledge that their parenting task requires special assistance and who view that help as inclusive, not intrusive, will create a more healthy adoptive environment.

Jon and Mary, adoptive parents of two children who are developmentally delayed, commented, "When it's the day for the speech therapist or physical therapist to come, we don't say, 'Oh no, those people are coming today.' They're our friends. When no one around us really understands what we are going through, they do. They are our support."

FACTOR FOUR: HEALTHY ADOPTIVE PARENTS KNOW THE IMPORTANCE OF CREATING A FAMILY ENVIRONMENT THAT OPENLY ACKNOWLEDGES AND COMMUNICATES ABOUT ADOPTION

When people think of openness in adoption, they most often think of the relationship between the family and birthfamily, but the openness that matters most is openness in attitude and communication about adoption. According to David Brodzinsky,

> Openness in adoption refers, first and foremost, to a state of mind and heart. . . . It reflects the general attitudes, beliefs, expectations, emotions, and behavioral inclination that people have in relation to adoption. . . . Its emphasis is on the adoption communication process, both informational and emotional, within the individual, between adoptive family members, and, for those involved in a structurally open arrangement, between members of the two family systems.[10]

Openness of heart and mind within the adoption relationship requires a willingness on the part of everyone to do the following:

- Acknowledge and discuss the role of adoption in their lives.
- Accept and trust the adoptive family as the child's true and permanent family.
- Explore, in age-appropriate ways, adoption-related questions that arise as the child grows and understands more about how she joined her family.
- Acknowledge the child's biological connection to his original family and accept and support the child in whatever level of interest he has in

his birthfamily.

- Acknowledge and seek support for any challenges the child may present due to abuse, neglect, or conditioning experienced prior to adoption.

This level of openness is lived out daily in the lives of adoptive parents and their children. What does it look like?

COPING STYLES WITH ADOPTION

Families develop healthy or unhealthy coping styles that will dictate how well they will do with the differences created by an adoption relationship. Examples of two coping styles follow.

Rejection of Adoption

With an impending move out of state, fourteen-year-old Judy was given the task of cleaning out and packing the family attic. On a cold, rainy February afternoon, Judy set about the task with less than minimal enthusiasm. She came across an unfamiliar box filled with all sorts of documents and memorabilia. As Judy related, what she found there set her adrift on a course of uncharted emotions and events.

> Before I taped the box, I decided to just go through it for fun. I found a large envelope that read, "Court papers." My first thought was that one of my parents had been in trouble and never told us. When I opened the envelope, a certificate of adoption fell out. It was a court paper finalizing the adoption of Judith Marie Walker. Adoption! I couldn't believe what I read. I didn't even know what to think or what to do. I put that paper back in the box and finished my job.
>
> I was very teary for the next week. My mother kept saying, "Judy, I know you are sad about our moving, but you will be fine." I finally couldn't hold it in any longer and started shouting at her, "You don't understand. I am not sad about leaving."
>
> I began to tell her what I had found in the attic. The only thing she could say was, "At least now you know the truth. We never wanted you to know."
>
> "Why didn't you tell me?" I pleaded.

Mother quietly told me, "We thought of ourselves as your family, your only family. I planned never to let you know." Later that afternoon, she told me more of the family secrets: My older sister, Katherine, was adopted, one of my cousins was also, and they didn't know either. Everything in my world changed for me that day.

This is an extreme example. Today, no adoption professionals advocate keeping adoption secret from the child, and very few adoptive parents choose that approach. But Judy's example does raise important questions. At the time of her adoption and in the ensuing years, her parents faced a critical decision encountered by all adoptive families. They must ask and answer key questions: As we raise this adopted child, how open will we be regarding the adoption? Is it better to avoid the topic and act as if the adoption never happened and this child is ours by birth? Will we deal with this adoption by hiding from it and ignoring the unique questions that adopted children often have as they grow up?

Parents who choose this approach send a message loud and clear that the child should forget about being adopted and everything that goes with it. This style of managing adoption communication breeds negative consequences in the future for the adopted child and family. It potentially blocks "the development of an accepting and trusting family atmosphere, an atmosphere conducive to open, honest exploration of adoption-related issues."[11]

Why do parents take this approach? One analyst suggested several underlying reasons:

- It is an attempt on the parents' part to minimize their sense of pain around loss.
- It is an attempt to protect the child from feeling the pain of loss and rejection.
- It is an attempt on the part of the parents to protect themselves from potential loss — not the physical loss of the child but the loss of the child's love, trust, and commitment to them.[12]

None of these motivations is served by secrecy. There is nothing to be ashamed of in adoption. Truth spoken in wisdom and love is the most successful approach.

Acceptance of Adoption

The approach that acknowledges the adoption is in direct contrast to hiding from adoption and creating a closed communication system in the family. Adoptive parents realize the importance of talking openly and freely about adoption. Children learn early that in their house, it is okay to ask questions and to explore their questions and feelings rather than going through life as if those issues didn't exist.

For one teen, Anna, growing up in a family that communicated openly about adoption meant developing a healthy identity and self-esteem.

> I always knew I was adopted. My parents shared my adoption story with me from a very young age. One special thing that my adoptive parents asked for from the adoption agency was to get a picture of my birthmother and a letter from her. I will never forget the day that my mom took me to lunch and gave them to me. I was probably about eight. What she did for me that day over nine years ago opened doors for me in terms of finding out what I needed to know about my birthfamily, my background, and myself. As I continue to occasionally deal with adoption stuff, I walk through those doors she opened for me that afternoon.

What does the acknowledging style within a family do for the parent-child relationship?

- It creates an atmosphere of empathy and sensitivity in which feelings, thoughts, and struggles can be not only expressed but also recognized as valid.
- It builds a firm foundation of trust between parents and child.
- It fills in the gaps of information that the child has about his or her past.
- It corrects fears and fantasies that a child may have developed.
- It provides a firm footing for the development of identity.

One particular concern of adoptive parents who understand the importance of open communication about adoption is that they may be talking about it too much. Parents have to create a balance between talking about adoption and living daily life. One way to do this is to ask yourself, *When was the last time we talked about adoption in this house?* If you don't remember, there is probably a need to address it in some way.

It's important for parents to follow the child's cue. Parents should not force adoption talk on their children, but they should look for underlying meanings in what children say and ask questions that make them feel free to talk about it. It's also important to be age-appropriate and not raise issues that children aren't ready to understand.

A FOUNDATIONAL REALITY

Jason and Kate stood before the minister, Jason proudly holding Chad, their six-month-old son. Chad wiggled in his father's arms, slightly uncomfortable in his crinkly white new clothes, sensing that his parents were a little nervous. As the minister began the christening ceremony, Chad began to suck his pacifier with renewed intensity. A brief sensation overtook Tiffany and she turned, looking at the empty space to her left and behind her. At the reception following the ceremony, when Jason asked Kate what she was looking for, she explained, "I felt her there, Jason. I can't explain it, but for a minute it felt like Chad's birthmother was standing right there beside me!"

Cassandra shifted nervously in the skimpy paper gown as she answered the nurse's questions, routine for an annual medical exam with a new physician. "How many children do you have?" This was one of the questions she always dreaded, one she always struggled to answer. Not to mention Kristy, the name she calls her first child, seems somehow unfaithful. Cassandra dearly loves Kristy although she hasn't seen her since the day she was born. There is never a week that passes without thoughts or questions about Kristy flitting through her mind. At the same time, mentioning Kristy has many other implications. She doesn't believe it is necessarily everyone's business that when she was fifteen years old, she made an adoption plan for Kristy. Cassandra swallowed hard as she heard the nurse ask, "How old is your oldest child?"

Julianna was turning eleven today. She wanted to ask her adoptive mother a question but was uncertain how to bring it up. She went out to the playhouse in the backyard and practiced how she would say it: "Do you think my birthmother thinks about me on my birthday? I think of her. I hope she thinks of me."[13]

Experiences like these just described are fairly common when adoption is part of a person's life. These accounts capture a phenomenon, a psychological presence, which has only recently begun to be understood and explored in the adoption world. Tiffany felt the psychological presence of Chad's birthmother. When Cassandra's doctor asked her certain questions, she felt Kristy's psychological presence. Psychological presence, simply put, refers to some person being in a family member's heart or on his or her mind. It is *"the symbolic existence of an individual in the perception of other family members in a way that influences thoughts, emotions, behavior, identity or unity of remaining family members."*[14]

One of the foundational realities of adoption that is crucial to creating an environment of open communication around adoption is this: Birthparents (primarily birthmothers) will be on the hearts and minds of adoptive parents (primarily adoptive mothers) to some degree, sometimes greater and sometimes lesser, throughout the course of their lives.[15] That birthparent is also psychologically present in the hearts and minds of most adopted children, spoken or unspoken.

How adoptive parents face this issue may dictate how openly they will deal with all aspects of the adoption relationship. In looking at how parents manage the reality of the psychological presence of the birthparents, researchers have described it in two ways:

1. *Adoptive parents deny the psychological presence.* For example, a child approaches his mother on his birthday and asks, "Mom, do you think my birthmother thinks about me on my birthday?" An adoptive mother in denial might respond, "John, I am your mother now, and I think about you. That is really all that matters." What John learns early in his life is that his questions and feelings about important things don't matter and are best if not brought up. It shuts him down.

2. *Adoptive parents acknowledge the psychological presence.* This response, although not always easy for adoptive parents, is healthier for the youngster. In this example, that same child approaches his mother on his birthday and asks, "Mom, do you think my birthmother thinks about me on my birthday?" An adoptive mother in a family that communicates openly about adoption might respond, "John, I don't really know for sure. I would think so since this is an important day. But you know what is also important. I think about your birthmother, and I bet you do too. Do you want to talk about it?

Do you want to send a letter or picture to the agency to give to her?" Now the lesson learned by the child is that he can be freely open about his feelings and questions without worrying about parental response.

Healthy adoptive families have explored their motivations and expectations in a realistic way. They demonstrate quality in interpersonal relationships and flexibility in the family system. They acknowledge the importance of creating an environment that deals openly with adoption. What else do healthy adoptive families do?

FACTOR FIVE: HEALTHY ADOPTIVE PARENTS UNDERSTAND THE CORE ISSUES OF ADOPTION THAT MAY AFFECT THEIR CHILD AND THE TRIGGERS THAT MAY CREATE CRISIS[16]/[17]

Much research and anecdotal evidence has shown that in the life of some adopted persons, certain issues arise during developmental stages and life transitions that are unique to adoption. Some adopted persons rarely encounter these, but others feel them deeply. Recognizing the possibility of these core issues in adoption is one way parents can be proactive and knowledgeable about what might be happening in the hearts and minds of their children. A brief description of each of these core issues follows.

GRIEF AND LOSS

When children have been separated from significant attachment figures, their emotional response can be one of grief and mourning. Even children who were adopted as infants may at some point in life experience the loss of the fantasy or dream parent they have never met and of "what might have been." Children adopted at older ages may grieve the loss of important attachment figures in birth, extended, or foster families.

LOYALTY

Having birthparents in addition to parents can create a conflict for children, whether the birthparents are known or fantasized. (This perceived conflict of loyalties is also frequently the case for children of divorce.) Children may feel that they are allowed to love only their adoptive parents and that closeness with and love for birthparents is an act of disloyalty toward the parents who are raising them.

CONTROL

Children who have experienced significant and traumatic losses may feel that they have no control or decision-making power over their own lives. This can generate feelings of frustration and helplessness.

They may try to regain control over their lives through one or more of the following behavioral indicators:

- Chemical dependence
- Depression
- Overeating
- Excessive control issues related to siblings, peers
- Compulsive need to manage their world; extremely organized; always planning (and worrying) ahead

REJECTION AND FEAR OF ABANDONMENT

Regardless of the actual circumstances surrounding the child's adoption, the child's perception is frequently that he or she was rejected and subsequently abandoned by the birthfamily. Some adopted persons feel that they are unlovable and unkeepable, and they may act out to test the commitment of the adoptive family. To avoid rejection, some adopted persons may not allow themselves to get close to others, or they will reject others before they themselves can be rejected. Some adopted persons continually seek acceptance and approval from others, being almost "too good."

Rejection ranks in anyone's life as a most anguishing experience. Especially in the vulnerable years of adolescence and early adulthood, an adopted person's feelings of rejection can diminish the benefits of the positive and nurturing love of their adoptive parents. The adopted person's perceptions of rejection can also interfere with building healthy relationships.

SHAME AND GUILT

A pervasive sense of shame is a painful feeling. It is the ongoing belief that one is fundamentally bad, inadequate, defective, unworthy, or not fully valid as a human being. Adoption presents circumstances that some adopted people experience as shame. Why? According to Lewis Smedes in his book *Shame and Grace: Healing the Shame We Don't Deserve*, the most devastating way for a parent to create shame within a child is to turn his or her back upon him, to fail to take responsibility for him. Another source of shame for some adopted persons is feeling that they were never what their adoptive parents had hoped for. They believe that they can never measure up to the child the parents did not or could not conceive. This belief may be a real or imagined situation within the adoptive family, leaving the adopted person with the incredible pain of not only never being that dreamed-for child but also never doing the right thing. In some families, adoptive parents do continue to grieve the ideal child and subtly communicate their disappointment to the adopted child. Shame may also be a major factor for the adopted child in a family with biological children who are living up to parental expectations or in a family with a "good adopted child" who is working extremely hard to live up to those expectations. Finally, guilt for the adopted person is also rooted in the feeling that he or she, even as a small child, caused the separation from the birthfamily.

IDENTITY

Some people who were adopted into their families feel that lack of information about their history and birthfamily make it difficult to establish their identity. Identity formation is a major task of adolescent development. Transcultural adoptive placements can also increase the adopted person's challenge in working out identity issues, particularly if the adoptive family lives in a homogeneous community with few families of the child's culture or ethnicity. Children who have suffered abuse or neglect prior to adoption may have difficulty forming their identity at a higher rate, while children adopted as infants tend to develop comparably to children raised in their biological families.

FEELING DIFFERENT

Some adopted persons at various stages in their life express strong feelings of being "different." They may look very different from others in the adoptive family in their coloring, body build or size, or even race. Perceptions of differences can feed identity confusion: "Who am I really?" and "Do I fit here?" are questions that can arise.

TRIGGERS

A trigger is something that creates an emotional reaction. For children who were adopted, some of the core issues discussed above can resurface around some of the following events:

- Mother's Day
- The child's birthday
- School transition (from one school level to another)
- School assignments (family tree, family history, genetics charts)
- Movies with adoption-related themes
- Going to camp
- Parent becomes seriously ill
- Parents go on a get-away weekend without any children
- Pet dies
- Parents divorce
- Being rejected by steady boyfriend or girlfriend
- Family moves
- Senior year of high school, age eighteen
- Holidays
- Medical crises of the child

The more adoptive parents are aware of the potential for an emotional response, the better they will be prepared to manage it if it arises. Of course, these significant events can be triggers for emotional reactions in nonadopted children as well.

FACTOR SIX: HEALTHY ADOPTIVE PARENTS UNDERSTAND THAT ADOPTION IS A LIFETIME COMMITMENT AND MAINTAIN THAT COMMITMENT THROUGH DIFFICULT TIMES

It is rare to hear of biological parents dissolving their relationship with their children when the going gets tough. Such should be the case with adoption. Biological parents do not really know any better than adoptive parents how their children will turn out. Adoptive parents should always keep their promise to love their child for a lifetime. Yet some do not. This is tragic and incredibly irresponsible.

Why do parents who once promised to be that forever family sometimes consider relinquishing their vow? There are many grave factors involved in termination of adoptive parental rights. One interesting perspective may pinpoint a partial reason why adoptive parents back down from the greatest challenge of their lives. It has to do with the attitudes of adults today.

People who were parents during the eighties and nineties form a unique generation. They are called the baby boomers, those people who were born between 1946 and 1964. In the process of development, baby boomers have redefined some basic life values. One of these is commitment. The adopting parents of today were raised by baby boomer parents and may have adopted their parents' perception of commitment.

Commitment took a negative rap with some parents of the baby boomer generation, according to researcher George Barna. They viewed commitment negatively "because it limits our ability to feel independent and free, to experience new things, to change our minds on the spur of the moment and to focus upon self-gratification rather than helping others."[18]

What does this belief have to do with adoptive parents? Some parents begin adoption with a dream of what it will be like. In fashioning their dream, they ignore realistic input. Not far into the journey, the dream begins to fade when reality is not what they expected. When the relationship stops feeling good, when the crises erupt, when tension and stress loom over the home, some parents question whether their relationship with their adopted child can continue.

Following this baby boomer approach to commitment, "people [some adoptive parents] willingly make commitments [to a child] only when the expected outcome exceeds what they must sacrifice as a result of that commitment."[19] Because adoption is based on a promise and because people can break their promises if they resent the circumstances they create, the adoptive relationship is at risk.

Healthy adoptive families maintain their commitment to a child even when the reality is very difficult. If circumstances require professional services outside the home, they look for care options such as a residential treatment home. They work through problems as a family and do not permanently terminate the relationship with the adopted child. When the pain threatens the pleasure, they opt for hope, not out.

Families who choose to adopt often face parenting demands unknown to parents raising their birth children. "You've got to be optimistic without denying what is happening," advised child advocate Susan Edelstein. "You've got to focus on strengths, keep perspective, set reasonable goals and get help when you need it. You have to be able to tolerate the unknown. You have to be able to say, 'I will love this child forever.'"[20] As one adoptive parent stated, "John is my son at four, fourteen, twenty-four . . . for the rest of our lives together, no matter what."

SUMMARY

Healthy adoptive families recognize six factors of success that can guide them through the experience:

1. Healthy adoptive parents have explored their motivations and expectations for adoption in an open manner and are in agreement.
2. Healthy adoptive parents demonstrate stability and quality in their interpersonal relationships.
3. Healthy adoptive parents demonstrate flexibility and openness in their family system.
4. Healthy adoptive parents know the importance of creating a family environment that openly acknowledges and communicates about adoption.

5. Healthy adoptive parents understand the core issues of adoption that may affect their child and the triggers that can create crisis.

6. Healthy adoptive parents understand that adoption is a lifelong commitment and maintain that commitment through difficult times.

QUESTIONS FOR SMALL GROUPS

1. What other traits of successful adoptive parents have you observed?

2. Of the factors mentioned in this chapter, what do you feel are your strengths? What do you feel are your weaknesses?

3. How do you feel about the baby boomer attitude toward commitment? In what ways, if any, do you think this attitude affects the adoption experience?

4. Has the promise you made to the child you adopted been tested? How have you handled the stress and ambivalence this testing creates?

Chapter Six

DEVELOPING A SUPPORTIVE ADOPTION ENVIRONMENT
How to Prepare Biological Children, Family, and Friends

By Elizabeth A. Tracy and Jayne E. Schooler

Natural child: any child who is not artificial
Real parent: any parent who is not imaginary
Your own child: any child who is not someone else's child
Adopted child: a natural child with a real parent, who is all my own
— *Rita Law*

Blending a family together, whether through adoption, birth, or marriage, is a journey down a road that will be filled with exciting twists and turns, thrilling highs, and, yes, a few bumps and potholes along the way. There are some people who believe if they adopt only infants, they will avoid the bumps and potholes. This is, however, not a guarantee. Whether biological or adopted, every child who joins a family is unique—an interesting blend of genetics, gifts, and personalities. Infants and toddlers who are adopted internationally may have spent time in orphanages or been exposed to war, famine, or other traumatizing events. Older children who have been in foster care may have lived through abuse, domestic violence, and multiple moves while "in the system." All these experiences come with them when they move into their adoptive homes.

Historically, when preparing for adoption, the focus has been on the adoptive parents. Are they prepared emotionally? Financially? Is the house big enough? Are they healthy? Who will the guardian be if the unthinkable should happen? While all that needs to be considered, preparing the home also means preparing the entire family for the adoption. If a family already has children in the home whether by birth, adoption, or marriage, they, too, need to be included in the process. Children already in the home are the ones who will experience the greatest long-term impact. They are the ones who will share their parents, extended family, friends, toys, rooms, schoolmates, and playgrounds. In fact, if a biological child and an adopted child are very close in age, they may rarely have a break from each other.

When considering adoption, parents should always remember their first obligation to their existing family. Parents may feel called to adopt, but they need to help their existing children feel right about the decision as well. Legally speaking, adoption is about providing parents for children, but it's really a whole family who adopts a child. Adoptive parents need to ensure not only their own successful adjustments but their existing children's as well.

Anticipating and preparing children for family changes is a critical task when creating a home environment that is not only supportive but also resilient to the challenges that may present themselves.

POTENTIAL POST-ADOPTIVE CHALLENGES FOR CHILDREN ALREADY IN THE HOME

POTENTIAL CHALLENGE #1: CHANGING THE BIRTH ORDER

The minute another child joins the family, someone's birth order is changed. For example, the baby may become the oldest, or the oldest may suddenly be a middle child.

Melanie and Todd Henderson have been married for twenty years. They have two biological children, Clarissa, age eleven, and Markus, age four. Three years ago they made the decision to expand their family through adoption. Three months after the paperwork was completed, an adoption worker called and said he had found the perfect additions to the Henderson family: Lisa, age fifteen, and three-month-old Lucy. Although the Hendersons hadn't pictured themselves adopting a teenager, they agreed to meet the girls and soon decided that Lisa and Lucy would be welcome additions to their family.

Shortly after the adoption, Mrs. Henderson contacted a therapist/adoption specialist and set up a family appointment. During their session Mrs. Henderson stated, "I just don't understand . . . nothing is going the way I pictured it. I thought the adoption would bring us closer together as a family, but now everyone just bickers and is territorial. Do you know that my eleven-year-old actually started marking her toys and furniture with her name and won't let anyone touch them? I am shocked at her selfishness; I thought I raised her better than that! My four-year-old is suddenly having potty accidents. Lisa, Clarissa, and my husband are constantly arguing about chores and house rules. The baby cries a lot, and I am drained by the tug-of-war I feel from the entire family."

Clarissa Henderson, with tears rolling down her face, echoed her mother's initial sentiment: "I just don't understand. I thought I was going to get a baby brother or sister and nothing would really change. When they asked me if I wanted us to adopt kids, I thought it would be fun. I *never* thought they would adopt a kid bigger than me! It's not fair! Now I'm not the oldest; she is. I'm . . . I don't know, it's like I'm second. I don't like being second; I want to be first again. I never thought they'd adopt a big kid, just babies I could play with."

Clarissa was grieving the loss of her status in the family. For eleven years she had been Mommy and Daddy's big girl, the one who set the example and helped with her younger brother. It was her identity until Lisa moved in, and suddenly Clarissa was relegated to "being second." Clarissa, in an attempt to recapture some of her prior status and vent her anger, began challenging everything her parents asked of her. She marked all of her belongings in an attempt to regain some control over the situation and show Lisa and her parents that she wasn't just second and that she deserved respect too.

Markus, on the other hand, was having difficulty after losing his "baby" spot in the family. At the table, Lucy's high chair was placed in his spot, and he was moved to the other side. His mother and father were busy feeding and caring for a loud baby who cried most of the time. Markus, feeling the loss of attention from both his parents, regressed in his potty training.

The therapist suggested that the Hendersons give Markus "big brother" jobs such as reading to Lucy and having chores like Lisa and Clarissa. This helped Markus begin to develop an identity within the new family unit. Resolving the table issue turned out to be simple: They returned Markus to his spot and placed Lucy on the other side between Melanie and Todd so both parents could attend to the infant. Markus's accidents stopped within a few weeks.

Today, Clarissa enjoys a closer relationship with her big sister and parents. Mr. and Mrs. Henderson attribute their family's success to open communication, creativity, patience, and time. Mrs. Henderson explained, "I expected Clarissa to be as excited as we were and share everything with her new sister.

I understand now that Clarissa needed time to adjust to all the changes. She needed us to listen to her concerns and then, as a family, figure out how to address them."

The Hendersons also discovered that in their haste to make Lisa feel like a real member of the family, they took away some of Clarissa's favorite activities with her parents. Again, they sat down with their daughters and decided to keep some of Clarissa's activities (going with Dad on Sunday afternoon to get dessert) and to create new family traditions (the oldest child lights the candles at dinnertime).

Once Clarissa's parents began listening and responding to her needs, Clarissa became less territorial and oppositional. Mrs. Henderson said, "I understand now that Clarissa was not being selfish. She wanted reassurance that she wasn't being replaced, and we needed to allow her to keep some of the activities that had defined her as the oldest child for eleven years."

Potential Strategies

- Discuss the birth order change with children prior to the adoption to assist with the transition. Ongoing post-adoption communication may minimize the impact from unplanned challenges when they occur.
- Keep as many things the same as possible.
- Assist the displaced child in developing an identity within the new family unit.

POTENTIAL CHALLENGE #2:
CHILDREN MAY WITNESS DISTRESS, SADNESS, AND ANGER WHEN THE FAMILY STRUGGLES

"I couldn't stand it when my parents worried about Peter," said twenty-one-year-old Bonny about her brother, adopted at age eight. "He used to sneak out and drink, I guess. I would hear them talk and cry about how frustrated and scared they were. One day when my parents left the house, my older brother and I cornered Peter and told him to stop because he was hurting Mom and Dad."

When asked about her own behavior as a child, Bonny replied, "I tried to never do anything wrong. I was always trying to make things easier for my parents. When I was younger I used to get so scared that Mom or Dad would die of a heart attack from all the worrying, so I tried not to add any more stress."

When parents cry, become angry, or have strong emotions, children feel out of control and frightened. Sometimes they take on a "good child" role and try to make things better for everyone in the house. For example, they may try to have perfect behavior or excel in school or sports. This is an attempt to offset the "bad child" and make the parents happy and restore harmony to the home.

Children will often be propelled into action when a new addition to the family is causing what they perceive to be pain to their parents. When they take action it is typically an attempt to alleviate the stressor (the behavior of the adopted child). This can sometimes take the form of intimidation, physical threats, or actually hurting the child they believe is causing the distress.

Potential Strategies

- The children's response is a direct result of how their parents handle the stress of the newly formed family. A support group or adoption therapist is an excellent option to assist the adults during the transformation.
- A calm, matter-of-fact presence will result in children who are confident that adults are in control and everything is okay.
- Children (including teenagers) should not be used as confidants for parents during times of struggle. They are often not well prepared to deal with their feelings.

POTENTIAL CHALLENGE #3: NEW BEHAVIOR MANAGEMENT (DISCIPLINE) TECHNIQUES AND HOUSE RULES

The Smith family had three biological children, ages seven, nine, and sixteen, and two adopted children, ages four and eight. During a support-group meeting, the discussion turned to challenges biological children face when an adoption occurs. "So," the facilitator said, "tell me something that has challenged you."

"Time-out!" the children yelled in unison and became breathless as they talked over each other to explain. "Time-out is when you do something wrong and you have to sit on the steps. We *never* had to do time-out before the other kids came."

Nine-year-old Jonathan said, "I told my parents it's embarrassing for me to have time-out and it's not fair that we have to do something because the new kids act bad." When asked by the facilitator what their parents had said, the three children sadly replied, "They said that now everyone has to be treated the same."

The facilitator encouraged the children to come up with a list of things to discuss with their parents. At the next support-group meeting, the children were delighted to tell how their family had switched to a system that included "getting privileges for good choices." Jonathan said, "I was surprised that Mom and Dad listened to us. Everyone is still being treated the same, but now it doesn't make anyone feel bad."

Mr. and Mrs. Smith initially implemented an effective behavioral management technique. However, until the adoption, their biological children had never even heard the phrase *time-out*. The Smith children were angry at the way their lives had changed.

Adoption may require a review of and possible changes to the household rules, depending on the age and special needs of the adopted child. The family needs to verbalize things that have always been a given, such as bedroom rules (Do we knock? How clean is clean? Can friends visit in there?) and food rules (Do we help ourselves? Do we need to ask first? If we don't like what's for dinner, can we make something else?).

Potential Strategies

- Focus on each child's individual and unique needs. Sometimes after adoption, parents feel pressure to treat each child exactly the same. However, treating everyone the same may actually cause more disruption than addressing each child as an individual. Some children need lots of limit setting as toddlers because they enjoy exploring and risk taking. Some teenagers are more responsible and can be relied upon to follow directions and make safe choices when unsupervised. Placing more limits on a child who doesn't need them may cause rebellion and frustration. Allowing younger siblings more freedom simply because their older brother or sister was mature may place them in risky situations.
- Explore behavior management techniques.
  - *Parenting with Love & Logic* is an approach that "helps children develop and grow in a healthy way, provides them with confidence and dignity, and teaches them how to become more responsible."[1]

- ■ *1-2-3 Magic* is a positive and effective approach to disciplining children without arguing, yelling, or spanking.[2]
- Encourage the whole family's attendance at a support group. Traditionally, post-adoptive therapy focused on helping parents relate to the adopted child and did not address the needs of biological children.[3] Thankfully this trend is shifting, and some agencies have begun providing pre- and post-adoptive support for the entire family.

POTENTIAL CHALLENGE #4: CHILDREN MAY BELIEVE THEIR OPINIONS AND FEELINGS DON'T MATTER

An exhausted and discouraged sixteen-year-old Jessica stated flatly, "It doesn't matter what I say. I didn't want my parents to adopt any more kids. I am tired of the chaos, having to explain the new kids to my friends, and sharing my parents. Look, my parents asked me, I told them, and they ignored me."

Children may feel ignored, especially when they are asked their opinion or they voice an objection and the adoption proceeds anyway. In an honest effort to include their children and get 'buy in,' some parents may ask if anyone has objections, thoughts, or opinions. The statement most often heard from biological children is, "Why should I tell them? It doesn't matter anyway. They do what they want to do!" When children are asked for their input, they have an expectation that their wishes will be respected.

Some parents feel that the decision to expand their family, whether through adoption or biologically, is theirs alone. In this case, parents usually 'inform' their children of the exciting news. Rebecca and Arthur said, "Our plan was to tell our children about the decision to adopt and honestly answer their questions. We did not ask their permission because we feel it is 100 percent our choice." Both Rebecca and Arthur admitted they learned a great deal by listening to their children's concerns. "Honestly," Arthur said, "we didn't think about some of the things that they brought up. Having preteen girls and planning to adopt a boy made privacy issues (friends, sleepovers, bathrooms) a big concern for them. Once we knew the issues, we could work to resolve them. I believe this allowed our six-year-old son to be fully embraced by his sisters from the beginning."

Other parents aren't sure how their children will react and want them to be just as excited about the adoption as they are, or they are just exploring the possibility and looking for input. Asking for input appears to work best if the parents are prepared to yield or negotiate after the discussion.

Yielding quite simply means accepting your children's wishes. For instance, they might want only younger children, just girls, someone their own age, or a sibling group of no more than two. However, they may also tell parents that they do not want any more siblings. Parents who have no preferences may find this easier than those who are looking to add a particular gender, age, or number to the family.

Negotiating with your children may include addressing concerns. Cassie and Max met with their biological children to explore adoption. Although they wanted to expand their family, they were prepared to yield if their children were adamantly opposed. However, during the discussion, they asked questions and discovered that their children were open to the possibility.

"Our children, whose ages at the time were four, nine, and fifteen, had different concerns. Our four-year-old wanted to know if he had to give away his toys. The nine-year-old wanted to make sure that his new brother or sister wasn't in the same grade or classroom as he was, and our fifteen-year-old worried that she might miss time with her friends when we needed her to babysit."

Encouraged by their children's responses, Cassie and Max worked as a couple to resolve the issues. Cassie said, "Max and I talked a great deal about how we might handle each child's concern without making promises we couldn't keep. We decided to reassure all the children that their things (toys, clothes, and so on) would remain theirs. If, however, they wished to pass something on to their new sibling as a welcome gift, they were free to do so. We agreed to choose a child of a different age and grade than any of our children, and finally, we defined babysitting for our fifteen-year-old. She would be asked to babysit (rather than told) and paid the same as a nonfamily member. We also agreed that if she didn't want to babysit because of previous plans, we would accept her decision and hire someone else. In our eyes, this was a win-win."

The parents of sixteen-year-old Jessica (mentioned previously) sought help through a family therapist and discovered that she thought her parents were asking her permission and was heartbroken at being dismissed. She felt unimportant and disrespected. Through family therapy and a support group for biological children, they discovered why she was opposed to the adoptions. Some of Jessica's issues were easily resolved because they involved spending uninterrupted time with each of her parents. Other issues, such as not having the money to go to expensive camps or buy the latest electronic gadgets, were not. However, Jessica's anger diminished greatly after she began to see the efforts her parents were making. At her last therapy session Jessica said, "I feel so special and important in my family. I don't resent my brothers and sisters so much either. The support group was the best thing because I got to meet other kids like me and we became friends for each other."

Potential Strategies

- Parents who decide to ask for their children's input may be more successful if, before approaching their children, they understand their own feelings and positions. Here are some questions for parents to consider: Have they made up their minds to proceed and are just trying to get their children excited about the idea? Are they asking their children's permission? What if the children say no? What if their children want to "pick out" their new sibling?
- If parents decide to ask for their children's input, being prepared to yield or negotiate may be an effective technique.
- If parents decide to inform their children of the adoption, being open to questions and addressing concerns may be a helpful response.

POTENTIAL CHALLENGE #5:
CHILDREN MAY FEEL TRICKED INTO SUPPORTING THE ADOPTION

"I remember my parents talking about how much fun it was going to be getting a new little baby from another country," said eighteen-year-old Paula. "They showed me on the news that the war was getting closer to where the orphanage was. I was told we would be *saving* a baby. I was fourteen, and I remember feeling panicked that all those babies were in a war. I wanted my parents to bring all of them home. I remember my dad telling me how I would be a big sister and how much fun we would all have together.

"When we knew it was a girl, my mom and I went shopping for little dresses. I felt as if our family was like 'God's angels' for the baby. But when they brought Monique home, everything changed. Suddenly I was like a built in babysitter. I couldn't go out with my friends because I had to watch her so my mother could go grocery shopping or work late. My parents told me not to be so selfish; they explained that they had to work extra hours because they spent a lot of money rescuing Monique. Don't get me wrong. I love my little sister and I am glad we saved her, but no one told me that I was going to have to give up my freedom."

Parents are sometimes overzealous in their efforts to convince their children of how wonderful the adoption will be, and they may unintentionally influence their children through a series of questions or statements akin to leading the witness. For example, "Would you like to have a little boy your age to play with? You will have a new brother and can teach him new things. He does not have anyone to love him or take care of him. You don't want him to be sad, do you?"

Children are generally told of all the wonderful things that adoption brings and therefore may not have realistic expectations. As a result, they may feel tricked into agreeing to an adoption because they did not understand all the implications.

Potential Strategies

This challenge can sometimes be disheartening for parents who are eager to add to the family. They sometimes react defensively and ask, "What are we supposed to say?" These parents express fear that a truthful approach may mean that they would never be able to convince their children to support the adoption.

The answer to the question is honest preparation. Give honest, age-appropriate information. Statements such as these may help:

- "Like all babies, your brother will need lots of attention and love."
- "Your new sister may need some practice being in a family who loves each other without hurting. She may also need to learn how to share."
- "They may have trouble talking about their feelings and may yell or have tantrums instead of saying, 'I am angry!'"

POTENTIAL CHALLENGE #6:
PARENTS MAY REGRET OR FEEL GUILTY ABOUT THE ADOPTION

During the first session with the Monroe family it was clear that Mrs. Monroe was filled with anxiety. She blurted out, "We were foster parents to the boys for four years. Andrew was only one and a half and Jude was two and a half when they came to live with us. How could we not adopt them? How could we say no? We are the only parents they have ever known."

Mr. Monroe added, "They had behavior problems at the beginning but are settling down. Finalizing the adoption has helped make them feel more secure. I think things are going okay."

"Okay? The girls are always mad at me!" shouted Mrs. Monroe. "I just don't know if we did the right thing. Now our biological daughters, Brandy, age thirteen, and Shelley, age fifteen, are demanding that the boys be kept away from their friends. They are always picking on the boys too."

"You do a great job with the children," said Mr. Monroe supportively. "I wish you would stop feeling guilty."

Mrs. Monroe responded, "I can't help it. The girls make me feel that way, and then I end up buying them whatever they want to make up for it. But when I do that, they get angrier with me and tell me to take the stuff back. What if we did the wrong thing by adopting the boys?"

Parents who are ambivalent or regret their decision to adopt may have the feeling that they are sacrificing the well-being of their biological children. They may be influenced by what they believe their children want and may give them inappropriate power in making decisions about whether to continue the adoptive placement. This may make the children bear a burden that should be the responsibility of the adults, resulting in feelings of guilt, shame, regret, or a sense of having done something wrong.[4]

In this case, the Monroe girls were reacting to their younger brothers as typical teenage girls. However, Mrs. Monroe, who was not confident in her decision to adopt, saw a normal sibling issue as potential for a lifetime of pain for her daughters. In an effort to make it up to the girls, she began buying them things. This made Brandy and Shelley angry and fearful that their mother would disrupt the adoption and they would lose the brothers they loved.

Potential Strategies

- Parents who have honestly prepared their children and feel confident in their decision to adopt do not need to feel guilty. This realization may help parents make better decisions during stressful times.
- It is imperative that parents understand that while children need a voice, they should not carry the ultimate power and decision in the family.
- It is important to establish open communication with all children in order to avoid negative behavior based on the fears that children may have as a result of misunderstandings.

Potential Challenge #7:
Children May Have to Explain to Friends and
Schoolmates About Adoption

"What's wrong?" asked Penny's mother.

"Charles said Katie was left on our doorstep because no one wanted her," cried ten-year-old Penny.

"What did you say?" asked her mother.

"I told him that Katie was adopted. We picked her to be my sister and I love her. He is such a dope," Penny huffed.

"Not everyone knows about adoption. You told him the truth and now he knows more," said Penny's mother.

Penny asked cautiously, "Mom, is it bad that sometimes I get tired of talking about how Katie joined our family?"

"No, it's not bad. Sometimes I get tired too. You can always choose not to answer their questions or change the subject by asking about their homework or pet," said Penny's mother.

People are naturally curious about adoption. Much of what people know they have gotten from the news or made-for-TV movies. Preparing children, particularly those who are school-age, to address the different types of questions may help reduce stress in the future. It's important that parents have open communication with their children. Parents need to feel comfortable bringing up difficult issues so that their children will hopefully feel comfortable reporting any questions they have been asked. This may give parents an opportunity to assist their children in developing helpful responses.

Children may be faced with more difficult questions if the adopted child has any learning or behavioral challenges. They may be teased about being the sibling of a "weird kid." They may be asked to explain why their adopted sibling behaves in certain ways.

Potential Strategies
- Invasive questions such as, "Does she have problems?" "Were they abused?" "I can't believe her mother didn't want her, can you?" will most likely be asked of parents; however, they are often times asked in the presence of their children. Children will learn how to handle questions by listening to their parents' responses.
- Some families do not mind answering general adoption questions.

Skilled families learn to carefully redirect and even educate inquisitive people when asked inappropriate questions about private family matters.

- Here are two solid guidelines regarding questions:
  - The decision to answer any and all questions about adoption rests with the person being asked. You have the right to refuse to answer any question.
  - The decision to tell the adopted child's "story" lies only with the adopted person.[5]

POTENTIAL CHALLENGE #8:
CHILDREN MAY BECOME INVISIBLE TO THEIR PARENTS AFTER THE ADOPTION OF A CHILD WITH SPECIAL NEEDS

Tashi, a twenty-one-year-old college student, stated, "Once they adopted my sister Andrea, it felt like I didn't matter anymore. My parents were so busy going to the doctors and talking to school counselors that it seemed like I faded away. I tried to tell them how unfair they were being, but they kept telling me how lucky I was to have them and that I should be thankful I wasn't handicapped. I think I learned to accept it and just kind of lived in the house. I felt like no one knew I was there because I didn't need to be 'fixed.'"

As discussed before, the journey through adoption for the entire family is like traveling along a road. There will be hills and valleys—moments of great joy as well as challenging times. Some people choose to travel a different type of road when they adopt a child with special needs.

The North American Council on Adoptable Children (NACAC) defines special needs as follows:

Conditions that make some children harder to place for adoption, including: emotional or physical disorders, age, race, being in a sibling group, a history of abuse, or other factors. Guidelines for classifying a child as having special needs vary by state. Common special needs conditions and diagnoses include attachment disorder, attention deficit hyperactivity disorder (ADHD), developmental delays or disabilities, fetal alcohol spectrum disorder (FASD), learning disabilities, and oppositional defiant disorder (ODD).[6]

The addition of a child with special challenges requires increased attention and focus from the parents in the home. Typically, the network of providers (therapists, doctors, social workers, and so forth) expands dramatically. Juggling appointments can become a full-time job, and sometimes the other children in the home get lost in the shuffle.

As illustrated by Tashi's story, "Many siblings experience feelings of bitterness and resentment towards their parents or the brother or sister with a disability. They may feel jealous, neglected, or rejected as they watch most of their parents' energy, attention, money and psychological support flow to the child with special needs."[7]

Potential Strategies

- Take advantage of respite and/or child care. Doing so may allow you to set aside one-on-one time with each child to help keep everyone connected, as well as to attend important events such as school functions, social activities, or sporting games.
- Discuss the changes that will occur in the day-to-day functioning of the home. For example, will ramps be added? Will alarms be added to bedroom doors or windows? Will the number of people visiting the home increase? Will there be physical or occupational therapists, behavioral support staff, or nurses involved?
- Consider finding a support group for the other children in the home or using strategies outlined in books about sibling relationships.
  - Sibshop is an example of a support group that can offer typically developing children an opportunity to meet other children whose siblings have special challenges.[8]
  - *Siblings Without Rivalry: How to Help Your Children Live Together So You Can Live Too* is an example of a book about sibling relationships.[9]

HOW TO GAIN SUPPORT FROM THE EXTENDED FAMILY

Dear Jack and Bonnie,

I feel I must write a few lines to make sure that you don't misunderstand our feelings concerning your adoption of the twins. I want you to know that we share in your joy, if it is for the best. I feel a real strain right now. I am afraid that you don't understand our concern. Do you think we are against you and that we can't talk things over?

This is a very big step you are taking right now — so much adjustment with two babies at one time. No doubt you can learn not to buy material things that you don't need so you will have enough money for a family of five. But what about the possible strain of adjustment with different dispositions involved? Also, what about your marriage and the strain it will feel?

We just pray for the best. Please don't forget that we love you. If you adopt these young children, they will be loved equally as our grandchildren.

Love,
Mom Wallace

When a couple or individual first thinks about adopting either an infant or an older child, there are usually special people whose responses hold great influence: their own parents. The approval or disapproval of parents and other extended family members is often used as a compass for couples as they determine the direction they will go.

Generally, extended family members hesitate in giving their full approval to a couple's dreams because of three major areas of concern. With the help of the agency or other support persons, couples can usually alleviate these apprehensions by offering further explanations to their family. Most often, enthusiastic support follows.

Here are two ways to communicate an adoption decision effectively.

1. *Introduce the idea as a tentative plan.* If the family has no hint that you have been considering this decision, don't present it as a finalized goal.

It took the Coles ten hours to drive to Oklahoma for a visit with Tim's parents. Every once in a while, Tim reminded Kathy, "Don't say anything about our plans to adopt from Korea. Let me handle it my way. I know Mom and Dad."

The first night at the dinner table, Kathy kept dropping hints to Tim to tell them the news. As the dessert was being passed, Kathy could wait no longer. "Guess what we are going to do," she said. "We are going to adopt a two-year-old from Korea."

Tim's parents looked at each other and then directly at Tim. After a moment's silence, his father simply inquired, "How are you planning to pay for it?"

The rest of that vacation week was spent in near silence on all sides. Tim's parents, who previously had no clue of their plans, felt totally left out of a very important decision. Because Kathy ignored Tim's request for handling the timing carefully, the young couple returned home without the initial and essential support of his parents.

2. *Develop creative ways to educate family members.* David and Jody shared their initial plans with both sets of parents. Because they were new to the whole process themselves, they couldn't answer some of the questions and concerns family members raised. They decided to do something unusual. They invited their agency adoption worker, two other prospective adoptive families, and their parents to a casual informational meeting.

During the meeting, the worker told the families how the process of adoption worked, what to expect from the child, and how to prepare for the arrival. Following that meeting, both sets of prospective grandparents joined their children in anticipating the new child. The education session about the entire adoption program eased many of their apprehensions.

WHERE DO WE FIT IN?

One of the uncertainties that can block grandparents from embracing the idea of adoption is their place in the child's life. Establishing this new relationship with an infant or toddler is not as threatening to grandparents as building an attachment with an older child or a youngster from a different race or culture.

Before their adopted son Daniel arrived, David and Jody Miller talked with the grandparents-to-be. They reassured them that they didn't expect love at first sight for either party, Daniel or the grandparents. Sure, it might happen, but more than likely it would take time.

Jody and David communicated to their relatives that building a family connection with an older child is a process that grows with "love actions," such as affirming conversation, kindness, and sensitivity. The Millers also suggested that their parents could do the following things to help bridge the gap:

1. Take pictures of the new child and display them with those of other family members. It would help them redefine the family unit.

2. Join the Millers in celebrating the adoption day. Encourage all family members to establish this anniversary as part of family rituals such as birthdays and holidays.

3. Establish a new tradition that is special just for the grandparents and the new child, for example taking the initiative to be the one who teaches the youngster to fish or to develop a new hobby or sport. This kind of tradition will long be remembered.

4. Choose the names the child will use for his or her grandparents. David and Jody did not assume that they knew what their parents wanted to be called. Choosing a special name for first-time grandparents of an adopted child would be treated the same way as choosing a name for grandparents of a biological grandchild.

Daniel was the first grandchild in the family, on both sides. It was a special honor for both sets of grandparents to come up with the name by which Daniel and the other grandchildren to follow would call them. When they met the four-year-old, they were introduced by those special names.

Will You Be Depriving the Other Children in the Home?

Although most adopters' parents fully support the adoption before as well as after, there is almost always a complete swing to full approval once the child joins the household.[10] For families with biological children already present, however, the initial support from grandparents is substantially less until the family integrates the new member. Grandparents tend to be very protective of their grandchildren.

When Ron and Charlene Williams decided to adopt, one of the first reactions of both their families was, "What about Robbie? Won't he be deprived? Won't these children take away time from you that belongs to him?"

The Williams were prepared for their parents' concerns. They discussed their considerations with them, legitimizing instead of diminishing them. They reassured their parents that they were keenly aware of their need to balance the new relationships in the home without neglecting Robbie.

Ron and Charlene's openness on these issues helped alleviate their parents' anxieties. After five years, the relationship between grandparents and their new grandchildren is energized by a deep love and acceptance. All the children hold equal importance. When this couple decided to adopt again, their parents asked the same question, only with a different slant: "What about Robbie, Patrick, and Lynne? Won't they be deprived? Won't this child take away time from you that belongs to them?"

As adoptive parents consider the adoptive environment within their extended family, they can prepare by making a promise to each other to forgive any insensitive, callous remarks or actions made by a family member. Long-term grudges will only weaken the whole family system.

It is important to grasp a significant concept that relates to potential responses from family members. Grandparents may value "blood ties" more than ties created by adoption. The relationship of promise creates a different connection for them as well. Their response is not intentional or planned. It is covert, possibly subconscious, yet it emerges through comments and behavior, as occurred in this incident:

> One woman, the oldest of three daughters, reminisced that her adopted son was the first grandchild for the parents. To all appearances, they were very pleased with the child. But when one of her younger sisters . . . became pregnant, the baby crib which had been in the family for several generations, and in which the three girls had also slept, was given to the couple expecting this baby.[11]

The prospective grandparents never thought of offering the crib to the adoptive family. This kind of behavior can cause resentment in couples who are desperately attempting to place equal dignity and position on their role as adoptive parents.

Covert sentiments also surface during family interaction surrounding holidays and birthdays. Adoptive parents should encourage relatives to be sensitive about giving gifts. Attempts at building adoptive grandparent relationships with an older youngster can be thwarted if a child perceives that he or she is valued as secondhand. Simple communication about this issue can head off potential problems.

ADOPTION WITHIN THE COMMUNITY — UNDERSTANDING PERCEPTIONS

One final group of people makes up the adoptive environment: the family's circle of influence in schools, churches, and neighborhoods. Adoptive parents often find that individuals in their local community view adoptive parenting differently than they view rearing a biological child. Even well-intentioned comments that are made without thinking can alienate members of the adoptive family from those very people whose support they need. Consider the following examples:

- "What a nice thing for you to do, adopting that biracial child."
- "What do you know about her background?"
- "How well you care for your baby boy — just like a real mother!"
- "Maybe the reason he doesn't do well in school is because he's adopted."

Adoptive families can successfully manage the outside world that affects them and their children by taking five positive steps.

First, *parents should use a vocabulary of accurate language for discussing adoption.* Words not only convey facts; they also evoke feelings. For example, when a TV or movie talks about a "custody battle" between "real parents" and "other parents," it reinforces the inaccurate notion that only birthparents are real parents and that adoptive parents aren't real parents. Members of society may also wrongly conclude that all adoptions are "battles."

Accurate adoption language can stop the spread of misconceptions such as these. By using accurate language, we educate others about adoption. We choose emotionally correct words over emotionally laden words. We speak and write in appropriate adoption language with the hopes of influencing others so that this language will someday be the norm.[12]

Second, *parents should make it a practice not to disclose private information about the child to anyone outside the trusted immediate family.*[13] Once information is given out, both the adoptive parents and the adopted child have lost any control over who knows it and whether it will be misunderstood or misused later at the wrong time or in the wrong way.

Third, as with comments from family members, *parents should not hold a grudge because of thoughtless statements.* One adoptive father said, "We simply

ACCURATE LANGUAGE	LESS ACCURATE LANGUAGE
Birthparent	Real parent; natural parent
My child	Adopted child; own child
Choosing an adoption plan	Giving away; giving up your child
Finding a family to parent your child	Putting your child up for adoption
Deciding to parent the child	Keeping your baby
Person/individual who was adopted	Adoptee
To parent	To keep
Child in need of a family	Adoptable child; available child
Parent	Adoptive parent
International or intercountry adoption	Foreign adoption
Child who has special needs	Handicapped child; hard-to-place child
Child from another country	Foreign child
Was adopted	Is adopted
Birth relative	Blood relative

made the choice not to let it bother us. If we responded emotionally to every inconsiderate or unthinking remark, we would be exhausted."

Fourth, *parents should educate those with whom the child has regular contact*, such as school teachers or Sunday school staff. Ask them to consider the child carefully when making assignments that have to do with families of origin. Usually at least once in the grade school experience, a youngster is asked to bring baby and family pictures. Children who were older when adopted are unlikely to have such photos.

Finally, *parents should ask professionals who regularly encounter the child to inform them if the child appears to be having any emotional difficulties*. During the middle school years, children experience a sense of loss regarding their genetic ties. Dr. David Brodzinsky found that some youngsters in these middle years appear to have more psychological and school-related behavior problems and more difficulty getting along with their peers than do their nonadopted peers.[14] However, even though these youngsters have more problems, the majority of them are well-adjusted and their difficulties do not require professional services.

SUMMARY

When a couple or individual decides to adopt, they must prepare not only themselves but also those in the adoptive environment. These individuals include biological children, extended family members, friends, neighbors, and professionals in their circle of influence.

Issues for biological children may include the following:

1. Children may experience a change in birth order.
2. Children may witness distress, sadness, and anger when the family struggles.
3. Children may experience new behavior management (discipline) techniques and may be expected to follow new house rules.
4. Children may believe their opinions and feelings don't matter.
5. Children may feel tricked into supporting the adoption.
6. Parents may regret or feel guilty about the adoption.
7. Biological children may have to explain to friends and schoolmates about adoption.
8. Children may become invisible to their parents after the adoption of a child with special needs.

Issues for extended family members include the following:

1. Gaining their support
2. Communicating the decision to adopt
3. Helping them understand where they fit in
4. Addressing the question of depriving other children in the home

Issues for friends, neighbors, and professionals in the local community include the following:

1. Using accurate vocabulary when discussing adoption
2. Disclosing information selectively
3. Managing and forgiving insensitive or unthinking remarks
4. Educating professionals and others with whom the child has regular contact

QUESTIONS FOR SMALL GROUPS

1. Of the eight concerns for biological children in the adoptive home, what have you identified as relating to your family? What additional strategies have you used to help your biological or other permanent children adjust to the newest addition to the household?

2. How have you prepared your biological children to manage comments and questions from peers or even strangers?

3. What issues, if any, have you encountered with your extended family members? How have you managed those issues?

4. What kinds of comments have you received from either family or friends regarding your decision to adopt? Have you experienced comments or questions following the arrival of your child, especially in regard to transracial placements?

5. What have you told school or church professionals about your child? How much do you feel they should know?

PART TWO

WHEN A CHILD
COMES HOME

CHAPTER SEVEN

BARRIERS TO ADJUSTMENT
Strategies to Ease the Transition

Adoptive parents who bridge the adjustment barriers understand two
things. First, their child has had a tremendous loss — loss of both parents,
genealogical ties, cultural heritage, to cite a few. Second, that child may
emotionally revisit those losses at crossroads on their journey through
childhood into young adulthood.

— *Family Ties*

Jerry was home from work the afternoon that the call came from the adoption agency. As anticipated, a teenage birthmother had decided on adoption for her newborn son. Would they be interested in discussing the child further? Could they come that evening? Jerry and Carol Smith had waited three years for this moment. Life without a child and the long weeks of roller-coaster waiting might finally be coming to an end. "Yes, we'll be there this evening," Jerry answered.

Sharon Ryan hung up the phone. She could hardly contain herself. The adoption social worker had just called, asking Sharon and David to come in the next day to discuss the possible adoptive placement of two siblings, a four-year-old boy and a one-year-old girl. Neither Sharon nor David slept well that night. Tomorrow they would face a decision that would affect them and two very special youngsters for the rest of their lives.

Every day in this country, prospective adoptive families receive such a phone call. It is an emotionally charged moment, and it creates an atmosphere of intense anticipation and anxiety. Questions flood their minds as they begin to wrestle with such a monumental consideration: Is this the right child? How can I prepare for him? Will we be good parents? Can we *truly* love a child born to another person? What if our parents won't accept this child?

There are two primary ways that couples can prepare themselves for the moment when a child moves in with them. First, they can learn as much about the child as possible from the agency and other involved persons. Second, in the case of older children who arrive through the foster care system or international networks, they can learn to recognize the potential adjustment barriers that may affect the initial relationship when the child joins the family.

This chapter will present an overview of the initial barriers to adjustment and will give suggestions for how to cope. Later chapters will discuss how to build a nurturing environment that responds to the attachment needs, behavioral adjustments, and long-term issues of many adopted children when they enter the home.

HOW MUCH CAN I KNOW ABOUT MY CHILD?

Jerry and Carol sat in one conference room at the agency; David and Sharon sat in another. Both families held pictures in their hands. For the Smiths, it was a beautiful picture of a three-day-old boy, eyes open and alert. For the Ryans, it was a picture of two beautiful children, Matthew and Katie.

Tears welled up in Sharon's eyes. She had dreamed of this moment for years. She had almost lost hope that it would ever come. Gwen, the Ryans' adoptive social worker, interrupted their thoughts. "Mr. and Mrs. Ryan, what questions do you have concerning the children?" she asked. "This is an important time for you prior to making the decision whether to pursue adoption of these children. We want you to have as much information about the children as possible and knowledge of what this means to you as you parent them."

David pulled from his pocket a list of questions that they had prepared well in advance of this occasion. Faced with a dilemma no biological parents ever consider, this young couple had to decide whether to take on the responsibility of parenting children not born to them.

During the decision-making time prior to an adoption decision, families will have the opportunity to talk with their child's caseworker. In the case of an older special-needs child, parents should also ask for the opportunity to talk with other professionals who have been involved with the child, including former foster parents, therapists, child care providers, and school teachers.

An important principle for prospective parents to follow is this: Prepare a list of questions for the information-sharing meetings with the child's caseworkers and other people involved in the child's life. Be proactive in gathering information. All adoptive parents need to do their homework.

The following are starter lists that parents can use when asking questions regarding their child.

Adopting a Child with Special Needs:

1. How complete is the social/medical history on the birthfamily, including the extended family? What is missing? Is it possible to obtain more information?
2. Is there a history of drug or alcohol abuse in the birthfamily?
3. Is there any history of mental illness in the birthfamily? How far back?
4. Is there any history of other genetically related illnesses such as diabetes or heart disease?
5. What is known about this child's prenatal care and birth history?
6. What is known about the birthmother's lifestyle and life experiences during pregnancy? How stressful were her life circumstances? Was there a lot of trauma due to domestic violence that the child would have been exposed to in utero?
7. What is known about this child's developmental history — physically, emotionally, and cognitively, including language development?
8. What is the child's current health? Does the child have allergies or ADHD related problems?
9. Why was the child removed from the biological family? If it was because of physical abuse, what kind, how often, and from whom? If it was because of sexual abuse, what kind, how often, and from whom?
10. What information do the caseworkers and other professionals have regarding the child's traumatic experiences? What age was the child when the trauma began? How long did it go on? What was the form of maltreatment?
11. What does the child understand about the reasons for removal?
12. When did the child last have contact with the biological family? What were the circumstances of that contact? Was it a planned "good-bye" visit?
13. Does the child have any brothers and sisters? What contact has this

child had with other siblings? Is it expected that these contacts will continue and to what degree? Who is responsible for making sure that it happens?

14. In what ways does the child manifest behaviors related to the abuse, separation, or other trauma? Are other children victimized by the behavior? In what ways?

15. How has this child functioned in foster care? How many moves has this child experienced in foster care, and why was he or she moved?

16. What methods of discipline does this child best respond to?

17. How does this child relate to his or her peers in the neighborhood and school?

18. What level of openness, if any, is possible with birthfamily members?

19. What special skills/abilities/talents/interests do birthfamily members have?

Adopting an Infant:

1. How complete is the social/medical history on the birthfamily, including the extended family? What is missing? Is it possible to obtain more information?

2. What is known about the birthparents' developmental history — physically, emotionally, and cognitively, including language development?

3. Is there a history of drug or alcohol abuse in the birthfamily?

4. Is there any history of mental illness in the birthfamily? Is there any history of other genetically related illnesses such as diabetes or heart disease?

5. What is known about this child's prenatal care and birth history?

6. Does the child have any brothers and sisters? What contact is planned, if any, with these siblings? How often and to what degree will these contacts be expected to continue? Who is responsible for making sure that it happens?

7. What special skills/abilities/talents/interests do birthfamily members have?[1]

Why is this so important? Gathering as much information as possible will enable the adoptive parents to fill in the child's memory gaps. It will enable them to answer the child's questions. Most important, the better adoptive parents understand the child's background, including the abuse, neglect, or trauma the child experienced, the more they will have realistic expectations for the child, themselves, and the journey ahead.

When an adopted child arrives home, there is great excitement, as well there should be. There are also adjustments everyone must make that are unique to the adoptive experience.

BARRIERS TO ADJUSTMENT WHEN ARRIVING HOME

Matthew opened the back door and ran through the living room, bubbling with excitement.

"Did Mommy Janet call yet?" he shouted.

"No, Matt, but the moment she does, I will call you to the phone."

Mommy Janet was Matt's foster mother with whom he and his sister had lived before moving to the Ryans' home. He had been in her home for almost a year. Wisely, Sharon knew that she had to allow Matthew to make the transition to their home in his own timing. Although she wanted Matt to see her as Mom, she knew it would take time. Part of that time meant she would welcome both the physical presence of Mommy Janet and Matt's need to talk about her and with her.

When the relationship with a child in the adoptive home begins, there are several dynamics that are a normal part of the process for the child. There are also dynamics for parents that may affect adjustment. Acknowledging and attending to these barriers can minimize their impact and smooth the transition for all family members.

From the Child's Perspective

Barrier One: Unfinished Business—Dealing with Separation and Loss

Matthew had experienced the loss of significant relationships in his young life. Often, excited adoptive parents fail to understand that when a child enters their home as an older adopted child, he carries with him losses from the past.

In Matthew's case, he experienced the loss of his primary vital connection when he was taken from his birthmother at age two as a result of physical abuse. Then he moved into his foster home and reestablished an attachment to another primary important person, only to face a second separation. His ties to his foster mother had been incredibly strong. When Matthew joined the Ryans at age four, he was not emotionally ready to transfer his attachment needs to yet another new mother. He was still in the stages of grieving his most recent loss.

Children and toddlers who experience circumstances like Matthew's usually progress through several stages in early reactions to loss. Adoption expert Claudia Jewett Jarratt, author of *Helping Children Cope with Separation and Loss*, along with other specialists in the field, outlines these stages within two general phases: early grief and acute grief.[2]

First Phase: Early Grief

1. *Shock and numbing.* When initially told of an impending separation or loss, children may respond with little emotion. This is numbness, the sense that it is not really happening to them and must be happening to someone else.

2. *Alarm.* There are physical reactions to the shock of separation, according to Jarratt. These reactions may manifest themselves in a rise in heart rate, muscular tension, sweating, dry mouth, bowel and bladder relaxation, and even shortness of breath. Insomnia has also been identified as a response to loss. Additionally, children appear to be susceptible to infection when undergoing the tremendous stress of loss and change. It is not unusual for a child to suffer a respiratory infection or gastrointestinal disturbance.

3. *Denial and disbelief.* Children in this stage of grieving appear to reject the reality of the situation completely. Annie, age six, moved into her adoptive home without having the opportunity to say goodbye to her birthfather. For a brief period of time she would run into the house, explaining, "My daddy just drove down the street. He still wants to see me." Because her father lived in another state, Annie's sightings were impossible. They appeared to be part of her denial and disbelief that her relationship with her father was really over.

Second Phase: Acute Grief

1. *Yearning and pining.* This stage in the grieving process is common to all who experience a significant loss. Matthew was at this point as he coped with the separations in his life. Deep inside he longed for the restoration of his relationship with his foster mother, yet at the same time he felt the conflict of a budding attachment to Sharon, his new adoptive mother.

   According to Jarratt, "Regression is a common companion to the conflict and fatigue that results from the yearning and pining stage." It had been years since Matthew wanted to be rocked to sleep, but now he demanded such attention at bedtime. And though he was long past the usual bed-wetting stage, Sharon found herself changing bedding almost daily.

   Some children may step back in time, shelving a developmental skill they mastered earlier in favor of returning to behavior from an earlier period in their lives. Adoptive parents who recognize such behavior in their child can be encouraged with the knowledge that this regression is only temporary. Children whose parents allow them to retreat to former territory will eventually establish a new perspective.

2. *Searching and bargaining.* A form of magical thinking can develop in a person who suffers the trauma of loss. Often children may consciously or unconsciously make a bargain. They may promise always to be good. They may promise never to love anyone else.

   A step away from yearning, this stage contains several elements, according to Jarratt.[3] One aspect of this stage is marked by children being absorbed in and passionate about the lost person. They often display a compulsive need to talk about this, dwelling on past memories. They will refuse to talk about the present and its realities.

   A second element of the searching and bargaining stage of acute grief emerges in children who demonstrate a sense of expecting something to happen. They may comment that the lost person might attend events they will be attending or might appear at places common to the child.

   A third element is restless or somewhat hyperactive behavior. The child may be unable to sit still or to focus for a period of time on tasks placed before her. Occasionally a child may be suspected of having behavioral problems when in reality she is working through tremendous grief issues.

Perhaps one of the most important assignments for adoptive parents caring for children at this point in their lives is to be patient in allowing them these expressions of grief. Some adoptive parents report a sense of rejection by the child in this stage. They comment that their own coping mechanism is to cut the child off in the midst of her expressions of grief by reminding her that those things belong in the past. Jarratt suggested that "curt remarks urging the child not to dwell on the past only cut off the sharing and make the bereaved child feel misunderstood."[4]

3. *Strong feelings of anger, guilt, and shame.* The Barretts had been told to expect Lorrie's outbursts of strong feelings. And sure enough, they soon broke the surface. "I hate you! I hate you!" Lorrie yelled at her adoptive mom. "Why did you ever have to come into my life?"

Facing this onslaught of anger without pulling away from a hurting child will demand strength, wisdom, and empathy from the adoptive parents. It requires them to realize that the anger isn't about them, although it is directed at them. It is impossible to predict the length of such a stage, but specialists say that it may take as long as six to twelve weeks for the worst of the pain to subside.

4. *Despair.* This stage can be most disconcerting to parents, who must watch their small child slip into a sense of hopelessness and helplessness. Although depressed children are not able to disclose any further what they are thinking or feeling, they will demonstrate behavioral changes such as extreme fatigue or changes in eating and sleeping habits.

What can parents do to ease the grief and transition for a child? First, if possible, adoptive parents should maintain post-placement contact with the significant people who came into the child's life when he entered foster care. Continued post-placement contact with significant people will ease a child's transition. Occasionally, adoptive parents and social workers agree that cutting off all contact and quickly disengaging a child from his "foster care past" will facilitate adjustment. However, children form significant attachments to adults and peers and need to transition out of those relationships. Abrupt disengagement is usually not emotionally healthy.[5]

Second, it is important for adoptive parents to understand loyalty issues. Even young children can struggle with feeling torn between loving adoptive parents and loving foster parents. Parents can help their newest child realize that she can love both her adoptive parents and her former foster parents. Early on she will get the message from her new family whether it is okay or not okay to talk about the other family, such as what they did and how they did it. The message may come in subtle ways. Parents need to allow her to say such things as, "My other mom did it this way" without feeling threatened. If parents respond with, "I know you really miss your foster mom. Tell me a little more about how she did it," it validates the feelings of loss and loyalty a child struggles with. If they respond by saying something like, "Well, in this house, we do it this way," they devalue not only her feelings of loss but her former relationship as well and set up barriers to adjustment for everyone. Asking questions about special memories with the former foster family, having a picture of that family in a visible place, and bringing them up occasionally will model acceptance and encourage growth in trust and attachment to the new family.

Third, adoptive parents need to allow the child to express his feelings of sadness, anger, or grief without relegating them to the past or negating their importance. Sadness about being separated from someone the child cares for is normal and even healthy. Children should be allowed to experience the grief and move on. Grief that is shoved under the rug will likely be uncovered in painful, more complicated ways later on.

Fourth, adoptive parents should keep the home schedule relatively free, avoiding excessive activity. Adoptive parents often attempt to help their children forget about the past by filling up their children's schedules. However, constant motion is not what these children need. Rather, they need an environment in which time for sharing and talking together is a priority.

Fifth, adoptive parents should remember the importance of physical touch. Researchers say that people need eight to ten meaningful contacts a day to maintain emotional and physical health. Children feel strength from a parent who sits close to them when they are sharing strong feelings. A touch on a shoulder or a lap to sit on reassures a troubled youngster of secure love and concern.

As a child makes her way through these initial stages of grieving, she eventually reaches the final stage.

5. *Reorganization.* Parents of children who are moving into the stage of reorganization notice a brighter countenance and a better frame of mind. Teachers report improved behavior and grades. For the most part, neighborhood conflicts disappear. After walking through the difficult stages of separation and loss, these children have now reorganized their lives without the missing adult at the core.

Barrier Two: Lack of Preparation of the Child

Moving a child into an adoptive family requires especially sensitive preparation if the youngster has formed a significant attachment to another adult. If age permits, clear explanations should be given to the child of what is going to happen to him and when it's going to happen. If he is old enough, he should feel a sense of contribution to the decision. Any child who is forced to move quickly may become shell-shocked and confused. Most successful placements of children begin with a preplacement time that is used by all parties involved as a period of preparation.

Tom and Terri Adams answered enthusiastically to the prospect of six-month-old Paul joining their family. Their desire was to rush over to the foster home where he was living and bring him home that night. However, wisdom and sensitivity guided them. During the first week, Tom and Terri began visiting Paul in the foster home, often staying two hours or more. Within that week, they took Paul on short trips and eventually on overnight visits. By the end of two full weeks, they were no longer strangers to this delightful youngster. He moved in with no major traumas to overcome. They also continued contact with Paul's foster parents, who visited regularly in the home for a number of months following placement. The foster parents still see Paul, now three, on special occasions and always have a seat at the birthday party. Paul's adjustment to Tom and Terri was greatly eased because they did not rush through the process of letting him get to know them.

For children who are verbal, preplacement visits provide them with space to integrate into their thinking what is happening in their world and to begin dealing with the changes and losses they will encounter. A significant barrier to adjustment is erected when children are forced to make a move into a new family with little information about the process or the family they are joining. Even very young children observe, understand, and absorb more than what they are usually given credit for. Many adoptive families prepare a welcome book that is used by agency staff to introduce the child to the family before meeting them in person.

Appendix 2 is a toolbox of resources and ideas on how to prepare children for adoption. These tools can be used during the preplacement time as well as after the child moves in.

Barrier Three: Cultural Differences

Susan was becoming increasingly worried about her new three-month-old Korean-born daughter, Kim. Kim cried every time Susan put her down to accomplish some work around the house. Susan wasn't getting anything done. More important, she wondered if something was wrong with the baby.

A short time later, Susan learned at an adoptive parents group that Korean mothers carry their infants on their back while they work. Kim's problem was that she wanted the closeness she was used to sensing. Susan thought she would give it a try. She learned how to wrap the child on her back. It was awkward at first, but she soon realized that she enjoyed the closeness. Best of all, Kim stopped crying.

This young mother discovered that even infants may require some significant adjustments. Families who adopt internationally should make the following inquiries to discover what kinds of adjustments may be necessary:

- What type of formula and food was the child given and in what manner? What type of eater (heavy, light, picky) was the child?
- When the baby fussed, what methods were used to console him?
- Where and how did the child sleep?
- Did the child demand attention, or was she content alone?

For parents adopting older children, the following suggestions may be helpful in making the transition:

- Be ready for some communication difficulties. If there is a person in the community who speaks the language of the child, arrange for that person to be in your home for extended periods of time in the early weeks following the child's arrival. Ask permission to solicit help in times of distress, even in the late hours of the evening.
- Accept the child's non-Americanized mannerisms and lifestyle. Eventually the child will adopt American ways. It is not necessary to push him.
- Be aware of talking down to a child. Often when children are

struggling with the language barrier, parents may treat them as far younger than their age. Or they may speak very loudly, as though the child cannot hear well.

- Learn some significant customs from the child's country. For example, some countries celebrate birthdays differently from what is common in the United States. This kind of celebration would be an excellent place to start.[6]

When children enter a new family, they face unforeseen barriers to adjustment. The same is true for their parents.

FROM THE PARENTS' PERSPECTIVE

Barrier One: Unmet Needs and Unmatched Expectations

Sitting across from a counselor, Holly and Jeff had nothing left to say. In the midst of the pain attached to the crumbling of their adoption dream, they couldn't believe what they had just said.

Only a year ago, they had worked hard to prepare for five-year-old Joey coming to live with them. Today, torn with frustration caused by their perception of Joey's inability to blend into the family, they felt like giving up. They had had enough.

What brought them to this crossroads? The answer lies in how Holly and Jeff began this journey. Two dynamics that are crucial to setting the course for building a relationship had been neglected:

- No one addressed this couple's needs for the relationship.
- No one addressed this couple's expectations for the experience.

Adoptive parents should consider their own needs during the process of deciding to parent a child born to someone else, because those needs will significantly affect the entire process. They will dictate a parent's response to adjustment issues. What are these needs? Here are some that adoptive parents have voiced. Notice who is the focus in this list:

- "I have a strong maternal/paternal need to nurture a child."
- "I have a need for this child to see me as the only mother figure in the

world. I need for him to forget his birthmother."

- "I have a need for this experience to be exactly the same as parenting a child born to me, since I can't have children of my own."
- "I have a need to feel a deep attachment to this child and she to me."
- "I have a need to give family membership to a needy child and to be appreciated for doing so."

And the list continues. Adoption is supposed to be about finding parents and families for children who need them, not about finding children for adults who would like to parent.

As they walk through the early months of the process, adoptive parents must not only identify their own needs for the relationship but also examine their own expectations.

Occasionally, such parents create in their minds an image of the child they hope to adopt. They enter the relationship with high expectations of performance and behavior for themselves and for the child. When those expectations go unmet, they find it difficult to invest in the child.

Unrealistic, wishful thinking can be dangerous in adoption. Unmatched expectations regarding the child and others involved in the adoptive environment often create unyielding tension on the newly formed family system. The ground underneath the promise begins to shift. What are some of those expectations? Again, here is what adoptive parents have said:

- "I expected my new child to appreciate all that I do for her. After all, look where she came from."
- "I expected my biological children to sacrifice for this new child in our home."
- "I expected my extended family to take to this new child as they would a biological child."
- "I expected the agency to be readily available to me with answers and support."
- "I expected that I would always feel happy and fulfilled because we've helped this child."
- "I didn't expect I could get so angry."

To greater or lesser degrees, many of these expectations will not be met. Parents who are unable to adjust their expectations of the child, their biological children, their extended family, and the agency will find themselves cornered in a maze of frustration without resources for finding their way out. They will find themselves broadsided by shattered assumptions.

Barrier Two: Marital Problems

A significant ingredient for a smooth adjustment in the new family centers on the health of the marriage, as was mentioned in an earlier chapter.

In hopes of fixing a troubled marriage, some couples feel that the addition of a child will be the determining factor. Instead of relieving a stressful situation, however, it will more likely compound it.

Occasionally, other couples in a more stable marital situation enter into the adoptive relationship without being fully committed to it as a team. Because they are not in agreement, crises or stresses precipitated by the adoption often cause marital difficulties.

Barrier Three: Reordered Family System

When a new family member enters the home, whether by birth or adoption, the entire family system shifts. A comfortable equilibrium disappears, replaced by momentary confusion and relational chaos. How families respond to the shift will greatly determine how smoothly everyone walks through the adjustment phase of adoption.

One primary task new adoptive families must accept is to create a new management system. Within that management system are new household routines such as getting more children out the door to school, packing more lunches, cleaning more rooms, and running more errands. Also part of that management system are new rules, often unwritten, such as how much time is allotted for TV, free play, study, and work. Setting up the new family system can be a physically and emotionally exhausting endeavor.

Steve and Darlene Miller adopted one-year-old twins, Bradley and Jonathan. Steve described the shock of change:

> We didn't realize how we would react to the loss of privacy and freedom we encountered when the boys first came. We were pretty much used to having time to ourselves and going when and where we pleased. We knew in our minds that those things would change. We didn't realize what it was like to live it. We were surprised that we would react in frustration to the change.

As soon as we perceived what was happening, we knew what to do about it. Instead of totally submerging ourselves in the children, we learned to balance time for them and for ourselves. We made plans for time together on a regular basis so that we could strengthen our own relationship, and we didn't feel guilty about it.

Barrier Four: Incomplete Resolution of Loss Within the Parents' Own Lives

Six years ago, Byron and Rachel Jones lost their only biological child to Sudden Infant Death Syndrome. Recovering from this tremendous loss proved to be a long and difficult process for them. Two years ago they adopted an infant, bringing her home straight from the hospital.

Following that adoption, Byron and Rachel moved from the community where they had lived to new jobs and new friends. They told no one of their loss. They told no one of Kayla's adoption. They had made an unconscious decision to block out the pain from their past. Kayla was their daughter, and that was the way it was.

This young couple is not likely to face adjustment difficulties with Kayla in their early years together. She is a happy, energetic two-year-old. But because the couple did not resolve their own loss, difficulties will likely emerge later when Kayla is eventually told of her adoption and Byron and Rachel must respond to her questions. Both parties in this adoption entered the relationship from the position of loss. Byron and Rachel lost a child. Kayla lost her birthfamily. As adoptive parents, Byron and Rachel will become the interpreters of Kayla's loss and more than likely will pursue it from the vantage point of how they handled their own—denial. Adoptive parents assume many roles in the life of their child. However, especially for older children, none is as crucial as the role of becoming their child's "interpreter of loss."

SUMMARY

Preparing for a child to come into the home requires two steps by adoptive parents: (1) Learn as much about the child's past history and family as possible, and (2) Recognize the potential barriers that may slow the adjustment of the adoptive relationship for all family members. These barriers include the following:

- From the child's perspective: unfinished business, separation and loss, lack of preparation, and cultural differences
- From the parents' perspective: unmet needs and unmatched expectations, marital problems, reordered family system, and incomplete resolution of loss in their own lives

QUESTIONS FOR SMALL GROUPS

1. What other questions, in addition to the ones provided in this chapter, can be helpful in learning about a child?
2. How assertive can and should adoptive parents be in getting this information?
3. What other barriers to adjustment have you experienced or observed other adoptive parents encountering?
4. How did you resolve these barriers?

CHAPTER EIGHT

ATTACHMENT, DEVELOPMENT, AND THE IMPACT OF TRAUMA

What Adoptive Parents Need to Know

BY TIMOTHY J. CALLAHAN, PSY.D.

> One of the most difficult things for adoptive parents to accept is the fact
> that nothing can change their adopted child's genes, early life experi-
> ences, or ties to another family. . . . Only by allowing a child this heritage
> from the birthfamily, and incorporating it into the current family, can
> that child really belong to the adoptive family.
>
> — *Bourguignon*

Every child has a story, and that story will have an impact on those who love him.

Johnny was born healthy and perfect to young Ashley, who hoped a baby would love her and make her life complete. Ashley felt unloved and abandoned by all who should have taken care of her, including her mother and Johnny's father. She would give Johnny everything she didn't get from her mother. Johnny would give her purpose. But Johnny cried and cried; the shrieks cut through her like a hot knife. Dirty diapers made her sick. She felt like the baby was sucking the life out of her. The baby was ruining her life, not completing it. She felt like throwing him out the window.

Ashley couldn't tolerate Johnny's neediness and left him alone crying in his crib. At first she would just go outside and smoke a cigarette, but she could still hear him wailing, so she went to a friend's house. It became easier to leave the baby. Johnny lay on his back squirming in distress and filth. No one looked at him. No one talked to him except to yell, "Shut up!" The only touch he received took the form of shakings and beatings. Ashley's shame overwhelmed her but only increased her resentment toward Johnny.

The authorities were notified by concerned neighbors three years later. When they arrived, Johnny was asleep by the dog with crumbs of dog food on his lips. He was taken from his mother and placed with a loving foster family. But Johnny would not respond to the love. He showed no expressions except when raging. He recoiled to touch. By age five he was found with a pillow over his infant foster brother's face; he showed no remorse. After he burned down the barn, the foster family sent him back to children's services. Johnny went through ten foster homes and two group homes. At age twelve, Johnny was adopted by a family who had the courage, patience, and knowledge to give Johnny a chance. His parents spent time with him and, rather than react to his efforts to push them away, they empathized with him and validated his feelings. They understood why he didn't trust anyone and why he acted the way he did. For the first time in his life, someone valued and understood him. Over time, Johnny felt connected, supported, and safe. He could finally relax and let others take care of him. He was no longer alone in a scary world.

Most adopted children attach to their new loving parents and families and make their transitions smoothly. However, it is important for adoptive parents to know about the potential effects of the abuse and neglect their child may have suffered prior to adoption. A child's ability to attach to his or her family can be seriously harmed by early maltreatment and lack of care.

UNDERSTANDING THE ATTACHMENT PROCESS

Attachment is our first act as humans and the key to our development and survival.[1] Minutes after our formation, we move down the fallopian tube and attach to our mothers. The attachment nourishes and anchors us. After birth, the anchor transfers from the world of the womb to the realm of the interpersonal. Over the next two years of development, the interpersonal attachment to the parents provides the necessary base from which to grow and thrive. It is from the security of the primary anchor that we learn about the world around us and about ourselves in relation to that world. The brain, as the grand regulator of all aspects of our organism, requires activation and definition through close interaction with the primary parents.

Attachment is not simply an interpersonal phenomenon; it is a biological one. It is the foundation for our neurological, emotional, behavioral, cognitive, social, and physical well-being. Early and chronic disruption of this attachment through maltreatment affects the ability of an infant to establish the necessary foundation and shapes the way he or she develops. Many children just like Johnny who enter adoptive homes as older children experience disrupted attachment.

Trauma affects how children interact and react to others, how they experience emotions, how they regulate themselves, how they adapt, how they remember, how they meet their needs, how they navigate through the stages of development, and how they comprehend themselves in the context of the world around them. Understanding the impact that attachment, and specifically attachment trauma, has on children's development frees us to be more attuned to them emotionally and to respond more effectively to their needs.

Once we begin to comprehend the pervasive impact of chronic early maltreatment, we find ourselves impressed and humbled by human resiliency and the drive to survive and adapt. We are forced to reevaluate our own theories about why our children do what they do. Behaviors begin to take on more meaning and make more sense. Behaviors that seem to us as performances designed to drive us over the brink of madness may in fact be attempts to influence a world expected to be unresponsive and unpredictable.

Understanding the survival function behind the behavior of maltreated children enables us to respond more patiently and more effectively. Parents of children who have suffered attachment trauma face special challenges in helping their young adapt, survive, and thrive. Knowledge and perspective give us hope by helping us see things clearly in a larger, more meaningful context.

This is a crucial area of understanding for adoptive parents, whether they are adopting children domestically or internationally. This chapter will explore how attachment influences development and what impact complex trauma has on attachment. The next chapter focuses on living with a child with attachment trauma.

The process of attachment appears to be similar across cultures.[2] Human development is rooted in the attachment experiences of the first years of life. The following are some specific aspects of our development that are affected by early attachment experiences.

GENES AND EXPERIENCE

We come into existence with a prepackaged set of potentials, collected over multitudes of generations. We inherit our basic set of potentials from our parents through genetic transmission. Genes carry the codes and blueprints that direct how we develop.[3] Our brains and nervous systems are the command centers that implement the genetic directives. It is estimated that 50 percent of who we are is inherited. The other half is formed through experience.[4] We start our lives with inherited brains that are whole but undefined. Experience carves and differentiates the brain, forming pathways and fresh connections. Early attachment experiences have the most impact because the infant brain is malleable and impressionable.

PRUNING

Our infant brains, containing over one hundred billion neurons[5] are actually more than whole. We are, in fact, born with more brain cells than we actually need. Pruning is one of the key mechanisms behind brain development.[6] Early interactions with parents not only activate our brain cells but also prune away potentials that are deemed not crucial for survival. If we were not able to prune, our brain pathways would be overwhelmingly cluttered and unable to function properly. If a trait or process is not mirrored by the parent during infant-parent interactions, it may be pruned away. Remorse, for example, often used as the true mark of sincerity, is a complex brain-based socioemotional capability that may be pruned away if not activated by loving empathic responses of parents. Children who have not been cared for properly may have lost this ability; therefore, judging their actions based on the apparent absence of remorse overlooks the role brain development plays in empathy.

THE BRAIN AND THE GAZE

The brain is essentially a regulator on an all-inclusive scale. The brain, along with interrelated nervous systems, controls, modulates, and monitors everything from breathing to reading the words on this page. Our basic regulatory processes, including the ability to regulate body temperature, which intuitively seem hardwired, are actually dependent on early interactions with parents.[7] The infant brain is essentially unable to adequately regulate on its own, so the attachment serves as a vehicle for coregulation.[8] A primary vehicle for the attachment experience is the face-to-face interaction between the infant and parents.

A parent holds her baby and is compelled to gaze into the baby's eyes, what neuropsychoanalyst Allan Schore refers to as the "mutual gaze."[9] Eye-eye contact is a critical symbiotic linkage that sets the brain toward balanced regulation. The mutual gaze leads to emotional attunement, a deeply satisfying experience of feeling harmonious oneness and completeness, not unlike the peace experienced in the womb. Without the attentive loving gaze and emotional responsiveness of the parent, the infant brain would struggle on its own to develop and mature.[10]

EMOTIONAL REGULATION

Interaction between the infant and parents activates and refines a myriad of complex regulatory processes, including such critical functions as emotional regulation and distress tolerance.[11] The capacity to tolerate and control distress is dependent on a parent's consistently satisfying a pressing need, be it hunger, thirst, discomfort, sleep, or touch during the critical first months.[12]

When distress is recognized and then soothed by parents, the infant feels acknowledged and gratified, returning to a state of equilibrium and comfort. Over time the infant's brain develops the ability to internally tolerate distress and tension. Over time the infant will come to trust that the world is essentially predictable, responsive, and manageable.[13]

Beyond satisfying a need, parents help differentiate obscure need states by putting words to them, helping to form the foundation for language development. Children who have been deprived of the opportunity to attach words to emotional experiences struggle in life to adequately communicate their needs and desires.[14] Without an adequately attuned, coregulating attachment, the infant is left alone and helpless with her unregulated impulses, needs, and distresses.[15]

SURVIVAL

Survival requires an effective reaction to a threat. Deep within the brain are structures designed to help us survive threats through fight (defend), flight (escape), or fright (play dead). When faced with a threat, our brain signals a cascade of chemical reactions that enables us to increase our chance of survival. The capacity to modulate and control these primitive survival strategies is dependent on attachment experiences that create deep sensations of safety and security. Without good attachment, the child's brain operates from the perspective of threat and responds in kind.[16]

SOCIALIZATION AND SHAME

Attachment facilitates socialization and behavioral control in a vast variety of ways. Healthy attachment not only activates cognitive processes in the brain that help override instinctual reactions to threat but also serves as the theater in which the baby learns about appropriate ways of behaving.

Healthy shame is a painful but naturally occurring emotion that results when we behave outside of acceptable boundaries. A child experiences shame when she transgresses and the parent responds with limits. The painful shame leads to a temporary break in the attachment relationship as the child withdraws from the parent.[17]

The key to healthy resolution of shame is the "interactive repair" experience in which the parent repairs the relationship by reuniting and ensuring that the bond remains intact.[18] In doing so, the feeling of shame is isolated to the behavior and not to the sense of self. Shame isolated to the behavior becomes the experience of guilt, a healthy and necessary driving force behind socialization and behavior control. Shame is a powerful influence in developing behavior controls but can be detrimental if left unresolved. If there is no "interactive repair," the shame is attributed to the whole self, not to the behavior, and becomes pervasive and overwhelming.

A parent who chronically allows the unresolved shame to grow out of control by shunning or ignoring the child during the critical window of opportunity for repair sets into course a lifetime of toxic humiliation and self-loathing.[19]

SENSE OF SELF

Autonomous sense of self is the unifying core of our personalities and is dependent on healthy attachment. In terms of a core sense of self, the infant during the first year is not fully differentiated from her parent.[20] Oneness through attunement and coregulation is necessary to anchor the infant to the world but must give way to individuation and formation of a separate sense of self.

A child who feels safely anchored can begin to define herself as independent and take risks to explore her world. The crown jewel of the "terrible twos" is the word *no*, a word that is the outward reflection of the necessary process of trying out the autonomous self.

Without oneness we have no individual sense of self; without a separate self we cannot function autonomously; without self-reliance we are at the mercy of forces beyond our control; once we lose control we lose the capacity to adapt. Having a coherent, meaningful view of oneself generalizes to experiencing the external world as coherent and meaningful. Without an intact sense of self, our life story is like a book missing chapters and in no particular order.

LANGUAGE AND EXPRESSIVENESS

Often to the dismay of those nearby, we are compelled to make baby talk, coos, and exaggerated facial expressions when interacting with babies. Babies elicit parent response and vice versa. The mirroring of facial expressions is crucial in activating the subtle facial muscles that are responsible for nonverbal expressiveness.[21] Babies and parents are prewired for baby talk and bright-eyed funny faces, primitive utterances that elicit responses from each other.[22] Language is formed out of these early infant-parent dialogues. Attachment experiences set the stage for the development of social awareness, including the capacity to read cues and understand humor.

PLASTICITY AND RESILIENCE

Our amazingly adaptive brains are able to reorganize and form new connections even after processes have been pruned away or damaged. Our brains have the capacity to compensate, a process known as placticity.[23] Infant brain processes that missed activation during critical periods may develop later but through different pathways.

For those whose development has been delayed or halted by maltreatment, hope remains because the association cortex is capable of making up for lost functions. Without plasticity, treatment and parenting would have no effect on helping the brain get back on the track of balanced regulation and adaptability.

Humans are resilient by nature. We are, for the most part, capable of tolerating enormous stress and strain and can adapt to trauma more than we think possible. Incredibly, children who have suffered severe maltreatment more often than not do not develop impairments in functioning, particularly when in stable, loving care.[24] But some children do struggle severely and suffer, and some may cause suffering to those closest to them.

COMPLEX TRAUMA AND ITS IMPACT ON ATTACHMENT

Masha was born in a dark alley and left to die. A soldier found her and took her to the authorities. The orphanage in which Masha spent her first eight years fed her, bathed her, and kept her warm but lacked the resources to provide her adequate security, comfort, and stimulation. She didn't talk much and never cried. Staff noticed that she rarely smiled and had a blank expression on her face. One male staff, in particular, noticed her and concluded that Masha's quietness could be a convenient protection against allegations; there was a good chance Masha wouldn't tell on him, and it excited him. He befriended her and spent time with her. He was nice and made her feel special. One day he brought her a piece of candy but told her she had to earn it. He sexually abused her over a two-year period. He prostituted her to his friends for bottles of liquor. When he was drunk he hit her and called her names. Then one day he left, and she was safe but alone again.

Masha lived mostly in her own world. She felt unreal sometimes and occasionally felt like she floated away from her body. She felt numb and could scratch through her skin without any sensation. Masha couldn't tell when her bladder was full and was frequently in trouble for wetting herself. When approached by staff she recoiled, and if touched she exploded in inconsolable rage. The inability to sleep except for a few hours of restless slumber left her edgy and irritable. When a family came to consider adoption, Masha was found in her room covered in her own feces; she felt like being left alone and knew no one would come near. Masha felt secure in her inner world; no one could see in, as if she was hidden behind boarded windows.

The American Psychiatric Association's *Diagnostic and Statistical Manual of Mental Disorders*, the diagnostic handbook for mental health professionals, describes posttraumatic stress disorder as a constellation of symptoms that stem from exposure to threatening and frightening experiences. A person suffering from PTSD persistently reexperiences the traumatic events, develops impairments in functioning, avoids and numbs to cope, and experiences persistent arousal, including irritability, insomnia, and/or hypervigilance.[25]

The concept of PTSD, previously referred to as "shell shock" or "battle fatigue," was developed out of literature on the effects of war. PTSD appeared in the 1980 edition of the *DSM* to respond to traumatized soldiers returning from Vietnam. The concept of PTSD is derived from circumscribed traumatic events, such as combat, disaster, and rape. Exposure to prolonged trauma over time or early in life, however, can have an even more pervasive effect on development than PTSD describes.

According to Bessel van der Kolk and Christine Courtois, PTSD as a diagnosis is not broad enough to capture the experiences of many victims of prolonged trauma, including profound changes in feelings of safety, trust, and self-worth.[26] Judith Herman, MD, developed and popularized the concept of complex trauma in her book *Trauma and Recovery* as a way to describe the experiences of those who have been prisoners of war, hostages, members of cults, and victims of early chronic child maltreatment.[27]

According to Herman, complex trauma involves totalitarian control over a prolonged period of time that has long-term effects on affect, consciousness, self-perception, perception of perpetrator, relation to others, and ability to make meaning and sense out of one's life. Totalitarian control refers to complete authoritarian dominance over another, which includes dictators, captors, and hostage takers; in the case of dependent maltreated children, the abusive or neglectful caregiver serves as the totalitarian controller. The key feature of C-PTSD is unpredictable and uncontrollable danger, and nothing is more dangerous to a developing infant than the absence of a parent who reliably and responsively protects and nurtures.[28] Infants and toddlers who have been abused, neglected, or exposed to violence may experience deep, broad, and lasting effects.[29]

A U.S. Department of Health and Human Services report states that there were 3.6 million referrals to child protective agencies in 2005; of these, 900,000 concerned children who were determined to be victims of abuse or neglect.[30] Early chronic maltreatment takes the form of emotional, physical, and sexual abuse; neglect and deprivation; exposure to domestic violence; and an array of experiences that disrupt the primary attachment. Babies left to cry unattended in orphanages, witnesses and victims of terrible violence, and used and abused babies left hungry and cold by uncaring parents are all examples of maltreatment.

Early chronic maltreatment is a deep source of injury because the trauma is to the attachment anchor, the main feed for coregulation and sustenance. Considering the role attachment experiences play in our development, any significant disruption to the link may have lasting effects in a wide range of domains, including the following:[31]

1. *Attachment*. Masha, from the story shared earlier, was rightly distrusting of people in authority, and she projected her suspiciousness onto all adults, waiting vigilantly for anticipated abuse. The lack of attachment, stimulation, and attention early in her life affected Masha's brain in such a way that she struggled to read social and emotional cues and lacked awareness of personal boundaries. Masha appeared to others as unpredictable, but in fact it was the world around her that was random, arbitrary, and confusing. Masha lacked remorse for her transgressions; her brain had pruned away the complex processes that control the ability to empathize because no one was there to love her during critical windows of empathy development.

2. *Biology*. Masha had difficulty reading and managing her sensory and physical cues, such as not knowing when her bladder was full or not being aware that she had scratched herself until bleeding. Complex trauma affects the very fabric of the child's biological being and makes her prone to health problems.

3. *Affect regulation*. Both Masha and Johnny had difficulty regulating their rages and feelings in general. Upon further investigation it was discovered that both children had difficulty describing feelings and internal states and struggled to communicate wishes and desires.

4. *Dissociation*. Dissociation refers to distinct alterations in states of

consciousness, including amnesia, impaired memory, and the feeling of being unreal. Masha felt as if she floated away and often felt like she was not real, "kind of like I'm dreaming but awake."

5. *Behavioral control.* Johnny struggled to modulate impulses, control aggression, and understand the impact of his behavior on others. He understood rules but did not feel they applied to him. He acted before he thought and felt little control over his actions.

6. *Cognition.* Complex trauma affects the child's ability to focus on and process information. Johnny and Masha had difficulty with executive functions, such as logic, reasoning, insight, and judgment; they struggled with planning, anticipating, and completing tasks. Complex trauma affects language development and may lead to learning problems.

7. *Self-concept.* Maltreated children may have difficulty experiencing themselves as continuous and fluid and instead view themselves as fragmented and unpredictable. Masha had a disturbed image of her body and self and described herself as "bad, ugly and like there's a big black hole inside me."

DOMAINS OF IMPAIRMENT IN CHILDREN EXPOSED TO COMPLEX TRAUMA[32]

The effects of maltreatment correlate with the very aspects of development that are linked to healthy attachment. Although there are other influential factors, including in-utero toxin exposure (nicotine, drugs), poverty, malnutrition, developmental disabilities,[33] and current environmental stressors, attachment trauma stands out as one of the most significant risks to the health and well-being of a child.

Early and prolonged trauma affects the developing being and reorganizes adaptive systems toward survival. What eventually appear as problems in functioning are, in fact, resilient solutions to adapt to a world expected to be unpredictable, unreliable, and ultimately dangerous.

When a maltreated child behaves in certain ways, ways that seem maladaptive, it is tempting to attribute the behavior to the child's personality. As Judith Herman observed, the concept of complex trauma prevents "blaming the victim" by clarifying and emphasizing that the victim's problems in functioning

1. ATTACHMENT	2. BIOLOGY	3. AFFECT REGULATION
• Problems with boundaries • Distrust • Suspiciousness • Social isolation • Difficulty attuning to other people's emotional states • Difficulty in perspective taking	• Sensorimotor development • Analgesia • Problems with coordination, balance, body tone • Somatization • Increased medical problems across a wide span (pelvic pain, asthma, skin problems, autoimmune disorders, pseudoseisures)	• Difficulty with emotional self-regulation • Difficulty labeling and expressing feelings • Problems knowing and describing internal states • Difficulty communicating wishes and needs
4. DISSOCIATION	**5. BEHAVIORAL CONTROL**	**6. COGNITION**
• Distinct alterations in states of consciousness • Amnesia • Depersonalization and derealization • Two or more distinct states of consciousness • Impaired memory for state-based events	• Poor modulation of impulses • Self-destructive behavior • Aggression toward others • Pathological self soothing • Sleep disturbances • Eating disorders • Substance abuse • Excessive compliance • Oppositional behavior • Difficulty understanding and complying with rules • Reenactment of trauma in behavior or play	• Difficulty in attention regulation and executive function • Lack of sustained curiosity • Problems with processing novel information • Problems with object constancy • Difficulty planning and anticipating • Problems understanding responsibility • Learning difficulties • Problems with language development • Problems with orientation in time and space • Two or more distinct states of consciousness • Impaired memory for state-based events

7. SELF-CONCEPT
• Lack of a continuous, predictable sense of self • Poor sense of separateness • Disturbances of body image • Low self-esteem • Shame and guilt

are a response to trauma and not caused by underlying psychopathology.[34]

Understanding the impact of trauma helps unveil the true cause behind a problematic behavior. For example, oppositional and defiant behavior in traumatized children may serve to protect them against a perceived threat by causing them to "freeze" in their tracks, a primitive but effective survival strategy. Freezing allows keener senses to scan for threats and can act as a "camouflage" to avoid attracting predators.[35]

Severely maltreated children may eventually display a constellation of symptoms and problems that cluster into an attachment disorder. For example, Johnny's story displayed a variety of disturbed and disturbing behavior including fire setting, inconsolable violent rages, and a homicidal attempt; Masha withdrew into her internal world where she felt secure and successful, and in doing so she became trapped in a world where smearing feces on herself seemed like a good idea.

SUMMARY

Attachment is the key to our development and our life-sustaining anchor to the world. Our lives literally depend on it. Attachment nourishes and activates us, defines and refines us. Fundamental features of our lives, such as how we feel, how we view ourselves, how we think and remember, how we relate to others, how we regulate ourselves, and how we find meaning are founded in the early parent-child attachment experiences.

When the attachment is disrupted by early chronic maltreatment, the course of the child's development is significantly affected. Attachment trauma affects the neurological, physical, emotional, behavioral, social, and cognitive well-being of the child. Attachment trauma affects everything in a child's world from family relationships to school performance to peer relationships and beyond. Children who have experienced early and chronic maltreatment need to be understood as survivors, resiliently attempting to adapt to an unresponsive, threatening, and unpredictable world.

Knowledge about what is truly happening to a developing child's brain and body provides us the necessary perspective and appreciation to effectively interact with our children. Perspective gives us hope because we can see our child's behavior in a meaningful context. Once we begin to fathom the complexities of human development, we can begin to appreciate our adaptability and drive to survive. Parenting children who have experienced such trauma is very challenging as well as deeply rewarding. The next chapter will discuss the journey and art of parenting a traumatized child who has developed an attachment disorder.

QUESTIONS FOR SMALL GROUPS

1. What do you think and feel when you read the statement, "Every child has a story, and that story will have an impact on those who love him"? How much of your child's story do you know?

2. What do you know about the early attachment experiences of your child? In what ways have you noticed that those experiences have affected your child?

3. Think about children in the foster care system in this country or older children in orphanages overseas. What life events have they possibly experienced that put them in "survival mode"? Now think about your child. Does he appear to live in the "flight or fight or fright" mode? How do his responses affect you as his parent?

4. What do you understand about the differences between posttraumatic stress disorder and complex trauma? How do these differences relate to you as a parent?

5. Think about your child again. Review the domains of impairment with complex trauma and the behavioral signs related to those domains. In what ways do you see your child reflected there? How have you been affected by these behaviors?

CHAPTER NINE

LIVING WITH CHILDREN WITH ATTACHMENT TRAUMA

Understanding the Terminology, Diagnosis, and Parenting Strategies

BY DR. TIMOTHY J. CALLAHAN

Remember, every child has a story, and that story will have an impact on those who love him.

Cindy dreaded the upcoming family reunion because she was convinced she would ruin it, again. Her parents reminded Cindy how she had behaved at the past reunions, as well as other family outings, in an effort to help her control herself better. But all she heard was that she was bad. She felt ashamed. She never planned to ruin anything, but she always did, whether it was fighting a cousin over calling her weird or knocking over the food table when playing hide-and-seek. No one seemed to believe her; even her loving parents looked at her suspiciously as if she planned to mess things up. Deep down, Cindy couldn't blame them; she didn't trust herself either. A sick, pressured dread would come over her sometimes, and she couldn't control what came out of her. Sometimes she felt as if she was watching herself from the side, a passive observer as embarrassed and mortified as her parents.

This time Cindy would try a different strategy; she would be invisible. She would blend into the background and scan the reunion in camouflaged silence. She remembered using her invisibility powers when her birthparents beat each other up and threw dishes. Her birthfather, when done with his wife, would look to the children for continued abuse. She learned to stay completely still and sit deep into the couch. Cindy believed the strategy would work again.

On the dreadfully quiet ride home from the reunion, she whimpered in the backseat. She couldn't believe she'd ruined it again. The invisibility backfired.

"Cindy, now don't be rude; tell your uncle about school, about your science project," her mother politely pressured. The word *rude* triggered a wave of rage that she could not hold back. She yelled, "Leave me alone; I hate you!" and ran off. She hid for hours in the woods behind the park. She planned out her apology, but when her father found her she felt frozen and unable to respond. Her parents were angry and said nothing to her all the way home. The coldness lasted for the rest of the week. Cindy was dumbfounded that she couldn't get it right. She didn't know how to act; it was hopeless. She heard a phrase once that seemed to describe her perfectly: *"I can't win for trying."* So she concluded to herself in a defeated, quiet way, *Then why try?*

To outside observers including parents, teachers, peers, and providers, behaviors of attachment traumatized children can bewilder and frustrate, frighten and unsettle. To outside observers, the child's apparently deliberate ruining of family fun, the compulsive need to control and lie, the explosive reactions to minor slights or demands, the hoarding of food, the stealing, the cruelty to animals, the bullying of siblings and peers, and the ever present manipulation stretch even the most capable person's patience.

Parents of children who display symptoms of severe attachment disorders often are perplexed by the purpose of such behaviors as putting raw meat in their bed, microwaving the kitten, and falsely reporting sexual abuse by their foster father. They observe their child acting charming and sweet to strangers but cold and hateful toward those that love her most.

Hope fades as the parents learn that the child's promises and apparent guilt over misdeeds never translate into behavior change. Some parents are so frightened by their child's sadistic behaviors and apparent lack of remorse or conscience that they conclude that the child is evil. But the child is not evil; he is misunderstood, untethered, and bewildered by an incapacity to adapt. His brain and being, particularly once safe and secure, will perform amazing feats of growth, but it takes time to heal. Understanding his experience as best we can helps allow and guide the healing process.

Understanding the experience of a child with attachment trauma, knowing the terminology used by the professionals with whom families will work, and gaining parenting strategies are three goals of this chapter.

Behaviors are outward reflections of underlying and unseen feeling states. Since we cannot read people's minds, we must interpret and infer a person's intent from observed behaviors. Road rage is inflamed when we attribute the slowness of a driver to an intentional desire to obstruct us; once we discover that the driver is an elderly driver just attempting to be safe, our rage fades. Understanding the child's world and seeing it from her perspective helps us make sense of our child's behaviors, even those that are bizarre and illogical.

Attachment traumatized children who display severe persistent behavior patterns appear to share some common feelings about themselves and the world:

- They experience themselves as bad and incomplete.
- They have a limited and fragmented sense of self and autonomy.
- They experience deep, obscure, and overwhelming shame.
- They have intense feelings of rage in the absence of an easily identifiable threat.
- They feel overwhelmed with pervasive anxiety in the absence of an easily identifiable threat.
- They experience overwhelming despair.
- They feel compelled to isolate themselves.
- They feel driven by destructive and self-destructive forces outside of their control.[1]

UNDERSTANDING THE CONCEPT OF ATTACHMENT DISORDER

The term *attachment disorder*, although frequently used, has "no clear, specific or consensual definition."[2] Increasingly, attachment disorder is used to describe an array of behavioral and emotional problems, but only the diagnosis of Reactive Attachment Disorder of Infancy or Early Childhood (RAD) is recognized. RAD was added to the *DSM* in 1980 and was refined in subsequent editions. The *DSM-IV-TR* describes RAD as a disorder that involves the following:

- "Markedly disturbed and developmentally inappropriate social relatedness in most contexts, beginning before age 5 years."
- RAD has two types of presentation: inhibited and disinhibited.
  - Inhibited type is evidenced by "a persistent failure to initiate or respond in developmentally appropriate fashion to most social interactions." A child with inhibited-type RAD, for example, is resistant to comfort, withdraws from others, is watchful as if anticipating a

threat, and shows a mixture of approach and avoidance toward caregivers and others.[3]

- Disinhibited type is evidenced by "diffuse attachments as manifested
  by indiscriminate sociability with marked inability to exhibit appropriate selective attachments." Children with this type will, for example, strike up a conversation in the waiting room with a stranger and
  in an engaging and charming manner discuss deeply intimate aspects
  of their lives, aspects they refuse to reveal to those who love them.
  Such children appear to be attaching to others, but the connection
  is superficial; such children make friends easily but cannot maintain
  them.

- The disturbance is not accounted for solely by developmental delays and
  does not meet criteria for Pervasive Developmental Disorder.
- The disturbance is associated with grossly pathological care, such as
  persistent disregard of the child's basic emotional and physical needs or
  "repeated changes of primary caregiver that prevent formation of stable
  attachments."[4]

RAD can be a stigmatizing label, and much care should be taken to rule
out other overlapping disorders, including conduct and oppositional defiant disorders, PTSD and other anxiety disorders, pervasive developmental disorders,
mental retardation, and severe forms of attention deficit hyperactivity disorders
before rendering such a severe diagnosis as RAD.[5]

There is a growing concern among clinicians, theorists, and researchers that
the way RAD is currently defined in the *DSM* is too narrow.[6] T. G. O'Connor
and C. H. Zeanah have suggested the concept of an attachment spectrum.[7]
An attachment spectrum includes RAD at the severe end but also contains a
range of other attachment related impairments along a continuum of severity
and type.

The following are behaviors that are typical for children who fit the severe
end of the attachment spectrum, including RAD. Caution should be taken to
avoid assuming that any one or cluster of symptoms indicates a disorder:

- Intense lying, often about obvious things
- Poor response to discipline
- Eye contact discomfort, except when lying
- Too much or too little physical contact

- Lack of mutual enjoyment with others; has difficulty having fun with peers and family members
- Body functions impairments, including eating, sleeping, urinating, and defecating
- Discomfort created by increased attachment
- Tendency to be indiscriminately friendly or superficially charming
- Poor communications
- Difficulty with cause and effect
- Lack of empathy
- Tendency to see things in extreme
- Habitual disassociation or hypervigilance[8]
- Desire to tease or hurt other children
- Innocent façade after being caught transgressing
- Dangerous behavior without any awareness of risk
- Deliberate destruction of personal or others' things
- No apparent guilt or remorse
- Cruelty to animals
- Stealing
- Sneaking, hiding, and hoarding food
- Inability to learn from experiences
- False reports of abuse
- Inability to feel pain when hurt or refusal to accept help
- Propensity to make demands instead of requests
- Bossiness with adults and peers alike
- Extended tantrums
- Accident-proneness
- Cute and charming actions in order to manipulate
- Overfriendliness to strangers
- Preoccupation with fires
- Preference of violent cartoons, TV, and movies[9]

There is much debate regarding the prevalence of attachment disorders for children who have been severely maltreated. Severe maltreatment is prevalent with victim rates of twelve per one thousand children reported nationally,[10] in addition to countless unreported, and so it is easy to assume that attachment disorders must be similarly prevalent. However, the *DSM-IV-TR* describes the prevalence of RAD as "very uncommon."[11] A 2006 taskforce report on RAD indicated that "a history of maltreatment should not imply any disorder."[12] The report suggested that "many emerge without any long-term mental disorders, let alone a disorder as severe as RAD. Resilience to trauma and adversity is not limited to the extremely healthy or robust. Rather, resiliencies are common and relatively normal human characteristics." Yet there is an apparent rise in the use of the diagnosis of RAD to describe troublesome behaviors by children in foster or adoptive care, a rise that may be due more to overdiagnosis than prevalence.[13] So what can parents do?

THE PROCESS OF ASSESSMENT

Attachment trauma can create problems in functioning along a wide continuum of severity and type of presentation. Our resilient nature and "plastic" brains help most maltreated children overcome many of the effects of attachment injury. For those children who display impairment in functioning and are suffering or causing suffering, much care should be taken to thoroughly assess and rule out nonattachment related factors, such as current environmental stressors (changes in placement, custody hearings) and other overlapping diagnoses.

A thorough assessment entails multiple sources of information, such as parent and school reports, as well as multiple observations of interactions with parents.[14] Assessment should take into account behavior patterns over time and across contexts and situations.

Attention should be paid to the family and caregivers, not solely to the child, and cultural issues must always be considered. A diagnosis of attachment disorder should never be given simply because the child was maltreated or grew up in an institution or in foster or adoptive placements.[15] A thorough assessment is crucial not only to clarify the nature of the presenting problems but also to point to the appropriate intervention.

Parents interested in seeking an assessment for their child should look for mental health providers who are licensed and have training and experience with children with attachment trauma. It will take some homework and networking to find the resources available in any community. The Association for Treatment and Training in the Attachment of Children's website, www.attach.org, is a good place to start to get a feel for what is current in the field and may be able to direct parents to local providers.

ATTACHMENT THERAPIES

The confusion and controversy regarding the term *attachment disorder* is minor compared to the current debate over so-called attachment therapies. There is no clear or agreed upon definition of the term *attachment therapy.*[16]

There are many different types of therapy that focus on attachment, ranging from the traditional to the radical, and websites touting the effectiveness of a particularly unique attachment therapy are on the rise. Holding therapies have drawn the most attention following the suffocation death of a ten-year-old girl during a therapy session in 2000; several similar deaths have occurred over the past seven years.[17]

A task force, put together by the American Professional Society on the Abuse of Children (APSAC), attempted to cut through the controversy and concern by setting guidelines and recommendations regarding attachment disorders, assessments, and treatments in a cautionary 2006 report. The report described the field of attachment as "young and diverse" and said that "not all attachment related interventions are controversial." The report also indicated that many treatments have not been scientifically determined to be safe and effective. The report was firm that the following treatments or attachment parenting techniques are unproven, potentially dangerous, and should not be used:[18]

- Physical coercion
- Psychologically or physically enforced holding
- Physical restraint
- Physical domination
- Provoked catharsis
- Ventilation of rage
- Age regression
- Humiliation
- Withholding or forcing of food or water
- Prolonged isolation
- Exaggerated levels of control and domination over a child

Holding in general, such as hugging, playing, and touching, is an essential aspect of a healthy parent-child relationship and should not be confused with risky coercive or compression holds. In addition, the report clarified that the recommendations do not include reasonable use of behavior management techniques, time-outs, grounding, rewards/punishments, and occasional restraint to prevent injury.

The task force recommended that prior to involvement in attachment-focused therapy, parents seek traditional first-line treatments that focus on "caregiver and environmental stability, child safety, patience, sensitivity, consistency and nurturance."[19] Many proponents of the intrusive attachment therapies argue that more traditional interventions, such as family therapy, cognitive-behavioral approaches, and parent-skills training are not as deeply effective as attachment therapy. Research, however, indicates that the common characteristics of successful attachment approaches include the core features of traditional therapy, namely short-term, behavioral, and goal-directed focus and emphasis on the parent-child relationship.[20]

The field of attachment treatment is in its infancy (or possibly toddlerhood), and the future looks encouraging, but for now much care should be taken to be discriminating consumers of all things attachment related. Although it can be argued that historically it has been a scientific challenge to determine the effectiveness of any psychotherapeutic interventions, consumers should look to attachment models that are grounded in research. Parents should look to approaches that treat the child with dignity, kindness, and respect. Attachment interventions should aim at helping the parents provide a secure and responsive base, increase attunement, and deepen the relationship; parents should avoid interventions that are designed to provoke rage or confrontations.

The task force report cautioned against any approach that predicts that a child may become a psychopath or predator if left untreated. Models that portray the child "as pervasively manipulative, cunning or deceitful are not conducive to good treatment and may promote abusive practices."[21]

We have discussed the language of attachment disorders and the need for the appropriate assessment. We are now going to turn our attention to parenting principles that lead to success.

PARENTING PRINCIPLES THAT LEAD TO SUCCESS

Mary and Todd adopted ten-year-old Billy late in their lives, having raised a birthfamily of three, with their youngest, Kim, still at home. Billy was affectionately referred to as "a handful" but in reality was straining the family, marriage, and well-being of all involved. Babysitters were no longer willing to tolerate the chaos. Friends and neighbors stopped visiting. Vacations were barely tolerable. Violence became unmanageable with him, and fixing holes in the drywall became a weekly chore. The power struggles were absurdly predictable, yet Mary and Todd felt helpless to avoid or win them. The school started calling meetings for behavior plans and intervention teams, and Todd noticed relief when he considered giving Billy back. The idea grew and preoccupied him, and he felt ashamed of his relief.

Mary and Todd sought support and knowledge, finding a community of parents and service providers dedicated to helping children with attachment trauma adapt and thrive. After years of reading, research, assessments, therapies, support groups, special classes, and programs, Mary and Todd learned how to parent more compassionately and effectively. They committed to having a family atmosphere of shared fun, peacefulness, and mutual respect, avoiding at all costs the lingering presence of rage, fear, or resentment. Matter-of-fact limits and clear expectations took months to fine-tune, but they eventually left the household free of the daily chaos. Assuming that Billy lacked the skills and the opportunity to practice being a member of the family instead of interpreting his resistance as defiance enabled them to create environments for Billy to learn self-control. Billy was difficult to understand at first, but by being open, empathic, and attentive, Mary and Todd found they began to feel more in tune with Billy's experiences. They learned that it was natural for Billy to occasionally behave like a toddler and sometimes act like a teen, that his life story still needed to move back and forth across chapters until past needs were resolved. Probably the hardest thing they had to do was learn to take care of themselves and keep their own joy, rather than allowing Billy to ruin their days. In the end, Mary and Todd were grateful that they hung in there; Billy turned out be an amazing person.

Parents face unusual challenges in parenting a child who has suffered attachment trauma. Extra care and support for all involved is crucial. Knowledge and perspective, understanding, and informed approaches are particularly necessary when helping children adapt and thrive in the family environment. In many ways, parenting a child with attachment trauma is similar to being a parent of a nontraumatized child, but in more concentrated form. The key appears to be a willingness to spend lots of time with the child interacting, playing, and guiding. The more time spent with the child, the more opportunities there are for reorganization and reactivation of the child's brain.

Mary and Todd made the leap to understanding parenting as an art form

that requires passion, disciplined perseverance, and adherence to certain principles. Daniel Hughes in his book *Facilitating Developmental Attachment*[22] outlined some key principles to consider:

- Family atmosphere. In Billy's case, his parents committed themselves to
  maintaining an atmosphere of relative peace and enjoyment where there
  is mutual fun and respect for each person's individuality and dignity.
  Mary and Todd learned strategies to keep resentments from accumulat-
  ing and to ensure that everyone went to bed free of anger and tension.
- Expectations and structure. Mary and Todd lived in chaos for years;
  they felt desperately out of control. Children who had no one to
  structure their world early in their lives tend to crave the security of
  limits yet fight to the death to push through or around the structure.
  Expectations should be clear and firm and enforced in a calm, consistent, and matter-of-fact manner.
- Emotional attunement. Mary and Todd listened carefully and observed
  Billy's patterns in a loving and curious way; they devoted themselves
  to attempting to understand his experience and empathize with his
  feelings. Since attachment trauma affects the child's emotional connection to the world around him, it is critical for parents to help rebuild
  the connection through attunement, understanding, and validation.
  Over time and through efforts to help their child identify and express
  his feelings, Mary and Todd helped Billy regulate his emotions more
  effectively.
- Practice. Mary and Todd consciously committed themselves to view-
  ing Billy as a person who lacked skills and needed practice rather than
  jumping to the conclusion that he behaved in purposefully resistant
  ways. Billy's failure to complete a chore, for example, was a source of
  much frustration for Billy's parents. Instead of employing punishment,
  Todd showed Billy how to wash and dry the dishes; next they did it
  together, and then Billy went solo. A natural consequence for not completing a chore is to practice it as many times as is necessary until the
  skill is developed.
- Regression. Attachment traumatized children may appear at times to
  act younger than their age, as when Billy talked like a baby and acted
  like he wanted to nurse. Mary and Todd learned that periodic regression was the way Billy's organism was attempting to work through the

trauma, and they used these regressions to provide him the nurture he did not receive when he was younger.

- Parental self-care. Mary and Todd initially struggled to implement techniques to attend to their own psychological and emotional needs because it seemed selfish. Over time, however, they realized that parenting attachment traumatized children can be grueling work, not unlike being a therapist, and if they were to be fully there for Billy, they must be healthy. Healthy parents attempt to maintain their joy and not let the child set the tone, despite the child's efforts to ruin the good times. Humor, patience, perspective, openness to support from others, and realistic expectations are key virtues for parents to practice.

Arthur Becker-Weidman suggested that parents take a PLACE approach to their children: Playfulness, Love, Acceptance, Curiosity, and Empathy.[23] One of the first things to go when there is undue stress in the family is the fun and play. Playfulness and humor are healing and can help reestablish the bond following tough times. Loving the child unconditionally accelerates and deepens the attachment process. Learning to accept the child's viewpoint and feelings as valid enables parents to understand and react more effectively.

A parent who can be constantly curious about the child is less likely to jump to false assumptions about problematic behaviors. Empathy is the capacity to share in another's feelings; it is the compassion we feel for our child's suffering, as well as her joy. By attempting to maintain such a stance toward our children (and each other, for that matter), we provide the fertile ground in which they can attach and grow.

Spending time with our children and investing ourselves fully in the art of parenting are the most effective ways to counter the effects of early chronic maltreatment. Children with attachment trauma need more of our concentrated time than children who have not been maltreated. Parents need to be constantly aware of themselves: what they say and how they say it. More so than we think, maltreated children listen attentively to what is being said between parents and remain vigilant to anticipated threat or abandonment. Parents are often the target but not the source of a child's wrath, so it is important to rise above the instinctual reaction to respond personally and emotionally to a child's attacks. Simple things, such as being glad to see the child when she comes home from school, playing games, reading bedtime stories, painting her fingernails, and brushing her hair have enormous impact on building attachment.

Parenting children with attachment related problems and serving as the critical anchor from which they develop can be very rewarding, but it can also be very exhausting. Parents need support and should not hesitate to seek assistance or therapy for themselves individually, as a couple, as a family, and/or in a group of other parents. Many children who display attachment related symptoms, whether intentionally or not, can be amazingly adept at pushing our buttons and provoking feelings of self-doubt, rage, and utter despair. They are often capable of creating in others the feeling states that preoccupy them, including hopelessness, bewilderment, fear, and hatred. Perspective and patience infused with knowledge can help us avoid reacting in unhealthy ways when provoked. Other principles to keep in mind are these:

1. Understand that the child's behavior isn't always about you. Monitor your responses and ask yourself, *Am I taking this personally?* If the answer is yes, your next question is, *What am I going to do to change my emotional responses to the child in my home?*

2. Pay attention to the messages you say to yourself. Self-statements such as, *I am a horrible parent, I am a failure, If anybody knew how I have failed, they would be horrified,* and so on are harmful and serve no helpful purpose.

3. Return to your initial motivation for adopting. Stop and take note of the improvements your child has made. Revise your unrealistic expectations for you and your child.

4. Continue to learn and study the key elements of healing for traumatized children: a safe environment, established boundaries (private spaces) for everyone, and the incredible importance of an established routine (in order to build trust).

5. Regularly examine and explore what is happening to each family member, especially the mother.

6. Do a role check. Is one parent carrying the load?

7. Take good care of yourself physically, emotionally, mentally, and spiritually.

8. Talk about your situation with people who understand. Don't run from connections.

9. Find balance in your life. There is no glory in martyrdom.[24]

SUMMARY

Children who have developed disturbed and disturbing symptoms from attachment trauma can be bewildering, frustrating, and even frightening to parents, teachers, peers, and therapists. The impact from early and chronic maltreatment can be deep and pervasive, affecting fundamental functions and processes.

Children whose symptoms cluster into a diagnosable syndrome share certain experiences and display common behaviors. Reactive Attachment Disorder of Infancy or Early Childhood (RAD) is the recognized diagnosis used by mental health professionals to describe the symptoms associated with attachment trauma. RAD is a rare and rather controversial disorder, frequently misapplied and overapplied to children who are suffering from other disorders or are simply acting out in foster or adoptive care.

As controversial as the concept of RAD is, it is minor compared to the debate regarding treatment for attachment disorders. Much care should be taken to research what types of interventions are available and to avoid any approaches that are coercive, dominating, humiliating, harsh, or that conceptualize the child as psychopathic or pervasively deceitful.

Parenting is an art with certain guiding principles. Parenting children with attachment disorders requires incredible patience, knowledge, passion, love, empathy, and skill. The family atmosphere needs to be relatively peaceful, mutually enjoyable, secure, structured, and a fertile ground in which to develop individuality. It is critical that parents take care of themselves emotionally by seeking support and keeping their humor and perspective. Because children are resilient and their brains are capable of incredible healing through compensation and reorganization, solid artful parenting in conjunction with support and intervention will enable the traumatized child to bond, grow, and thrive.

QUESTIONS FOR SMALL GROUPS

1. Why is it important for you as a parent to understand the life experiences of a child with attachment trauma?
2. Why is it important for you as a parent to understand the common feelings shared by attachment traumatized children?
3. Looking at the list of behaviors that are typical for children who fit the severe end of the attachment spectrum, do you identify any of

those behaviors in your children? How have you tried to manage these behaviors? What do you need the most help with?

4. Before seeking assessment or treatment for a child who might have an attachment disorder, what other steps and actions should be considered? Have you taken any of these in your family?

5. Discuss the key principles of parenting to consider when parenting a child with attachment trauma. What principle might be most helpful to you right now?

PART THREE

COMMUNICATING ABOUT ADOPTION

HOW DO WE FEEL ABOUT ADOPTION?

Understanding the Different Perspectives of Parents and Children

I couldn't talk to my parents about adoption; I didn't want to hurt them.
They wouldn't talk to me about it either. I learned early on to keep my
thoughts and feelings about my adoption to myself. I grew up feeling
alone, isolated, and different.

—Sarah, age twenty-five

Kellie, age nine, wandered into her parents' bedroom one morning.
"Mom," she said, "I've been wondering. Why do you think my birthmother got rid of me?"

Her mother, Beth, was surprised by this "out of nowhere" question. She
and her husband, Jake, had always maintained open lines of communication
with Kellie about her adoption. They shared with Kellie all they knew about
the circumstances of the adoption plan her birthparents had made and how she
came to join their family right from the hospital. They thought their open and
truthful responses had satisfied her need to know. Evidently, they didn't. There
were more questions and more feelings yet to be faced.

Children like Kellie, who are adopted in infancy, obviously form their primary attachments with the adoptive family. Their emerging comprehension
of what adoption means grows slowly with each passing cognitive developmental stage. An adopted child may begin to ask penetrating questions that
parents knew would be coming, but when the child does, parents often feel
unprepared.

Communicating about adoption is not a one-time event. It is a process cul-
tivated by the fulfillment of two parental requirements. The first requirement is
that parents comprehend how their child feels and thinks about being adopted
as he or she moves through the developmental stages of understanding. The

second requirement is that parents have a clear understanding of how they see their family and what adoption means to them.

HOW MIGHT A CHILD PERCEIVE ADOPTION?

The most reliable generalization that can be made about how children handle adoption as they pass through their many stages of growing up is that it is difficult to generalize. Just as every child raised in a biological family is different, likewise every child raised in an adoptive family is different. Many biological children go through challenging times in their identity formation. Adopted children can too, and they have additional issues and revelations to deal with. Some adopted adolescents and adults attribute their psychological struggles to being adopted. But most adopted children, especially children adopted as infants, have no more difficulty dealing with identity formation than do children raised in biological families. The extent to which adopted children as a whole group may exhibit identity issues more often is a function of abuse and neglect suffered by some of them, not a function of being adopted. Still, it is important for adoptive parents to understand the kinds of struggles that some children experience as they deal with growing up adopted.

Adopted children cannot fully understand adoption until they understand conception. As they grow up, their understanding of adoption dynamics also matures and potentially changes over time. Each developmental stage ushers in a deeper perception of the experience. Children ask more questions that invite parental sensitivity. Although these developmental stages are linked to chronological ages, every child is different. Some progress rapidly from one stage of understanding to another; others may remain at a particular stage much longer than expected. When adoptive parents understand the sensitive nature of adoption through their child's eyes, they'll be better prepared to communicate effectively during each stage.

STAGE ONE: PRESCHOOL (AGES THREE TO FIVE)

Adoption is a very abstract concept. While children at this age are too young to understand the concepts of adoption, parents can begin foundational work to assist children in developing positive attitudes about adoption, their birthparents, and themselves during these early years.[1]

Preschool-age children are capable only of concrete thinking. They love to hear their adoption story and often ask to have it repeated as a favorite bedtime story. By the age of three or four, many adopted children can repeat the story verbatim as it was told to them.

While children under five have acquired some language to talk about adoption, they are repeating words they really do not understand. For example, the concept of growing inside the birthmother's tummy and living with another family is very abstract, essentially unintelligible to the young child. Children under the age of five rarely have the cognitive ability to understand the concepts behind the words in their adoption story. While they can parrot the words, the lightbulb of understanding has not yet "clicked" on.

During this developmental stage, the parents' job is to create an open environment in the home where it is normal and natural to talk about adoption. Parents can encourage questions and answer concretely and simply. Parents can listen for cues about incorrect information or perceptions a child might have about adoption or his or her story. This is an important time to create a positive environment where everyone is comfortable talking about it.

STAGE TWO: EARLY ELEMENTARY (AGES SIX TO EIGHT)

As adopted children enter this period of their life, their understanding of adoption goes through significant change. Children at this age become more reflective, analytical, and logical in their thinking. "As a part of this growth in cognitive and social-cognitive reasoning," David Brodzinsky explained, "children's knowledge of adoption also undergoes changes."[2]

Because school-age children understand the concept of adoption for the first time around the age of seven or eight, they realize at that time that they joined their family differently. If they were adopted as infants, the children are now mature enough to understand this as a loss.

Children may perceive that they have lost connections and a relationship with their birthfamily, knowledge of their own history and roots, and perhaps cultural understanding and continuity. Even if adoptions are open, children have still lost the lives they would have lived with their birthfamilies. Because they become more aware of the concrete significance of adoption in their lives, a mental and emotional reorientation may begin, even though several years may have already lapsed since the separation.[3] They may view adoption not only in terms of family building but also in terms of family loss.

As always, children's interest in their biological past varies greatly, but it is at this age that questions can begin to surface. Parents can encourage questions and answer them honestly. Difficult issues may be omitted (but never changed) until the child is older. Parents can tell the adoption story as a favorite bedtime story. Parents can use this period of time in their child's life to use and add on to the life book. The life book, which is more fully explained in chapter 11, is a book that contains stories and pictures from the child's past. Most important, parents can reassure their child that God makes families through adoption and that she is right where she belongs. She will not lose her adoptive family.[4]

When Doug, who was adopted as an infant, was eight, he went through a stage of asking his father, Cliff, at bedtime, "How do I know you are my real parents?" Cliff would be very consistent in his answer: "Well, Doug, there are lots of ways you can know we are your real parents. We're responsible for you. We take care of you. We love you like crazy, with all our hearts. We would die for you, do anything for you. We buy you lots of toys and spend all kinds of money on you. Your birthparents say we're your parents. They loved you, but they knew they could not give you what you needed and deserved: a married, loving mom and dad. Our adoption agency says we're your parents. And there is a legal document in our file cabinet and in the county courthouse that says we are your parents."

Doug was impressed by all those reasons and believed them, but interestingly, the one that tied it all together for him and made him feel very secure about it was the legal document. In addition to the love he felt from his parents, the certainty of the law helped make him feel secure in his family; it helped assure him that he was where he belonged and where he would remain.

When Doug was thirteen, he asked the question again. Cliff started to answer it the same way as before. Doug interrupted, "No, I know that. I mean, 'How do I know you're not some aliens from another planet?'" In his ornery, early-teenage way, Doug was clearly comfortable with being adopted.

STAGE THREE: LATE ELEMENTARY (AGES NINE TO TWELVE)

When heading into the "tween" years, many adopted children seem to "go underground" about adoption issues. They cease to ask questions and seem relatively unconcerned about the past. It is so important at this stage for parents to really know their children and continue to maintain an environment of openness about adoption. All adopted children think about adoption, but they vary greatly in their questioning of it and in their need to know about and connect with their biological past. Some children, once they begin to understand adoption, have many questions, but they may or may not bring them up, depending on how much "permission" they feel they have from their parents. Other children react to their new understanding with simple acceptance.

If a tween seems to have gone underground about adoption, much may be happening inside. The adopted youngster may be beginning to understand that his situation is different from his classmates. The nine- to twelve-year-old begins to consider not only that he gained a family through adoption and lost one in the process but also that he was actually "given away." He may wonder about but never discuss a potentially damaging thought: *People don't give away valuables; I must not be worth much.*

Whether raised in a biological or adoptive family, almost everyone wonders about his or her self-worth at times. Many of an adopted child's or adolescent's self-esteem issues may have little, if anything, to do with adoption. But adopted children who perceive their placement as abandonment clearly have an additional challenge to overcome in achieving a healthy sense of self-worth.

According to Elaine Frank from the Child Welfare Information Gateway,

> The full emotional impact of that loss comes to children, usually between the ages of 7 and 12, when they are capable of understanding more about the concept of being adopted. It happens because they live more in the world outside of their families and are more tuned in to the world inside their heads. While this is a giant step toward self-reliance, it leaves parents in a quandary about when and how much adoption information to share, and uncertain about whether their child is wanting or dreading to hear it. It is especially difficult at this time to decide what to do or say to children who do not inquire about their birthparents.[5]

Some children do not inquire because they do not feel a need to know; others feel a need to talk about it but are afraid. Lynn, a fifth grader, knew she was adopted. She never expressed much interest in knowing much about it, so her parents didn't pursue the topic. Although Lynn was quiet about adoption, her insecurity about it manifested itself in her behavior. Her mother commented,

> We noticed that Lynn starting doing something that was noisome. She
> began to pull out her eyelashes. It was an increasing nervous habit. I
> quizzed her about what was going on and she always replied, "Nothing,
> Mom, nothing." One evening long after we thought she was asleep,
> Lynn tiptoed into the living room with tears streaming down her face.
>
> "Mommy, I want to ask you something, but I don't want to hurt
> your feelings. What does my birthmom look like? I forget. What did I
> do to make my birthmom get rid of me?"
>
> I knew to expect these questions sooner or later. I asked Lynn to
> come over and sit down next to me on the couch. I encouraged her by
> affirming that she was okay in asking those things of me. As a family, we
> sat down to look through the box of pictures we had of her birthfamily.
> She needed this discussion at a different level from before. It was an
> extremely positive experience and just reminded me that I need to see
> Lynn's needs as they change over time.

Parents can help their children through this stage by realizing that when
children are not talking about adoption, it doesn't mean they are not thinking
about it. A parent's task is to find a balance between talking about adoption and
not emphasizing it. Parents can develop sensitivity regarding how much their
children may want or need to talk about it at any given time.

Because children at this stage are concerned about fairness and loyalty, they
are likely to believe that they are being disloyal to the adoptive family if they
have feelings, or even questions, about their birthfamily. Children need to know
that they can love both their adoptive parents and their birthparents. They do
not have to choose. Explaining to the child that adults are allowed to love more
than one child in a family can alleviate some of that struggle. When additional
children join a family, parents do not have to stop loving the children who were
already there in order to start loving the children who have just arrived. In the
same way, children are able to love both those who gave them life and those
who parent them and give them a loving, permanent family. They do not have
to stop having feelings about their birthfamily when they become part of their
adoptive family.[6]

Stage Four: Early and Later Adolescence (Ages Thirteen to Eighteen)

An adopted teenager who has not experienced an adoptive family environment that embraces openness in communication about adoption can spiral into some negative attitudes about adoption, his family, and himself. This early adolescent, capable now of sophisticated, abstract thought, may be confused about the reasons his birthparents have abandoned him. His understanding of adoption progresses at this age. The adopted teen has moved from gaining a family and losing a family to being "given away" to possibly arriving at the conclusion, "I was rejected."

The teen who has not experienced a healthy adoptive family environment may be angry about a lack of control in his adoption, and he may look for someone to blame for earlier separations and the lack of information about his history. Often, the adoptive parents are selected to be the scapegoats for the child's rage and confusion. If his history has not been discussed since the child was a preschooler, as happens in too many adoptive families, the child may have used fantasy to create a web of new information, implicating the adoptive parents as kidnappers responsible for the separation. The adopted youth may firmly believe that his adoptive parents have complete information about his history but, in collaboration with social workers, have chosen to withhold the information or even actively lie about it.[7]

As a result of the internal struggles faced by maladjusted adopted adolescents, parents and professionals note behavioral changes that go beyond normal adolescent behavior. Due to the complexity of needs for some adopted teens, especially those who have suffered multiple placements, abuse, or neglect, this subject will be explored in chapter 12. That chapter discusses the adopted adolescent in greater detail and gives parenting strategies for navigating this period of a child's life as it relates to adoption. Most adopted adolescents who have had a loving, stable adoptive family life experience no more tumult than does the average teenager raised in her biological family.

As mentioned earlier, the first requirement for adoption communication is that parents comprehend how their child may feel and think about being adopted as he or she moves through the developmental stages of understanding. The second requirement is that parents have a clear understanding of how they see their family and what adoption means to them.

HOW PARENTS FEEL ABOUT ADOPTION

Chapter 5 contained a thorough discussion of two ways parents deal with the issues of adoption. One was rejecting the role of adoption in the family's life and stifling communication about it. The other was accepting and acknowledging the role of adoption and openly communicating about it.

Professionals assert that there are many benefits in the acknowledgment approach. Both parents and professionals point out that this style is especially valuable in creating an environment of empathy and sensitivity in which feelings can be expressed and recognized as legitimate.

Five other advantages to the acknowledgment approach are noteworthy.

First, it builds a trusting relationship between parent and child. Lauren, now twenty-one, didn't learn she was adopted until her parents told her at age twelve: "I was traumatized by that disclosure, not so much about the adoption part but that they had kept secrets from me. I have grown up wondering what else they haven't shared."

Second, this open style integrates missing pieces from the child's past. For many adopted children, lack of information creates a sense of void in their life. Some say it's like trying to put a puzzle together knowing you don't have all the pieces. Research has shown that children whose parents were open about adoption issues are generally more satisfied with the quality of family communication and relationships.

Third, open disclosure corrects erroneous views of the past as, fourth, it helps the child sort out realities and fantasies. "One of the greatest fantasies I maintained as a school-age child was that one day my now-rich birthparents would regret getting rid of me and come back for me," commented twenty-seven-year-old Diane. "I think I embellished that fantasy because I didn't have any clue of what was reality."

Fifth, this straightforward approach helps create a foundation for identity formation. A broader discussion of this critical adolescent need is addressed in chapter 12.

Approaching the issue of adoption directly by asking a child to sit down and talk about it will probably be an unsuccessful effort, cautioned David Brodzinsky. Finding less direct methods will result in a more positive response. Brodzinsky encourages parents to plant seeds. For example, a parent might open with the following: "I was watching a TV show last night. It was interesting. It had a story about a birthmom who planned an adoption for her child. It reminded me a lot about your story. I've been thinking about it and wondering if you have had any thoughts or questions lately that we need to talk about." This plants in the child's mind the idea that it's okay to talk about adoption.

A second suggestion (discussed more fully in the following chapter) is the use of books. A parent might say, "I was at the bookstore the other day and there was a book about adoption. It is for kids your age. I bought it for you. Would you like to sit down with me and read it together, or would you like to read it on your own?"

In the early years of family life when the primary job is to incorporate the child into the family and build connection and trust, a hiding-of-adoption style may serve the family well, Brodzinsky said. But later on, as the young person matures and struggles to find meaning in being adopted and of being relinquished, an acknowledgment-of-differences pattern offers a clearer choice to ensure openness, honesty, and the meeting of needs.[8]

One final approach, the insistence-upon-differences approach, is found in some adoptive families. It differs from the first two in its consistently negative effects. Consider the following three statements, which reflect this third coping style:

- "Carrie is an LD student because she is adopted."
- "Joe was suspended a third time. I think the reason he's always in trouble is because he was adopted. He's a bad seed."
- "If we had never adopted him, this family wouldn't be in such chaos. He came from such a terrible family."

This management technique is found in families in crisis. Brodzinsky commented in an interview, "This pattern often leads family members to view adoption as the basis for family disharmony and disconnectedness." It also relieves everyone, except the adopted child, of responsibility for any problem.

Of the three coping patterns potentially integrated into the family, this paradigm builds walls between parent and child and between adopted child and biological child. It reinforces to a struggling youngster that in this home he is expendable. This view often leads families not into therapy but into either an emotional disengagement or a courtroom to dissolve the adoptive relationship.

At age seven, Jesse is back in the foster care system. At age nine, Bonnie was returned to a foster home. At age seventeen, Todd walked out of his adoptive home. He will soon move into an independent living program and eventually move on into adulthood with very few stable family ties.

These three children were adopted at an early age. However, for a variety of reasons, their families were never able to incorporate and love them unconditionally. Symptoms of potential disruption occurred early because with every problem or crisis, the family would insist upon the differences.

In good times, Bonnie's parents introduced her as their daughter. In difficult times, an adjective was added: their *adopted* daughter. Their personal needs as parents and their inability or unwillingness to see the issues in the light of the whole family system brought heartache and disruption. Eventually, the walls that had been built over a period of time became insurmountable. No one had energy left to keep the relationships intact.

"We usually find very little of this insistence on differences until the kids begin to act out," said Brodzinsky. "We find it mostly with families of teenagers who have a long history of parent-child conflicts, not necessarily around adoption issues, just a lot of acting out."

When a family begins to look at all the problems in the family through the lens of adoption, that is when they get into this insistence on differences pattern. Adoption becomes the only mechanism for explaining problems. It then comes as no surprise when an underlying message is given to the child: "You are adopted — of course you will have problems."[9]

Within this kind of family system, members internalize a belief system that takes on a life and energy of its own. That belief system is that adoption creates problems. Brodzinsky suggested, "Insistence on differences is not what created the problem in the first place. But once the problems begin to emerge, the belief system begins to become a larger part of the parent and child relationship. This perception helps to maintain an atmosphere of nonacceptance and therefore helps to maintain a level of ongoing conflict."

In most cases, this pattern does not lead to a formal dissolution of the relationship. More often, it leads to unrelenting conflict and a dissolution of any real sense of relationship and intimacy between the parents and child, unless professional help is sought. Professional intervention in adoptive families in crisis is crucial. It helps the family approach the problems as a unit and separate those actions and behaviors that initiate conflict from the deeper belief system that maintains the struggle.

In this chapter we have looked at the issues and concerns for parents and children as they journey through the adoption experience. The beautiful thing about adoptive families is that they are just like biological families in the fact that all families face difficulties as their children grow. Healthy families learn how to work through those problems and help their children grow into successful, well-adjusted adults.

The following are statements from kids who wanted to let the world know how it feels to be adopted.

How do I feel about being adopted? Most of the time, I really feel okay. It is not a big issue for me. My mom, dad, and two sisters are my family. Every once in a while I feel sad just for a little while. Just lately I have been thinking about being adopted. I sometimes wonder what my birthmother looks like. When I have questions, I want to go to my mom and ask her. She tells me all the time that she is fine with my questions, but I don't want to hurt her. I wonder, *Do I have other brothers and sisters?* Maybe I can find out someday.

—VALERIE, AGE ELEVEN *(adopted at four weeks)*

How does it feel to be adopted? I feel like I have always lived with my parents since I was born. A lot of people ask me how it feels and what I think. It is a normal family. I know that I am safe and secure. My parents love me lots. I don't have to worry as much or be embarrassed as much. I didn't get to go to school before, and now I go all the time. And now since I am adopted, I don't have to worry about being a foster kid. That's how I feel. I never really think about my birthparents unless someone asks me.

—NICKI, AGE THIRTEEN *(adopted at nine, leaving behind a history of severe neglect)*

We have some pictures of the day I arrived in New York from Korea. My parents told me I came with five other kids and that social workers took care of us on the airplane. I have a picture of my mom at the airport hugging me and looking very happy. I was three. I wish I could remember my real-real-real parents and know what they look like. My mommy is the one I love a lot.

—SOO-MAE, AGE EIGHT *(adopted at three from Korea)*

I love being adopted. I feel safe and I know I will never leave here, at least until I am a lot older. This will always be my family. At first I was scared. After four years of staying here, I know this is my family. I have fun here. I don't have as many problems as I used to have. I love my mom and dad.

—TINA, AGE ELEVEN *(adopted at seven, leaving behind a history of abuse and neglect)*

I love my family.

—ALEX, AGE SEVEN *(adopted at three)*

SUMMARY

When creating a home where talking about adoption is a normal part of conversation, it is important that adoptive parents understand two important requirements:

1. They need to understand how their child thinks and feels about adoption at various developmental stages.
   - Ages three to five—Children learn their story but do not understand the concept of adoption.
   - Ages six to eight—They understand they joined their family differently and may understand they have lost connections.
   - Ages nine to twelve—Children seem to go underground about their adoption issues, but many are thinking about it and forming feelings around those thoughts.
   - Ages thirteen and above—The teen, now capable of abstract thought may have strong feelings about his adoption and the meaning of it. A teen may feel his adoption meant rejection.
2. They need to honestly evaluate what adoption means to them as parents and how they see their family. Do they deny the role of adoption in their lives and stifle communication about it? Do they acknowledge adoption and encourage open communication about it? Or do they blame adoption and the adopted child when confronting problems within the relationship?

QUESTIONS FOR SMALL GROUPS

1. What are your needs within this adoptive relationship? Will you deny the role of adoption in your family in order to meet them?
2. What can you do to balance being openly communicative about adoption and being too pushy in communicating about it?
3. What have you observed in adoptive families who blame adoption for their problems?
4. Have you observed your child or other adopted children experiencing any of the developmental stages discussed in this chapter?

CHAPTER ELEVEN

TALKING TO CHILDREN ABOUT ADOPTION
When and How

Children will ask the questions they feel they have the permission to ask. They have to be grounded enough and whole enough to ask questions that they don't have permission to ask.
— *Dr. Jane Hoyt-Oliver, LISW, PhD*

What would it be like if you were Katie?

Katie, now sixteen, was adopted as a two-year-old. She knew it, of course. Everyone knew it. Everyone also knew why she was adopted — everyone but Katie. One afternoon she was sitting by the family pool when a visiting cousin asked her what it felt like to know that her birthfather killed her mother and was in prison. Katie was stunned. Why wasn't she told?

What would it be like if you were Justin?

Justin, an energetic eleven-year-old, knows he was "given up" for adoption, but he doesn't know why. The truth is that his birthmother was only sixteen when he was born and made an adoption decision because she was too young to care for him. The problem is that no one talks to him about it. Justin received an unspoken message from his parents early on not to ask many questions. He believes something is terribly wrong with him and that is why he was "given up."

Perhaps the most delicate dilemma of the adoptive parent-child relationship is the need to communicate to the child about the adoption and the circumstances surrounding the child's past. If the child enters the family as an infant, creating an environment of openness regarding adoption issues is the primary task. If the child is older at the time of the adoption, the parents must inform their child about the facts of his past and also aid in the healing of his heart and mind.

Why do parents struggle with talking about adoption? When should parents tell a child she is adopted? How much should they tell her? How do parents deal with their child's past? These questions present parents with a task that is unique to adoption. However, as parents understand the reasons behind what they must do and gain the tools to accomplish the task, it can be a process that binds the relationship tightly together.

WHY PARENTS STRUGGLE WITH TALKING ABOUT ADOPTION

There are a number of reasons why adoptive parents struggle to talk to their children about adoption and the issues of their past. Here are just a few:

- "I fear my child might feel a lesser part of the family."
- "I fear I will lose his love."
- "It isn't the right time."
- "It will devastate her self-esteem."
- "I don't feel I have the skill."

"I FEAR MY CHILD MIGHT FEEL A LESSER PART OF THE FAMILY"

One adoptive mom expressed her concerning in talking about adoption with her child when she commented, "I am fearful I will cause the child I love to think that I see her as "always different" by talking about adoption. I wonder if she will feel more isolated rather than included within the family. If I don't talk about it, I don't have to worry about it."

"I FEAR I WILL LOSE HIS LOVE"

It was once common practice to not tell a child of his adoptive status. It was believed that the child could be fully integrated into the family and the parents could pretend there was a biological connection and not have to worry about sharing the heart of a child with birthfamily members. Regretfully, although that was not uncommon thinking decades ago, it still occasionally happens today too. Withholding the fact of the adoption has never been a good strategy for a healthy adoptive family. It has been proven through the painful stories of scores of adopted adults that secrecy doesn't work. Family secrets are almost always found out.

Adoptive parents need to know that a child can love both his family and his birthfamily. When adopted children have the support of secure adoptive parents, they learn early on that they do not need to choose. They learn there is room in their heart for both those who gave them life and those who gave them a permanent family. By giving a child permission to have thoughts and feelings for his birthfamily, adoptive parents are in reality strengthening their relationship with their child.

"It Isn't the Right Time"

At a meeting of adoptive parents, Madeline introduced herself. "My name is Madeline, and I am the adoptive parent of our son, Michael, who is twelve. However, he doesn't know he is adopted yet."

The response from several in the group stunned her: "Why doesn't he know? "When do you plan to tell him?"

Somewhat embarrassed, she replied, "The reason we haven't told him is that he isn't ready yet."

One adoptive parent tactfully asked, "Do you really mean that you are not ready yet?"

When is the best time to start talking about adoption? The best time is the beginning. The task for adoptive parents of infants is to create an environment where adoption is a normal part of conversation. That can begin early by reading books to toddlers about adoption or reciting the story of the child's arrival. We read or tell other stories our children do not fully understand, so why not read stories about adoption? By talking about adoption even before the child can understand, the child becomes familiar with the word *adoption*, and the parents become comfortable and practiced in talking about it.

Adoptive parents need to know that children will grow in developmental understanding of their adoption story. It is important that the process of telling follows that developmental understanding, as discussed in chapter 10.

"It Will Devastate Her Self-Esteem"

It was believed in the past that if a child knows her negative family history, it will erode her self-esteem. She will feel badly because of her negative family circumstances. However, much worse happens when children are told nothing.

Adoptive parents need to know that when significant truthful information is kept from a child, that child will develop an image of herself, her family, and her story that is based on misinformation and imagination.[1] Often times what is imagined by a child or teen is far worse than the original story. Adopted adults have told us that they may not have liked the truth, but it was better than the slippery slope of fantasy.

How and by whom the child is told about her negative family history is important. When she was an adolescent, Carol found out about the sexual and physical abuse she suffered as a very young child. She found out against her wishes from a confidential intermediary who was working for a birthfamily member who sought to have contact with Carol, also against her wishes. The disclosure experience was traumatic for Carol. If she had been told this information lovingly by her parents, rather than having it forced on her by a stranger working for someone else, she may have accepted it more easily.

"I Don't Feel I Have the Skill"

Sometimes the truth of what an adoptive parent must relate is harsh and difficult. Feeling a lack of competency to share such information is not uncommon. Adoptive parents need to know that the assistance of skilled adoption professionals or an adoption therapist can be used when they feel overwhelmed by negative and what they perceive to be potentially harmful facts. While secrets are often harmful, open communication rarely is.[2]

Recognizing barriers to communicating about adoption is a step forward. Gaining an understanding of five principles in talking to children about adoption and their past will help solidify the adoption relationship.

PRINCIPLES IN TALKING TO CHILDREN ABOUT ADOPTION AND THEIR PAST

BEGIN EARLY

Parents who choose to disclose adoption early, during the toddler and preschool years, set the tone for a lifelong journey on a firm footing. This attitude promotes a healthy parent-child relationship in three ways.

First, the parents are the first ones to create awareness of adoption within the context of their love and commitment. They know that although a toddler will not understand the words, he or she will understand the spirit in which they are said.

Second, they will offer honest, accurate information, thus avoiding the necessity of attempting to undo someone's mismanagement of the facts. The child then knows that he or she can come to the parents for "real" information rather than feeling that everyone else knows and can tell the child's story.

Third, and perhaps the most important, is that parents will not have to live under the shadow of secrecy and the fear of accidental disclosure.

BE HONEST AND OPEN AND DISCUSS THE ADOPTION STORY APPROPRIATELY BY AGE

Discoloring the truth about a child's birthparents, adoption history, or other concerns related to how the child joined the family generates serious trust issues when the truth comes out. The truth may be revealed by a slip of the tongue or by a careless relative, or it might be discovered in family papers. When that happens, what was viewed as an attempt to protect the heart of the child or teen ends in an undermining of trust and intimacy in the relationship.

It is critical for parents to know that being open and honest also means that omissions are okay due to the developmental stage of the child. What a parent would tell a ten- or twelve-year-old is not the same information a parent would share with a five- or six-year-old. Parents know their child's developmental understanding and will have a discerning sense of when to relate the needed information.

DON'T PLACE VALUE JUDGMENTS ON THE INFORMATION

Often what may seem to parents like devastating information about the child's past may be interpreted differently by the child. As mentioned earlier, a child's history should never be changed, and important facts should not be omitted when talking with an older child. What parents think may devastate a child may be the one thing that provides understanding.

Cameron's story demonstrates this truth. Cameron was conceived as the result of a rape. He was placed as a six-month-old infant with Debbie and John. Cameron had never been told the circumstances surrounding his adoption, and as a preteen he became more and more obsessed with knowing his story. His family wanted to protect him from learning that his birthfather was a rapist as his own awareness of sexuality was emerging. Not wanting to lie, they simply told Cameron that his birthmother had been unable to raise him. Cameron interpreted this to mean that his birthmother had been a horrible person who had rejected him and found him so repulsive that she could not care for him. Seeking out the help of an adoption therapist, the family went together to hear Cameron's story as it was told to him by that therapist. When told the actual circumstances, he expressed incredible relief: "My mom was not a slut; she was a victim. Now I understand why she couldn't keep me." He truly understood that his mother had rejected the rape, not him. His imagination had created a far worse scenario than the actual one.[3]

THE CHILD KNOWS MORE THAN YOU THINK HE DOES

Dennis and Carrie went to a workshop on talking to their children about their past. Their twins, Micah and Lacey, now eight, had been with them for almost three years. They were adamant that they would never talk to their children about the physical abuse they had experienced at the hands of their birthfather in the first three years of their lives.

Dr. Greg Keck, international attachment expert, asked the question, "Why wouldn't you talk to a child about a life experience they lived through?" Parents often forget or choose to deny that the children they have grown to love may have experienced incredible trauma, even preverbally, and may have unconscious memories and emotional pain that must be addressed. Addressing that pain can happen only in an environment that faces the past, age appropriately, with proper support and understanding.

THE CHILD SHOULD HAVE CONTROL OVER THE TELLING OF HER STORY

A child's story is her story. If friends or extended family members ask about sensitive information, simply tell them that the information belongs to the child and when she is old enough to answer their questions, she may choose to do so.

It is helpful for parents to assist the child in developing her own cover story and model it for her when the opportunity arises. The following example demonstrates this principle. Liz, Mick, and their two beautiful children from Korea sat in a restaurant waiting for their food order. Patrick, seven, and Megan, five, attracted attention wherever they went. Liz knew that as a transracial adoptive family, they were conspicuous and that she needed to prepare the children for questions and comments that would come. That particular evening, a woman came over to the table and began to ask questions. "How old are your children? How long have they been with you?" Then the bomb dropped. She looked at seven-year-old Patrick and said, "Why did your mother not want you?" Both children stopped their chattering and looked at their mother. Liz, modeling what she hoped the children would learn, understand, and later do themselves, simply replied, "We just talk about that at home." She felt no obligation to answer the woman's intrusive question.

CREATING AN ENVIRONMENT WHERE QUESTIONS CAN BE ASKED AND ANSWERED: TOOLS FOR THE TELLING

Whether children are adopted as infants or as older youngsters, there will be multiple periods in their life when they will deal with separating from their first family.

For an older child who has memories of that family, a keener awareness of that loss is apparent and is occasionally recalled. A supportive approach in walking the child through those periods of questions and confusion can be found in the use of a number of communication tools.

USING LITERATURE TO EXPLAIN ADOPTION

Bibliotherapy simply means helping with books. It refers to the use of selected literature to help children broaden their total development.[4] As children read the stories of others, they can view how other youngsters in similar circumstances confronted difficulties and overcame them. They can also see how children who had the same life experiences faced loss, disappointment, separation, and fear.

It is important when selecting books for children that parents consider the following criteria:

- Developmental age, as well as the child's reading level. Preschoolers enjoy stories with colorful pictures and simple conversation. Older elementary children enjoy stories with mystery, plot, and intrigue. Teens usually pick books that are relevant to their concerns, such as identity, dating, decision making, and parent-teen struggles.
- Selection of reading material or videos that address a child's apprehensions. Those apprehensions could include leaving a foster family, loss of birthparents or siblings, or living in a transcultural family. Dr. Vera Fahlberg pointed out that most G-rated movies for children deal with loss.[5] Movies such as Bambi or Annie, just to cite two, can open up discussion between parents and children about feelings of separation and loss. Parents should learn how to explore feelings and attitudes by asking appropriate and timely questions. Those personal questions can be couched by asking how the child thinks the hero or heroine felt and how he or she would feel in the same position.[6] A suggested reading list can be obtained by visiting Tapestry Books at www.tapestrybooks.com. Adoptive Families of America also provides an extensive reading list for children at http://www.adopting .org/AdoptiveFamilies/.

THE LIFE BOOK: THE BRIDGE FROM AN UNKNOWN PAST TO A PROMISING FUTURE

"I don't have any memories of the important people in my past. I wonder if the important people in my past have any memories of me."[7]

Each child reacts to the separation from his family of origin with his own set of unique, individual responses. But these painful feelings weave a common thread throughout the lives of older adopted children. For children whose memories of former relationships smolder vaguely in their minds, frequent themes revisit during the healing process:[8]

- Feelings of abandonment accompanied by feelings of humiliation and worthlessness
- Anger at the person who deserted them either by surrender, death, or divorce
- Feelings of being responsible for the desertion, in total disregard of reality
- Shame or guilt about the terrible deed they believe caused the separation
- A need to punish oneself for such a deed

For children to move from a painful past to a promising future, they must have an understanding of past and present events and why things happened as they did. According to Marian Parker, a retired veteran in adoption services with the Hamilton County (Ohio) Department of Human Services, "This understanding is vital for [the child's] sense of identity, his sense of continuity, and most all, his sense of worth." An effective tool for helping children integrate their past into their present is a life book, a retrospective of their life in words and pictures.[9]

The Purpose for the Life Book

The basic purpose for the life book is to provide answers to questions that have not yet been asked. Therefore its content must contain clear, accurate information. Marian Parker made the following recommendations:

> It is essential that we tell the child the truth — at least, as much of the truth as he is able to understand at his level of development. It is crucial that the truth be told with compassion for all those involved. In describing the negative aspects of a child's life, words must be chosen with great care and sensitivity. Sensationalism must be avoided at all times. The child may well wish to share his life book with people important to him . . . and we must make every effort to ensure that he is able to do so with reasonable comfort and minimal embarrassment.

This is not to say that the realities of his life should be sugarcoated . . . but rather that our manner of narrating these realities should show compassion for the human limitations that caused him to be neglected, abused, abandoned, or whatever. We need to convey to the child that the bad things that have happened to him are not a reflection of his worth, and most important, that they were not his fault. Above all, we need to convey to him our hope that better things are coming.[10]

What Goes into the Life Book?

The exact content of a child's life book should reflect her unique life story. Most public agencies now provide adoptive parents with a child study inventory that includes a nonidentifying social and medical history of the parents. Adoptive parents should ask for such information if it is not made available. In foster care adoptions, foster parents are often acquainted with the birthfamily and have access to more extensive information. In private infant adoptions, comprehensive details, except for medical histories, rarely are gathered about the extended birthfamily.

Whatever portion of it can be obtained, the following information will become valuable to the child with a fully disclosed adoption at some point in the future:

1. Child's birth information: date, time, location (city, state, hospital), weight, and length
2. Child's family tree or genogram (A genogram resembles a family tree. It is a more detailed description of family members over an extended period of time. It can be helpful in preserving information such as births, deaths, separations, ethnic backgrounds, and medical history.) The genogram should include the date of the parents' birth, a physical description of the parents, education and employment of the parents, and known health problems of the parents, grandparents, and siblings.[11]
3. Foster homes or relatives' homes where the child has lived
4. School-related information: list of schools attended, dates, teachers' names, report cards, comments from teachers, and sample work
5. Medical information on the child
6. Letters and mementos from parents, relatives, or significant others

7. Anecdotes about the child: developmental milestones; favorite activities, hobbies, or sports; favorite friends; cute, "naughty" behaviors; special trips or outings with the foster family; religious experiences

Who Contributes to the Life Book?

The contents of the child's life book can come from several sources, according to Marian Parker. Primary contributors to the life book in its initial stages are foster parents. They play a significant role in compiling, collecting, and preserving pictures and other documentation. They are usually the ones who carry the ongoing development of the book. A second participant is the social worker. This person serves as a facilitator to the entire process and generally has access to the needed information. The child, if age appropriate, should also be an active participant in what he or she wants in the book. Comments and drawings included in the book will have meaning later in the child's life. Finally, other participants can be the birthparents and other birthrelatives. The social worker is often able to gather content for the book from relatives of the child. Frequently, a birthparent writes a letter to the child that shares the circumstances of difficulties that arose or decisions that necessitated the transfer of parental rights.

Using literature and creating a life book are just two powerful tools in talking to a child about her past. Appendix 2 offers a brief description of other tools and resources parents can use.

HOW TO ADDRESS SENSITIVE ISSUES

Lisa, Robin, and Terri joined other adoptive mothers at the life book workshop. Their assignment that day, with the help of agency staff, was to update their child's life book. For Lisa and Robin, the job was simple. Both of their children came into their families as infants, straight from the hospital. For Terri, the task was fragile, and it concerned her. Dale, their bright, happy two-year-old, came into their family as a result of a harsh reality. His mother was dead. His father had killed her. How does one write that in a child's life book?

Adoptive parents are genuinely concerned about dealing with sensitive issues regarding their child's past. So much of a child's sense of worth can be tied to his family of origin. How a child perceives that family can shape his opinion of himself.

When wrestling with the fear of stirring things up, parents should be aware that it's not what is shared openly and honestly that agitates problems; it's the unknown that can leave a child unsettled and insecure.

The following suggestions may prove helpful when constructing a child's life story amid negative circumstances. In each situation, adoptive parents must emphasize and reemphasize that the child is not at fault regarding his circumstances, that he did not create his birthparents' problems, and that he is not in any way responsible for them. Parents can also lead the child into an attitude of forgiveness. They should not condone or sugarcoat the behavior of the birthparents; however, in an effort to avoid bitterness taking hold within the child, they can encourage the child as he matures to "hate the sin but forgive the sinner."

Realities are sometimes hard to face. Following are some of the difficult realities that many adopted children must confront, with sample ways to explain them to children.

EXPLAINING MENTAL ILLNESS

"Your father was upset in his feelings and behavior. This often left him very confused. Because he couldn't handle the problems of his own life very well, it was impossible for him to provide you with a happy and safe home."

EXPLAINING ALCOHOLISM OR SUBSTANCE ABUSE

"Your parents had many sad feelings that made life difficult for them. Because of those unhappy feelings, they would drink too much alcohol (or use drugs) to help them forget their problems.

"They did not have control over their drinking (or drug use) and would often leave you in a dangerous situation. Because of their drinking habit, they could not guarantee a safe family home."

EXPLAINING LAWBREAKING

"Sometimes adults make bad decisions about how they will behave. There were times when your first mother chose to break the law. She thought that (name the crime) would help her solve some of her problems. It did not. Because of her bad choices, she had to spend time in jail. The judge decided that it was best for your mother to spend time in prison so that she could learn to make better decisions. Another judge decided that the jail term would be too long a time for you to wait to be with a family, so he asked a children's services agency (or whoever was responsible) to make an adoption plan for you."

Explaining Mental Retardation

"Some people are born with a thinking handicap that prevents them from learning as well or as quickly as other adults. Your mother had this problem. It was difficult for her to learn things like cooking, cleaning, and taking care of her personal needs. Many adults had to help her care for herself. It was too difficult for your birthmother to take care of herself and learn how to care for you. She was unable to do both. Because of her inability to learn new things, she could not provide a safe home environment for you."

Explaining Abandonment

"Your parents were very confused about how to care for you when you were born. They were frightened at the task of raising a baby because they were still very young themselves (or they didn't have any money) and weren't married. They decided that it was best to leave you in the hospital (or whatever they did) when you were born so that more responsible adults could make good decisions about your life. They knew that these people would do a good job of caring for you and that they would find a loving home for you."

Explaining Child Abuse

"Your first parents often became frustrated, impatient, and angry over things. Instead of learning how to deal with what was bothering them, they took it out on you and hurt you. It is possible that their parents did the same things to them as they were growing up. Because of the times they hurt you, the court officials decided that they were unable to be good parents and asked a children's services agency (or whoever was responsible) to make an adoption plan for you so that you could grow up happy and safe."

EXPLAINING SEXUAL ABUSE

"Your father touched you in ways that were not right. He knew that what he was doing was not right for children. He and other adults may have told you to keep it a secret or that you were just imagining things. You were in no way responsible for his behavior. It was a good thing that you shared this secret with people who could help you get away from it."

HOW ONE ADOPTIVE FAMILY HANDLED A DIFFICULT REALITY

Following the workshop, Terri felt more confident in writing about her son's history before he joined their family. This is what she wrote about the circumstances of his mother's death:

> Your father and mother had a great deal of trouble getting along with each other. They would often argue so loudly that neighbors worried about you.
>
> Eventually your father moved out of the house that you lived in. He had problems dealing with his anger. He needed help from a counselor, but he didn't get it.
>
> One night, very late, he came over to your house. Your father became very angry with your mother. He began hurting her so badly that she died. Because of what he did, he will be in prison for a very long time. Maybe he can get the help he needs while he is there.

Terri and her husband also kept newspaper clippings of the tragic affair. If Dale wishes to know more information about the whole matter when he is older, they will share it with him. They plan to do so because it was a highly publicized event in a small community, and therefore many residents know Dale's story.

Whatever circumstances created a difficult past for their child, it is crucial for parents to deal with those realities. Facts create an environment of healing.

Secrets block it. As children face the facts of their past, they will occasionally need to deal with the memories from those events. Those memories may spark mood changes and alter behavior.

HELPING THE MEMORIES HEAL: RECOGNIZING ANNIVERSARY REACTIONS

Jackie came in from school one November afternoon and went straight to her room. She had been doing this all week. Her parents had become increasingly concerned because normally she was a perky, happy-go-lucky junior high student.

Jackie had joined their family four years earlier when she was eight. Periodically, she had gone through these same withdrawal behaviors. It was time to find out what was happening inside her. They contacted her counselor the following morning.

What Daryl and Ruth found out resulted in real understanding, not only on their part, but also on Jackie's part. Jackie was experiencing an "anniversary reaction." She had been part of the foster care system since the age of three when she had been removed from her birthfamily on a cold, dreary November day. She went to a foster home where she lived about a year.

On a snowy day just after Thanksgiving, Jackie's social worker came to the home and moved her to another foster family. From that point, Jackie was put through three additional moves, and all but one occurred in late fall.

Because Jackie and her parents had no knowledge of the dates of the moves, they never recognized the corresponding reaction. Now they knew that Jackie was responding emotionally to the anniversary of major separations in her life. When the weather turned cold, Jackie identified it with a move from one home to another and the onslaught of more grief and confusion.

Jackie's story is not unusual, according to Cincinnati psychotherapist Deborah Joy:

> Children often create distance in their close relationships in an unconscious attempt to avoid further loss. This frequently occurs at anniversary times of separation or trauma in their lives. Some children feel anxious and begin to act out their feelings. Others become tearful and depressed.

Healthy adults who experience a major trauma, death, or separation often revisit grief in the years to come on the anniversary of when the crisis occurred. Imagine how these youngsters, who have not been responded to early in their times of deep suffering, deal with it.[12]

Joy said that these reactions are not limited to dates. Feelings and behavior can be triggered by such things as a person, an object, or an action. For example, the sight of a firefighter or police officer might remind a child of the person who removed her from her birth home. A particular type of discipline used in the adoptive home may send a child into an unexpected response.

When eighteen-month-old Lindsay came from her emergency foster home into her adoptive family, a critical piece of information was not given to her parents. Up until the time she entered foster care, Lindsay spent seven to ten daylight hours stuck in her crib. When her adoptive parents used the crib as a disciplinary measure during the daylight hours, Lindsay reacted hysterically. Had the parents known what the crib signified to Lindsay, they would never have used it.

In handling anniversary reactions and eventually helping the child's memories heal, Joy suggested the following:

- Obtain as much specific information about the daily life of the child as possible. Find out what time of year major events such as moves and separations occurred.
- Remember that negative behavior may signal emotional distress. Parents who understand what problems the behavior might be signaling will respond more appropriately.
- Work with a therapist who understands adoption issues. A third party is often very helpful for a family who may lose objectivity in the middle of a crisis.
- Use a life book. It is one of the most helpful tools in bringing memories to the surface so that they can be dealt with and their negative power can be defused.

Confronting issues of a child's past through a life book and through therapy takes a great deal of sensitivity and work. One might ask, "Does all the work make a difference?" Ask an adopted teenager.

IS THE LIFE BOOK WORTH THE EFFORT?

Mindy was adopted in 1978 at age five. At that time, life books were not routinely suggested. Her adoptive parents saw the need and constructed Mindy's story for her as she entered adolescence. The following is her perspective in the form of a letter written to her birthparents:

Dear Mom and Dad,

Do you remember me? You held me many times before you gave me up for adoption. I do not remember you at all. I was only a year old when I knew you. I only know what my life book says about me, about you, and about my past.

You see, my parents adopted me when I was five. They also adopted two of my brothers. They were really patient in trying to help us accept them — they had as many fears as we had questions. When my older brother turned sixteen, my parents prepared a life book for us. At that stage in life, we were all teens and our insecurities had set in. We wondered why we were adopted and who you were. We wondered if we had any siblings and what our preadoptive life was like. We even wondered what kind of medical problems were in our birthfamily.

My adoptive mother felt that the life book was so important to us that I remember she stayed up all night and had to call off work the next day in order to finish it. She was scared that the truth would turn us away from her. She now knows how wrong she was.

The life book answered so many of my questions about you and even sparked interest in things that I had not known about myself. Within the pages of this book, I was able to discover and accept a secret part of my past that otherwise might have kept me troubled and confused for life. Reality crept in as I was able to put an end to the fairytale dreams that many adopted girls have of being a long-lost heiress or princess. I finally came to terms with who you were. I found out that I had an older brother and sister also, and the book informed me some about them.

My life book also told me of my medical past, with copies of doctor visits while in foster care and some of the medical past of my birthfamily.

The book explained reasons why we were removed from your home.

That answer was so important to me. I no longer wonder why we were adopted. Before the life book, I would cry, wondering if I was just given up, unwanted, or abandoned. That book put an end to my tears.

I'm very glad my parents took the time to make the book for me so that I could know about you and my past. I am now able to accept who I am and seek out a better future because I know my past.

Love,

Your daughter,
Mindy

SUMMARY

One of the most important tasks undertaken by adoptive parents is communicating to their child about the past. They are faced with a decision to postpone the telling or to initiate it early in their child's life. There are two specific tools, among many, that parents can develop for the task: using literature and the life book. In addition to talking to their children about the facts of their past, parents always carry the awesome responsibility of helping their children through the process of healing any hurts that resulted from the wounds of their past.

QUESTIONS FOR SMALL GROUPS

1. When do you think children should be told that they are adopted? Why?
2. What do you think are the strongest reasons supporting the "tell them early" approach?
3. What other kinds of comments or explanations are helpful for assisting children in understanding the realities of their past?
4. What other materials can you think of that could be added to a child's life book?

PART FOUR

GROWING UP ADOPTED

Chapter Twelve

WHAT'S INSIDE AN ADOPTED ADOLESCENT?

Helping Teens Resolve Five Crucial Issues

By the time I was fourteen, I felt angry, alone, and left out. All my friends
knew their backgrounds, knew about their past. They all knew where
they were born. I didn't have one clue. Everyone in my world kept me
guessing.

— *Beth, age twenty-five, adopted as an infant*

Not many teens feel like Beth — "angry, alone, and left out" — because
they were adopted. But it is important for adoptive parents to be familiar
with the full range of attitudes they may encounter in their adopted adolescent.
Of course, the emotions Beth expressed are experienced by many teenagers at
various times during adolescence. The adopted person's lack of knowledge of his
background does not necessarily cause this anger and loneliness, but it may con-
tribute to it. And it may make adoption an easy target for blame. This state of
mind can certainly be caused or made worse by neglect or abuse suffered prior
to adoption too. In any case, whatever negativity adopted youth suffer as they
go through their potentially turbulent teen years, we can be sure that they are
almost always better off with a healthy family through adoption than in foster
care or an institution or living independently.

Whether an adolescent is raised in her biological family or an adoptive
family, it is somewhat unpredictable how she will "turn out." We've all known
parents, biological or adoptive, who seemingly raised their children beautifully
but saw them go wild in their teenage years. "Growing Up Adopted," a study
by the Search Institute, has shown, however, that adolescents adopted as infants
develop in psychological well-being roughly equally to nonadopted adolescents.
This study of 715 families and 881 adolescents adopted as infants concluded,

On a series of measures about the formation of identity, we find little evidence that adopted adolescents [adopted as infants] are particularly vulnerable. Some are, of course, but at rates no more pronounced than those for adolescents in general. . . . When asked to compare themselves to others their age, adopted adolescents report satisfactory resolution of identity concerns at rates as high or higher than their peers. And on an index of self-esteem, adopted adolescents compare favorably to a national sample of 12-18 year olds. For most adopted adolescents in this study, adoption is seen as a fact of life that is accepted with relative ease.[1]

This "ease" is reflected in how adolescents adopted as infants answered the following question in the study: "Below are four different ways young people might feel about adoption. Which one is most true for you?" The answers are followed by the percentage of participants who answered that way.

- "Being adopted has always been easy for me." 68 percent
- "Being adopted used to be hard for me, but now it's easier." 15 percent
- "Being adopted used to be easier for me, but now it's harder." 12 percent
- "Being adopted has always been hard for me." 5 percent[2]

This positive report does not mean that parents of adolescents adopted as infants can put parenting on autopilot during the teen years any more than biological parents can. As we will see in the stories in this chapter, feelings about adoption can be a significant factor as adolescents struggle with forming their identities. Moreover, according to the Search Institute study, for more than a quarter of adolescents adopted as infants, adoption "is a big part of how I think about myself."[3] Of course, prior abuse or neglect and multiple placements can make parenting adopted adolescents more challenging. But parents can be encouraged that with continued sensitivity in parenting and openness in communicating about adoption, they can help their adopted adolescents sort out their identity issues to the best of their ability.

A FAMILY CRISIS

Melinda was meeting with her supervisor on Tuesday morning when a call from the high school counselor interrupted them. "Where's Kathy this morning?" the voice inquired. "No one called to report an absence, and Mark says he doesn't have any idea where she is."

Puzzled, Melinda muffled an excuse and hung up. Immediately she called home. No answer. Explaining to her boss that she had a family emergency, Melinda rushed home. Throughout the ten-minute drive to their home, Melinda kept telling herself that she was overreacting. "Don't worry—everything's fine," she reasoned. "Kathy's probably just running late."

Going in through the garage, Melinda walked into the family room. On the kitchen counter was a note:

Mom and Dad,

I have been so mixed up lately. I am so confused. I don't know who I am and what I am going to do with my life. I know that you've been concerned about me and that I've been a real problem lately. I thought if I just leave, then you won't have the problems anymore.

Melinda was dumbfounded. She had no idea that Kathy was struggling to that degree. She never dreamed in her wildest imagination that Kathy would run away. It was so unlike her. Melinda called Ron at work and asked him to come home right away.

As Melinda sat anxiously waiting for Ron to get home, her thoughts sped back to the day when Kathy had entered their lives. Five years into their marriage, Ron and Melinda had encountered a harsh reality—they would never conceive a child. Unexplained infertility stole their dreams. Determined to raise a family, however, they decided to adopt.

After months of waiting and then working through the lengthy homestudy, they had a glimmer of hope. The adoption agency called them about the possibility of adopting an infant girl. Within five days of that phone call, Kathy entered their lives. The Barkers began their adoption journey.

Six months after Kathy arrived, they stood before the judge to make a life-long vow to her. They promised to love her, nurture her, and provide a permanent family for her. That promise was full of high expectations for themselves as parents. That promise was full of dreams for the child. Up to this point, it seemed that their dreams had been fulfilled. Yet beneath the surface lay a reservoir of untapped concerns.

The Barkers made their promise first to Kathy and then later to a son, Mark, with little or no understanding of the broader issues of adoption that confront every adoptive family. They did not know that resident within the adoptive relationship are special considerations unique to the adopted child. They did not realize that these questions can reach a fever pitch in adolescence. They found out only when they crashed headlong into the difficulties their teenage daughter was facing.

WHAT IS AN ADOLESCENT?

Adolescents undergo the most dramatic period of change that they will ever experience in their lifetime. A twelve-year-old boy who began summer vacation short and stocky may return to school in the fall towering over many of his classmates. In addition to incredible physical changes, adolescents go through turbulent mental and emotional transformations. They begin to see the world differently. As thinking processes deepen, they shift from the tangible preoccupations of middle childhood, in which they were focused only on things they could see or experience, to a view of life on a higher level. Adolescents begin to ask profound questions such as Who am I? What am I going to do with my life? and even What is the meaning of life?

Adopted teens such as Kathy are no different from other adolescents. They struggle with the same questions. However, for some, the weight of such complex issues can be heavier because as they struggle with life's normal transitions, they do so with a history they do not fully understand.

IS ADOLESCENCE A MORE COMPLEX JOURNEY FOR ADOPTED TEENS?

According to Deborah Riley, MS, author of *Beneath the Mask: Understanding Adopted Teens*, "The overall adjustment of adopted adolescents is, in fact, good. The emotional health of adopted adolescents was found to be statistically better than a comparison group of adolescents from single parent families and comparable to the adjustment pattern of adolescents born in intact families."[4] There were only a few exceptions to this generalization:

- Adopted adolescents ran away from home more frequently than the control group adolescents.
- Adopted adolescents had a greater incidence of academic and school problems.[5]

As a result of her clinical experiences working with adopted teens, Riley noted that although research points to generally successful outcomes for adopted adolescents and their families, it comes after parents and teens go an extra mile. "Adoption does complicate the necessary developmental progression," Riley pointed out. But, she continued, "adoption should not be confused with psychopathology. Adoption is not something that is wrong. It is not the problem. However, it is a factual circumstance of great emotional importance. It cannot be ignored."[6]

Families facing problems in the adolescent years should examine other sources for the causes of those issues. Before labeling the crisis as adoption-related stress, parents should take a look at what's happening within the family, at school, and in peer relationships. The household disruption might have nothing to do with adoption issues or past events; it could be related to current family functions, problems at school, or difficulties with friends.

IDENTIFYING ADOPTED TEENS' MOST VULNERABLE ISSUES

The story of Kathy Barker is the story of a loving adoptive family who thrived on the relationships they had developed with their children. It is also the story of a family who was completely unaware of the sensitive life issues that their adopted adolescent needed to bring to the surface. Taking steps toward recognizing these issues and responding to them provides an important bridge as the teen separates from her adoptive family to form new relationships and a new life as a young adult.

As mentioned earlier, adopted children gradually understand the meaning of adoption on a developmental scale. By the time the child reaches adolescence, he may perceive his adoption in a different light from what his parents believe he does. As an adolescent, he is preoccupied not only with normal identity struggles but perhaps also with more unsettling questions such as Who am I really? Can I have a future if I don't know my whole past? What is the truth about my separation from my birthfamily? What will happen to me when I separate from this family? and Will I still be part of the family?

As a result of the internal struggles, professionals and parents may note behavioral changes that go beyond the normal confrontation of issues in adolescence. These behavioral changes could be signals of a child's struggle with one or more of several primary adoption issues.[7]

In providing counseling to adopted adolescents, Dr. Alan Dupre-Clark, a clinical counselor, urges parents to define the primary issue with which the teen is struggling. Dr. Dupre-Clark describes this primary issue as "that one which provides the obvious handle on what the child is expressing about his birth origins through his behavior."[8] Once a primary issue is identified, parents and counselors have much more insight with which to help their young person.

HOW DOES A PARENT RECOGNIZE A CHILD'S MAIN ADOPTION ISSUE?

A child's main adoption issue can be recognized primarily by paying close attention to repeated behaviors and noting patterns of events that seem to trigger distress. Teens are often not fully aware of what is happening within them. Their attitudes and behavior may be as confusing to themselves as they are to their parents.

What are those issues or concerns felt by some adopted adolescents?

"A PART OF ME IS MISSING"

"It's so difficult to describe how I feel. It's like a part of me isn't here. I feel empty."

Some adopted adolescents describe a feeling of being incomplete, empty, or like a vacuum inside. They credit that perception to their lack of birthfamily ties. They also say that they have been unable to fill that void with a substitute, no matter how loving and nurturing that person has been. For some adopted kids, the feelings of emptiness and loss are so strong that it causes them to turn inward and blocks their ability to give and receive love.

In looking at grief and loss in adoption, Riley stated that the losses in adoption are unique from all other losses: "Loss in adoption does not have closure as in death. . . . It is less socially recognized."[9] Continuing, she said, "As a society, we embrace adoption in a celebratory way because we believe all children have the right to be in a permanent loving family. Adoption is embraced as a happy event that should be celebrated, not mourned. Looking clear-eyed at the many losses behind this happy scene might spoil the warm and fuzzy glow. However, not looking will lead to later and greater pain."[10]

What Should Parents Look For?

A deep sense of emptiness or incompleteness can result in serious behavioral problems. Sorting out what is related to the circumstance that led to adoption and what is related to what is happening in the teen's world is a challenge that can be met with the assistance of other adoptive parents or professional counselors. When adolescents troubled by some aspect of their adoption are not able to address their issue, they can exhibit behaviors that other troubled teens resort to:

- Chemical dependence
- Depression and multiple suicide attempts
- Attempted, successful, and recurrent pregnancies
- Overeating or anorexia
- Seeking mother figures

What Can Parents Do?

According to Betsy Keefer Smalley, adoption expert with the Institute of Human Services in Columbus, Ohio, the issue of loss and emptiness is perhaps the most serious of all adolescent issues, and it can best be resolved by attempting to remove a portion of the child's source of grief: the sense of loss of birthparents.[11]

How is this accomplished? In some cases, adoptive parents have been able to secure a letter or video from a birthfamily member by contacting the agency that acted as a liaison between the adoptive family and the birthfamily. In some extreme cases, where the grief has created very serious, even life-threatening adjustment problems, a possible reunion between the child and his or her birthfamily may alleviate the pain.

Adoptive families generally have many concerns about attempting such a drastic measure for their teenage child. They question how a reunion will affect their child and the relationship they have with him or her. However, for a child and family bordering on a life-threatening crisis or torn apart by drug or alcohol abuse, there isn't much to lose. This was the case for seventeen-year-old Andrea Mitchell.

In her preteen years, Andrea showed little interest in the subject of adoption. She knew that she had entered her family at birth directly from the hospital. She had been informed of her circumstances, and her parents were readily available to answer any questions she might have. She had grown up in a loving family. She knew she was their pride and joy.

However, as she neared her middle teen years, Andrea began to ask more penetrating questions. Her parents noticed a dramatic change in their sensitive child's behavior. She became increasingly depressed and withdrawn. Attempts at getting her to talk were unsuccessful. Andrea just didn't know what was the matter.

Andrea's problem then hit a crisis level. One morning when Andrea failed to get out of bed for school, her mother, Cynthia, knocked on her door. When there was no answer, she cracked the door open to find her daughter apparently still asleep. As she walked over to awaken her, her foot crushed a pill bottle on the floor near the bed. Attempts to rouse Andrea failed. Cynthia rushed out to call for emergency help and then called her husband, Peter, at work.

Fortunately for Andrea and her family, her suicide attempt was unsuccessful. Following her recovery, the entire family entered therapy. The theme that consistently recurred from Andrea was, "There's this feeling inside, like a huge, gaping hole that always has been there. It just doesn't go away. It feels like a part of me is missing. I just got so tired of feeling that way."

One strong recommendation from the therapist, which the entire family was willing to pursue, was to initiate a search for Andrea's birthfamily. Her parents contacted a regional organization that specialized in such undertakings. Their questioning brought to mind some old information that Peter Mitchell had long stored away.

Two months prior to Andrea's birth, when the Mitchells were sitting in their attorney's office, an apparently unrelated phone call interrupted their meeting. Following the conversation, the lawyer wrote down the name of a Patricia Smith and her expected due date. The information caught Peter's eye. On impulse he made a mental note of the name and the woman's due date and later placed it on a piece of paper in Andrea's adoption file at home.

When Peter went to that old file at the suggestion of the search group, he pulled out the note he had kept. The woman's due date was within five days of Andrea's birth. Perhaps this was a lead.

Following a four-month search, Andrea's birthmother was located just an hour's drive from the Mitchells. She agreed to a meeting, and the family met her in a park in their area. Since that day, Andrea has kept in contact with her birthmother sporadically. She doesn't intend to establish a close relationship with her at this point in her life. She said,

> The Mitchells are my parents. They have loved me and cared for me. Meeting Patricia was the most important thing I could have done, for it enabled me to close the book on the past I never knew. It filled in an incredible sense of emptiness that was gnawing away at me. I feel complete and whole.

In the next chapter, we will discuss crucial steps parents need to take in dealing with search and reunion. Another issue that appears for some adopted adolescents is control.

A Cry for Control

Fran felt like slamming the phone receiver down, but she didn't. It was the high school principal again. Their fifteen-year-old son, Steve, was sitting in the office, suspended from class for the third time that month. This suspension meant he would be ineligible for the next three basketball games. *What has gotten into him?* she wondered. Steve's father had attempted to talk with him, but Steve just mumbled meaningless responses, so Mike decided to drop the subject.

Until this year, Steve hadn't experienced any major problems at home or at school. Of course, he'd had his share of detentions for minor infractions, but nothing as disruptive as what he was doing currently.

Steve had been a delightful youngster to raise — compliant, cooperative, and fun loving. He had become part of the Rossburg family at the age of three and a half. His history painted a sad picture of extreme neglect and abuse, but Steve never seemed bothered by it. He generally did whatever was asked of him.

Struggling with confusion about her son's behavior, Fran made a decision. She called one of her friends, another adoptive mom of an adolescent, to ask her advice. After Fran described Steve's behavior, her friend suggested that perhaps Steve was calling out for some control in his life.

One common issue for adopted teens revolves around the need for control. Many feel that their lives have been overly managed or mismanaged by adults in their world. The mismanagement might have begun with their birthparents' decision to relinquish parental rights—or, even worse, their birthparents' loss of parental rights due to abuse or neglect.

Following that series of events, decisions were made concerning future foster or adoptive parents, how much information would be available to them, and expectations regarding the child's behavior and acceptance of what life was handing to them. For some youngsters, years of frustrated feelings build up from their belief that they have had no control in their lives. A strong need to govern their own lives erupts in adolescence.

What Should Parents Look For?

The following behavioral signals may indicate that teens are struggling for a sense of control:

- Extreme limit testing of authority figures
- Lying
- Behavior tantrums and verbal abuse of authority figures
- Breaking rules
- Chemical dependency
- Eating disorders
- A compulsive need to manage their world (for example, being extremely organized or always planning ahead)

What Can Parents Do?

Teens struggling with lack of control can best move toward resolution as they are given more opportunities for choice, according to Smalley. "Parents who can provide more opportunities for the teen to handle decision making may discover fewer power struggles in the home," said Smalley.

For example, within the framework of established boundaries, parents can give teens plenty of latitude in selecting clothes. A youngster who is given a specific amount of money to spend on three pairs of pants, four shirts, and five pairs of socks will gain a sense of control in his life when he is allowed to choose his purchases.

Another opportunity for choice is in the assignment of chores. Parents are encouraged to offer the teen a number of options regarding what chores need to be completed, along with a time limit to complete those chores. Teens are reminded again of the variety of choices they have but are also cued into the possibility of consequences should they not exercise those choices.

Loss and control are two issues some teens may face. A sense of rejection is another.

Rehearsing Rejection and Abandonment: "Am I Permanent Here?"

"I can't imagine any kid being so bad that his parents dump him like a piece of trash."

"I'm not going to get too close to anyone—that way, I'll never be discarded again."

"My birthparents rejected me. When is this going to happen with my adoptive parents?"

"I have always had the fear that some morning I will wake up and nobody will be here. They will all have mysteriously disappeared."

Rejection ranks as one of life's most painful experiences. For some adopted children, especially in the vulnerable adolescent years, feelings of rejection and abandonment from their birthparents can override the positive and nurturing love of their adoptive family.

Teens' perceptions of rejection can spill over to affect them in building healthy relationships. They can develop a pattern of pursuing acceptance and backing away from it when emotional intimacy appears close.

Robin, the beautiful sixteen-year-old daughter of Paul and Beth Clark, never dated a boy for very long. Robin was thrilled with the amount of attention she received from the young men in her school. She chatted enthusiastically with her mom about possible dating prospects. However, after a few dates, Robin invariably began refusing phone calls and rejecting further invitations. Her behavior stumped her parents.

Robin's confusing behavior is typical of a young person dealing with rejection issues. Robin was adopted by the Clarks at six weeks. Their openness about how she was separated from her family gave her information that was helpful to her. But she repeatedly asked two questions that the Clarks could not answer: "Why did they get rid of me? Why did they just leave me?" This theme of rejection was so strong with Robin that in most of her relationships, she rebuffed girlfriends and boyfriends before they rejected her. Essentially, she planned to quit relationships before she got fired.

Not only is rejection a theme for some adopted teens, but the sense of permanence is as well, especially for those adopted youngsters who entered their homes as older children and had previously experienced multiple moves.

John, who was adopted at ten, had always been an average student. Academics were not a major issue for him. However, it was John's senior year and all of that changed. John was failing, and his parents were stumped. As teens move into the final year of high school, graduation may represent parental loss and perceived abandonment.

The fear of growing up and leaving home triggered in John an unconscious reaction and fear— *"If I leave here, am I really a permanent member of the family?"* Overcome with a deep sense of a lack of permanence, John was sabotaging his senior year. He convinced himself if he didn't graduate, he wouldn't have to leave.

A suggestion for parents sensing this type of reaction from their teen is to plan that teen's departure from home in gradual steps. If a teen plans to attend college or technical school, parents can suggest he spends his first year living at home and commuting.

For young adults who are planning on working right after graduation, completing a plan for independent living may take up to two years. (For information on how to prepare an adolescent for independent living, see Casey Life Skills, www.caseylifeskills.org.)

What Should Parents Look For?

Characteristic behaviors in teens grappling with the perception of rejection and permanence include the following:

- Successive cycles of pursuing friendships or relationships with abrupt termination of them; rejecting others before they can be rejected
- Negative behavior that sets up a pattern of perceived rejection responses from the adoptive family
- Expressing fear of being close to people

- In serious cases, depression and/or suicide attempts
- Resistance to the transition of teen to young adult with the expected emancipation from home
- Getting in trouble with the law
- Clinging, dependent behavior
- Truancy

What Can Parents Do?

Because the fear of rejection or abandonment can be so strong, teens may attempt to create a reenactment of the felt rejection by distancing themselves emotionally from the adoptive parents. Throwing rejecting messages at adoptive parents such as, "You're not my real dad" or "I don't want to be in the family" can easily pull a hurting, frustrated parent into returning similar rejecting messages. "If you don't stop this behavior, you are not going to be part of this family anymore," parents may retort.

To help a youngster deal with deep feelings of rejection and pain, Smalley suggested that parents monitor their responses to their teen's acting out. In heated moments, parents have two choices: to respond in anger with rejecting remarks or to remove themselves from the conflict momentarily in a kind of parental time-out. Most rejecting messages come in the midst of heated conflict.

Parents can also examine their own communication skills to determine what messages they are subtly, or not so subtly, sending to their child. Are they available to listen? Do they listen beyond the surface words? Are they able to ask questions that will get below the surface? Do they allow their teen to express feelings without judging her or reacting defensively? Good family communication sends a message that the teen is accepted in their family.

Preteens and some older teens occasionally respond to the deep emotional scars of rejection and abandonment when changes in normal family living occur or during transitional periods of their lives. If a parent becomes ill or plans a long trip, abandonment fears may prompt negative behavior. These times require special awareness and an effort to communicate about the teen's fears. Although youngsters in this age range understand cognitively that a parent will recover or return, they may stumble emotionally, said Smalley.

As mentioned earlier, as teens move into the final year of high school, graduation may represent parental loss and perceived abandonment. The fear of growing up and leaving home triggered an unconscious reaction in eighteen-year-old Brian, who attempted to sabotage the last semester of his senior year. Somewhere inside he was clinging to the thought, *If I don't graduate, my parents won't make me leave and go to college.*

One suggestion for parents sensing this type of reaction from their son or daughter is to plan their teen's departure from home in gradual steps. If teens plan to attend college or technical school, parents can suggest that they spend their first year living at home and commuting to a nearby school. For young adults who are planning on working right after graduation, completing a plan for independent living may take up to two years.

INVESTIGATING IDENTITY

A recurring comment made by some adopted adolescents, especially in later years, is, "Who am I, really?" The identity crisis commonly attributed to the adolescent years is compounded for some adopted teens. Adoption experts give this the label "genealogical bewilderment." It is described as the "feeling of being cut off from your heritage, your religious background, your culture, your race."[12] Giving this experience of some adopted adolescents a psychological label may be excessive; it is not a pathology. But unlike their nonadopted peers' usually thorough knowledge of their genetic roots and identification with a family, adopted children usually lack information about their beginning.

Dan's tremendous musical talent was the pride and joy of his musical parents. Just like his adoptive father, Dan could pick up a trumpet or sit at the piano and play superbly. Dan's confusion as he matured was, "Who am I really like—my birthfamily or my adoptive family?" Dan took on the characteristics of his adoptive parents. He knew what they were. He saw them every day. But what about the characteristics of his birthparents? Were they musical? Was he more like them? He had no idea.

Casey, age seventeen, was nearing graduation and trying to decide what direction to take in her life. Casey knew the circumstances of her adoption. She was born to an unwed teenage mother who lived on welfare. Struggling with attempting to find some identity, Casey made some poor decisions. Just before graduation, she announced to her parents that she was pregnant. In spite of her parents' acceptance of the crisis and willingness to help, Casey moved into the apartment of her baby's father. She had chosen an identity on which to build her life. In some respects she was identifying with her birthmother.

What Should Parents Look For?

Teens grappling with identity generally signal their distress in one or more of the following ways:

- Easily giving in to peer or group pressure to be like others
- "Trying on" different identities, including those they perceive might be characteristic of their birthparents
- Being moody and brooding
- Acting in a clingy or manipulative manner with adults in their world
- Displaying a sense of helplessness
- Association with troubled peers

What Can Parents Do?

First, Smalley suggested that parents return to the agency that arranged the adoption and attempt to get as much information as possible. Even nonidentifying information about birthparents that gives a physical description, ethnicity or cultural information, and interests can help guide a child toward identity formation.

For parents in the early stages of the adoptive relationship who are far from facing the adolescent years, Smalley recommended that they return to the agency to obtain similar information before the "trail gets cold. Get everything in writing so that the young person can read it for himself," she advised.

Second, parents should monitor how they feel and think about the child's birthparents. Adoptive parents occasionally feel threatened by the invisible presence, also known as the psychological presence, of the child's birthparents. They may have a tendency to criticize them to the child. "A child cannot feel good about himself until he feels good about where he came from," offered Smalley. "Parents should be realistic, while at the same time as positive as possible."

"Being Adopted Is Different, and It Feels That Way"

"Sometimes I look around the dinner table and think to myself, *I don't look like a single person here.* There are times I feel like I really don't belong here."

"I get so tired of people asking questions about my past, like, 'Don't you want to meet your *real* mom?'"

What Can Parents Do?

To help a child with the issue of feeling different, parents can look outside their own family circle to other adoptive families. As they cultivate friendships with families in similar circumstances, their children will see others who are just like them.

Support groups provide a positive resource for families facing this need. More and more support organizations around the country are providing opportunities for adopted children to meet with each other through age-based groups and recreational activities.

"MY PARENTS HAVE DONE SO MUCH FOR ME"

On the bright side of the issues confronting teens during the upheaval of their adolescent years is the common theme of gratitude. Their words say it best:

> I know how important I am to my parents. All throughout my growing up they told me in so many ways. One of the hardest things I struggled with was going to them and asking for information about my birthparents. Their response was overwhelmingly positive. I know it came from a heart that felt some pain, like I would reject them or something. But they helped me in spite of their concern. Their response was born out of sensitivity to me and my needs. I am deeply grateful for the home in which I grew up.
>
> —ANNA, AGE NINETEEN (ADOPTED AT THREE MONTHS)

> I don't remember a whole lot about coming to my family. What I do remember were the problems that erupted when I was in late elementary school and junior high. I was some mixed-up kid. Late at night, after I had gone to bed, I would hear my parents talking about me while sitting in the kitchen. I heard such words as, "Richard has so much to offer. He is a talented young boy. With help, I know we will see him through this. Our family will make it." I never heard words that gave me any idea that they were ready to dump me.
>
> I can't express enough how much I love my parents and hope someday I can repay them. I know when times get tough for them, I'll stick right by them.
>
> —RICHARD, AGE TWENTY (ADOPTED AT FIVE)

The most meaningful experience I have had with my parents was the trip we took to Korea when I was fifteen. They had always been so open about my special issues—cultural things like that.

Although we couldn't locate any specific information about my birthfamily, I was able to see how they would have lived and what it would have been like for me. Our trip there provided me with much more information. However, it gave me something else. It deeply impressed upon me how much my parents love me. I hope someday they will truly know how very much I am grateful to them for all they have been to me.

—Kimberly, age eighteen (adopted from Korea at five months)

AN EPILOGUE

On the evening of Kathy Barker's disappearance, she called her parents from a friend's home in another town. She had walked to the bus station that morning and caught a bus to her friend's town. Crying, she told them that she felt so mixed up and lost. She wanted to get help. Ron and Melinda were deeply relieved after Kathy's call. The following week, the Barkers made an appointment with a counselor in their area who specialized in adoption-related issues.

Following almost six months of family counseling, the Barkers have stronger relationships today. They now are more aware that their children, special miracles in their lives, will have issues that other teens will not. They also learned that the issues may possibly surface and resurface during transitional phases of their children's adult lives. They know that Kathy and Mark will still need their adoptive parents for support because adoption is not an isolated event; it is a relationship that begins, grows, and is sustained by a lifelong promise. It can best be explained by this:

Each of us has things to which we return now and then to work on and worry over—things from the past and present that occasionally resurface. . . . It may be a relationship to a sister, it may be a fear of flying, it may be a tragic first love affair. . . . We tuck these issues away in a hatbox, in a closet, in a far-off corner of the house.

Every now and then, something makes us search out that far-off corner, open the closet door, take down the box, and deal with the issue for a while. Eventually, we feel finished with it, at least for the time being, so we put away the box and go back to living our lives. Some day in the future, though, we'll go back to that closet again, and deal with the issue in the box for a while longer.

That's what the adoption issue is like for most [adopted people] — no more, no less.[13]

SUMMARY

Most adopted adolescents mature in psychological well-being roughly equally to their nonadopted peers unless prior neglect or abuse complicates their adjustment. For some, however, being adopted is something they experience as an additional challenge to identity formation and self-esteem.

It is important for adoptive parents to know the potential thoughts and feelings about adoption that their teens may experience and understand how to deal with them should they arise. It is also crucial for these same families to evaluate how their own family dynamics may be affecting their children.

There are five key issues that may confront adopted teens:

- "A part of me is missing" — emptiness, loss, and grief
- A cry for control
- Rehearsing rejection and abandonment
- Investigating identity
- Feeling different

QUESTIONS FOR SMALL GROUPS

1. What issues do you feel are confronting your teen?
2. What behaviors have you found confusing or even disturbing?
3. What steps have you taken, if any, to work on these issues?
4. What have you found to be valuable in helping your teen?

CHAPTER THIRTEEN

SEARCHING FOR A PAST

Why Adopted Children Seek Their Roots and How Parents Can Respond

The letter was fragile and yellowed with age. It was written by my birthmother at the time I was born. She was only sixteen. The letter expressed
love and concern for me. For the first time in my life, I felt worthy of
love. I knew my adoptive parents loved me, but I never felt worthy of it.

— *Marcia, age thirty-two*

Randy hesitated on the cracked sidewalk bordering the front yard. Then
she stepped carefully through the litter-cluttered lawn and climbed the
uneven steps to the door. She was apprehensive, scared. Did she really want to
go in? It was hard to believe this day had come. All her life she had tucked away
questions about her birthparents. Today she would finally get some answers.

Randy had been only four years old when she and her older sister walked
out the door of an orphanage hand in hand with two strangers. Those two
strangers were to be their new mother and father. The children were given no
further explanations. They just left.

By the time she was five, her parents had finalized her adoption. Randy's
parents believed that when a child is adopted at such a young age, the door is
shut on the past. They believed that it was as if all issues surrounding Randy's
earlier life were erased and she entered the new family with a blank slate.

However, Randy's separation experience brought questions: "Why did my
birthparents leave me? Do I have other sisters and brothers? Who do I look
like?" These questions gnawed away at her feeling of well-being, attacking sensitive and deep issues in self-esteem and personal identity. "Although I knew my
adoptive parents loved me," she said, "I felt that pieces of my life were scattered
and no one knew where they were. I had to find them."

Do adopted young adults want to know more about their past, and do they think about adoption and meeting their birthparents? The answer is that many do and many do not, at least not to a significant extent. The Search Institute research project "Growing Up Adopted" reported the following data (notice the difference between boys' and girls' responses in some cases):

- Forty percent of the adolescents studied wanted to know more about their birth history (45 percent of girls, 30 percent of boys).[1]
- Sixty percent thought about adoption never, less than once per month, or about once per month; 20 percent thought about it every day or two to three times per week.
- Sixty-five percent would like to meet their birthparents if possible (70 percent of girls, 57 percent of boys);[2] far fewer actually ever search.
- For those interested in meeting their birthparents, the primary motivations the adopted adolescents gave were these:
    - To find out what they look like: 94 percent
    - To tell them I'm happy: 80 percent
    - To tell them I'm okay: 76 percent
    - To tell them I'm glad to be alive: 73 percent
    - To find out why I was adopted: 72 percent[3]

The researchers interpreted their data as follows: "Though adolescents tend to have few concerns about adoption in matters of cognition and emotion, there is still a desire to know about one's biological origins. This desire is not driven by emotional turmoil or identity confusion. It simply reflects, in all probability, a healthy curiosity."[4]

Tom and Chris's father-son steak dinner out is a good example of a typical adolescent attitude. Tom said, "Chris, it's been awhile since we've spoken about this, so I just wanted to ask you if you ever think about your birthparents." Chris replied, "Occasionally." Tom went on, "Well, I just wanted to make sure you know that whatever you decide about contacting them—" The seventeen-year-old assertively interrupted, "I know. You'll support me in whatever I decide." Tom, a little flustered, replied, "Well, that's right, but let me finish my sentence because it's important for me to say it. Yes, Mom and I will support you in whatever you decide." In confident teenager fashion, Chris looked Tom in the eye and said, "Dad, you have butter in your hair." Tom was right to want to make sure Chris knew, and Chris sent the message, "I got it, Dad, and everything is just fine."

However, for some adopted adolescents, when the teenage turmoil increases, the interest in biological origins can intensify and the curiosity can grow into a longing that becomes intertwined with the search for identity in various ways. For many teens, especially those nearing the end of adolescence and moving into young adulthood, there are other reasons to consider a search and actually move forward.

WHY THE SEARCH?

Randy's yearning to find a connection to her birthfamily is not an unusual occurrence for adopted people. Activating a hunt for one's origin and history can be motivated by many reasons, ranging from a need for medical and genealogical information to a deep desire to unite with family ties from the past.

NEEDING MEDICAL HISTORY AND INFORMATION

Chuck excelled in high school and earned a four-year science scholarship to a well-known university. He dreamed of one day pursuing a career as a medical missionary. He had never really thought about tracking down information about his birthparents before, but when a crisis hit, it became a necessity.

Over the course of his junior winter semester, Chuck noticed a dramatic deterioration in his vision. He immediately sought the care of a specialist, who told him that his problem was potentially critical and most likely genetic in nature. At that point, some answers about Chuck's genetic heritage were imperative. He began the search only for genealogical and medical information. He was not interested in developing a relationship with his birthfamily.

Chuck's hurried and dramatic investigation brought heart wrenching results. Although he never wanted or obtained specific information identifying his birthparents, he did obtain medical records revealing a history of blindness on his biological father's side. His father had been completely blind by age thirty. The report Chuck obtained offered him some hope, however, because it enabled his physician to offer potentially preventive treatment.

Shelly initiated her research for an entirely different reason. By the time she turned twenty-five, both of her adoptive parents had died, leaving only Shelly and her younger sister. She had never taken the opportunity to make inquiries about her past out of concern that her parents would misunderstand. Spurred on by a yearning to connect to her roots and a need for a parental relationship, Shelly began attempts to locate her birth family. She has not located her birth parents, but she did discover two sisters who were adopted prior to her birth. All of them live within the same state and enjoy getting to know each other.

NEEDING MORE INFORMATION AND COMMUNICATION

One primary factor that activates the search is the lack of communication around adoption issues.[5]

Jenny was adopted in 1963 as a two-year-old. She remembers being told of her adoption status perhaps twice prior to adolescence. She stated, "No one ever mentioned the word *adoption* around me, so I couldn't ask anyone about it. In the sixties people just didn't talk about it, like it was a horrible secret. By late elementary school, I knew I was different and adoption wasn't normal. I began wondering then, was it bad?"

Thankfully, it is unusual today for children not to be told about their adoption. But Jenny's example illustrates the importance of how parents choose to deal with adoption communication from a wide continuum of options. Some parents desire to keep the matter a closed subject, virtually denying its reality. These parents have adopted the coping style of rejecting the role and reality of adoption in their lives (see chapter 5).

In contrast, other families communicate openly and honestly about the details of the entire adoption experience. In this acknowledgment-of-adoption coping style, parents allow themselves and the child to explore the many facets of adoption. They are open with the information they have concerning the child's life. They accumulate adoption-related books and other literature and make it accessible to the child.

When parents understand the value of openness in relating information to their adopted child, it seems to lessen some trauma and stress related to the child's experiences. Finding out the whole story is one factor that might compel someone to begin tracing the past. Finding birthrelatives in order to identify family resemblance is another.

Who Do I Look Like? Who Do I Act Like?

When Penny, a thirty-year-old with auburn hair and freckles, opened a manila envelope from the adoption agency, she certainly didn't expect to find what she did. The letter ended a lifetime of wondering, *Do I look and act like anyone in my birthfamily?* (At least the following level of detail in birthfamily medical and social history is generally provided at placement to the adoptive parents in domestic infant adoptions.)

Dear Ms. Wright,

I am enclosing the social medical information that you requested. We have the following nonidentifying information concerning your birthfamily:

Social and Medical History of Penny Carter Wright

Father: Your birthfather was a single white Protestant young man and was twenty-one years old at the time of your birth. He had dark hair, green eyes, and a medium complexion. He stood five foot nine and weighed 160 at the time of your birth. He was described by close friends as quiet and reserved. He shared many of the same interests as your mother. He enjoyed art and music and played both the piano and the guitar. He did enjoy some outdoor activities, particularly horseback riding. He was in college when you were born, majoring in music. He reported no medical problems.

Mother: Your birthmother was a single white Protestant young woman who was twenty years old at the time of your birth. She had auburn hair, brown eyes, and freckles. She was five foot four and weighed 145 prior to pregnancy. She was described by friends as warm, giving, and responsive. She also had a strong interest in music and art and played the piano. At the time of your birth she was a sophomore in college, also majoring in music. She wanted to become a concert pianist. Learning and accomplishment came easily to her. Her health problems included eye correction for nearsightedness and moderate difficulties with allergies.

Penny was overwhelmed with the similarities. When she joined her new family at two years of age, she was the only adopted child in the house. She grew up with a loving, gracious family of light-complexioned blonds, even down to their blond cocker spaniel. As she grew into adolescence, the differences widened. Her two sisters and brother all grew to over five foot nine and never struggled with problems of being "short and fat," as she described herself. Her own perceptions of herself made her wonder if she really fit in this family.

As is the case with many adopted people, Penny's perceived lack of similarities with her adoptive family was the significant motivator in her birth search. Because she resembled no one in the household, she felt a sense of frustration, embarrassment, and insecurity. The driving desire to find a genetic similarity was the thing that motivated Penny during the ten months it took to receive information. Upon obtaining that information, she said,

> For the first time in my life, I felt physically attached to someone. I look like both my father and mother, suffer with her allergy problems, and now understand why I have such an interest in music. My adoptive family are all sports enthusiasts, and I never could get interested. I am not such an oddity after all. In many ways, I am like my birthparents.
>
> My reason for the search was not to hurt my relationship with my parents. They are fantastic. I just wanted to know who I looked like and who I acted like. I wasn't interested in meeting them or even in seeing them. I just wanted to know if someone else out in this world looked like me. That information was all I needed to put my search and my questions to rest.

WHERE AM I ON MY GENETIC FAMILY TREE?

Connie was adopted at age four, and by the time she entered fifth grade, she was well aware of it. In fact, reminders of the difference followed her even into the classroom. Memories of confusion and pain from one particular school assignment still surface occasionally:

> I recall one afternoon when our teacher gave an assignment that set off questions no one had answered for me.
>
> "We're going to build a family tree," she told us. "I want you to bring in your baby pictures and pictures of your grandparents, aunts, and uncles."

Baby pictures, I remember crying inside. *Don't you know that some adopted kids don't have baby pictures? And besides, other than my sister, I don't know another person on this earth who has the same flesh and blood as I do!* I can remember the fear I felt. What reason could I give to my friends why I didn't have those pictures? No one had ever fully explained it to me.

It was at that point that Connie first acknowledged an experience of feeling different. The block to her past seemed to immobilize Connie emotionally. She couldn't see any continuity from her past relationships to her future ones. As an adult, an overwhelming need to find her place in the narrative of a family's story persuaded her to seek information about her birthfamily. Did she have genetically related aunts and uncles, grandparents and great-grandparents? Who were they and what were they like? Connie's search, which included a genealogical survey through historical records, satisfied her need. She found her place on her birthfamily tree.

Chuck's need for medical information, Penny's need to find genetic similarities, and Connie's desire to find a place on a genetic family tree are three reasons for the search for birthfamily members. Adoption experts and adopted adults cite even more specific issues that initiate the walk into the past.

A Need to Connect

By the time Shelly turned twenty-five, both of her adoptive parents had died, leaving only Shelly and her younger sister. She had never taken the opportunity to make inquiries about her past out of concern that her parents would misunderstand. Spurred on by a yearning to connect to her roots and a hunger for a parental relationship, Shelly began attempting to locate her birthfamily so that she would at least have some family ties. She has not yet located her birthparents, but she did discover two sisters who were adopted prior to her birth. All live within the same state.

A Need to Forgive

One of the most painful burdens an adopted person may carry is the perception that the person was given away. Robin Henig explained, "For [some] adopted children, part of them is hurt at having once been relinquished. That part remains vulnerable to grief and anger for the rest of their lives."[6] Without assistance to deal with the anger and grief and move toward forgiveness, some adopted people are likely to find bitterness a close companion in adulthood.

This issue compelled Randy to unravel an unknown past. Her story of healing and completeness offers hope to those in similar situations:

> As I entered adolescence, damaging thoughts took root in my heart and mind. I convinced myself that since my family life was different from anyone else's I knew, I wasn't as good as the rest of my friends. Tremendous feelings of inadequacy barred me from trying new things or from branching out into friendships.
>
> By the time I was nineteen, I was still plagued by feelings of deep resentment. I had a lot of anger toward the parents who had rejected me as a two-year-old. I became more and more bitter all the time. I don't know how many times I thought to myself, *Mom and Dad, you left me. You were never there for me.*
>
> I felt stuck in a downward spiral of negativism that drained me of happiness and peace. I had to put the fragmented pieces of my life together.
>
> I know that from the beginning, my birth search was directed by God. As I searched through records in a large metropolitan county courthouse, a clerk volunteered to help.
>
> "This is highly unusual," she informed me. "Just two weeks ago, a man was in here looking for the same information. Over two months ago, a young woman asked me these same questions. I gave them this address."
>
> Out of the multitude of personnel at the courthouse, this clerk helped all three of us. That afternoon, I learned I had a birthsister and brother, and I had a way to make direct contact with my birthfamily.
>
> Like many adopted kids, I had manufactured fantasies about my birthparents. I imagined them as wealthy people who deeply regretted giving me away. As I stood on the front porch of a small house that summer day, looking at the disheveled woman who had given birth to me, all sorts of emotions welled up within me. I spent three hours with her. Our conversation was empty and strained. What I heard and saw jarred me to reality. It was obvious that alcohol still permeated this

home, just as I had been told. When I walked out the door, I left my fantasies behind.

The process of healing began that day as I encountered the desperate, tragic state of my birthfamily. Their lives were empty—ravaged by alcohol, drug abuse, and poverty. God had spared me such a life.

Compassion filled me. I did forgive those who had left me with so many missing pieces. Now I could go on with my life, stronger with the reality of what my life has become and with a deepened relationship with my adoptive parents.

WHAT HAPPENS AS A RESULT OF THE SEARCH?

Results from reunions vary greatly. Some reunions are joyful and lead to healthy long-term relationships. Other reunions may not lead to ongoing relationships but still satisfy the searcher's longing for understanding of the past. Some can be unpleasant and contentious, especially when they are not mutually consensual. In all cases, adoptive parents who assist their children in searching should insist that they follow the law and not force themselves on birthparents who do not want to be contacted.

Randy, Connie, and Penny conducted successful searches for information about their past and experienced positive results. Many adopted people who search report finding what they were looking for, resolution of inner conflicts connected to their condition and circumstances, filling the emptiness created by an unknown past, and establishing a sense of identity. Many adopted adults even indicate that one of the strongest positive results is a new level of closeness and intimacy with their adoptive parents.

A study of adopted people who had completed some portion of a birth search found that all respondents experienced considerable improvement in their lives as a result of changes brought about by their search. References to significant improvements in self-esteem, self-confidence, and assertiveness appeared frequently. Others reported that they had finally acquired feelings of connection, which had previously escaped them. Still others alluded to increased peace of mind, a sense of calmness, and a greater ability to handle and express feelings.[7]

One important piece of the adoptive relationship that adopted people should know is that most adoptive parents are willing to support their adopted young person in whatever he or she decides about searching for his or her past, as long as it is ethical and legal. To one degree or another, parents understand that people want to know their roots. However, in responding to this desire, parents can encounter feelings that are considerably complex. For some parents, cognitive recognition that this is a normal issue for an adopted person stands miles apart from the psychological and emotional impact it incurs.

Randolph Severson, author and therapist, portrayed the ambivalence encountered by some adoptive parents as they support a search, enduring some confusion and even pain along the way: "Adoptive parents—some with joy and some with anguish—are awakening to the fact that roots, however twisted, are as vital to the leafing of the tree as is the gentle nurturing of the sun and rain."[8]

Although some parents understand the desire for their adopted teen or young adult to seek his or her birthfamily, others react negatively and fearfully. For some parents, the probe into the past resurrects painful dormant memories.

Reminder of Failure and Loss

When Sandy's twenty-year-old daughter, Ali, approached her with the news that she wanted to find her birthparents, Sandy was devastated. Once again Sandy was reminded that she was different. Once again she suffered the distressing memories of her inability to conceive a child. Old disturbing emotions surrounding her own infertility and inadequacy surfaced—ones she thought were resolved long ago.

Sandy's halting response to Ali's question, "Will you help me?" was strained and cool. "If I can find the time," was all she could muster.

Inadequacy and Rejection

Linda's negative response to her son Keith's interest in conducting a search was rooted in another cause. Years before, sitting in a counselor's office, she had asked about this very issue. She was told by the counselor, "If you are the right kind of mother, your child will never want to search."

Today Keith had asked the question. Today a crushing sense of failure as a mother consumed Linda. She simply couldn't support Keith's intentions. His request only confirmed her perceived deficiency as a parent. Carol Demuth, in her book *Courageous Blessing: Adoptive Parents and the Search*, said adoptive parents were given the message, "If you were loving, nurturing parents who acknowledged your child's adoptive status early, there would be no need on his part to know anything else."[9]

All that came to mind for Robert and Susan when their son informed them of his search and impending reunion was, *Aren't we good enough for you any longer?*

> We felt we had given everything we could to our son—support, love—everything. But all those feelings of doing a good job as a parent came crashing down the day he told us of his plans. We don't know why it affected us so emotionally. We know he needs to do this, but it doesn't feel good for us. We just don't feel good enough for him any longer.[10]

Being reminded of loss related to infertility and feelings of inadequacy and failure are two reasons parents do not assist in the process. The third is fear.

Overwhelming Fear

Parents have two primary fears: loss of the relationship with their adopted child and the potentially harmful impact of the discoveries on the young adult. "Some adoptive parents feel threatened by the desire to search," commented an adoptive mother of eight. "They fear that they will lose their child's affection. They are apprehensive about encouraging the child's birth search due to the frightening possibility that the discovery could permanently dissolve their family relationship and leave them childless again."

Some young adults (eighteen to twenty-one) are still unrealistic about what they will discover. They expect to find out that their natural parents now have it all together and will welcome them with open arms. This rarely happens.

Another fear for parents is that the child's discovery of possible negative origins may have long-lasting effects, especially concerning identity and self-worth issues. If young adults discover the complete truth of their family of origin, it could escalate feelings of inadequacy and worthlessness. But for some, it is a risk that must be taken.

HOW PARENTS CAN RESPOND TO THE NEED TO SEARCH

When faced with the prospect of a son's or daughter's appeal for help in the search, parents must choose whether or not to give it. Adoption specialists concur that the most healthy response, which will keep family communication open, is to provide support. Involvement is vital, although the level may vary.

The first step that adoptive parents must take in supporting their adult child's search, according to Lois Melina, is to grant permission. This means letting their child know that it's all right with them if the child decides to search. "Related to this," Melina wrote, "is the sharing of information the adoptive parents have about the birthparents or the adoption. It is hypocritical for us to say it's okay with us if the [adopted person] searches, but withhold information that could assist her in the search."[11]

Parents often ask for practical suggestions on how to deal successfully with birth search issues. The following suggestions are intended to provide insight and encouragement for families who have yet to confront the issue as well as those who are in the midst of assisting their adult child in a search.

1. A family must be comfortable with the reality of adoption. They must be willing to understand and accept, without personal threat or guilt, the lifelong dynamics that appear, disappear, and reappear.

2. Parents should share information about the child's adoption early. They should disclose the information they do have on a gradually increasing basis.

3. Parents must realize that a lot of groundwork needs to be laid before the search begins. This can be accomplished by communicating as a family and through an adoption-sensitive counselor, if necessary. The adult child may open up a Pandora's box of painful uncertainties or shattering realities. Adoptive parents may be needed to pick up the pieces.

4. Parents must realize that the intensity of the search may be more than their adopted child expected. The following describe basic issues resident within the search that when validated will help their searching young person.

   a. *Know the emotions they may encounter.* The searcher may experience intense anger and rage, a resurgence of painful memories, and/or incredible sadness and depression. The searcher also is likely to experience any or all of the following fears:

1. Fear of the unknown
2. Fear of rejection
3. Fear of ruining a birthparent's life
4. Fear of losing control
5. Fear of finding nothing—dead ends or death

   b. *Check in on their expectations.* Often searchers expect to be immediately transported into a fantasy family they've carried in their imaginations. These fantasies of a perfect reunion are intensified by media accounts glorifying emotional and instantaneous reconnections. Sometimes adopted people expect to be instantly healed emotionally. Others expect to find unconditional love from their birthmothers.

   c. *Realize what they might find.* Some searchers discover overwhelming acceptance, which is often unfortunately accompanied by intrusiveness and control from the birthrelatives. Other undesirable outcomes include criminal history, abandonment, or dead ends or death.[12]

5. Parents should not fear sharing their own personal concerns with their adult child. Honesty builds a stronger foundation for any family dealing with these issues.

6. Parents can communicate specifically what they are willing to do to help in the search. From attending how-to workshops to thumbing through phone directories, adoptive parents can choose the level of assistance they agree to provide.

Conducting any portion of the birth search is usually a highly emotionally charged process for all parties involved. If it is handled with sensitivity and openness from all participants—the child and the adoptive parents—it can be a time of growth for everyone. It can also be a time when the efforts of molding and shaping the promise throughout many years find their greatest, deepest, and most meaningful rewards.

SUMMARY

As with many issues in adoption, the issue of whether to search and the reasons behind the decision could not be more diverse and personal. Some adopted children ask few questions about their past. Others, however, not only raise many questions but also vigorously seek answers. For adoptive parents facing this issue in the life of their adult or adolescent child, it helps to recognize several primary reasons why children search for their roots:

- To obtain medical information
- To obtain more information and communication
- To discover who they look and act like
- To find out where they are on their genetic family tree
- To make a connection
- To forgive

Occasionally, adoptive parents experience emotional difficulty in supporting the search, usually for the following reasons:

- Issues surrounding their own infertility
- Feelings of failure as a parent
- Fear of losing their child's affection
- Fear that the adult child's discovery of negative origins may have long-lasting effects, especially concerning identity and self-worth issues

QUESTIONS FOR SMALL GROUPS

1. What changes or additions, if any, would you make to the reasons listed in this chapter for why adopted adults choose to begin a birth search?
2. As an adoptive parent, what are your personal feelings regarding the existence of your adopted child's birthfamily members? How have you dealt with their psychological presence?
3. In your opinion, how open can and should an adoptive family be toward the question of searching?

4. What can families do if their child wishes to meet his or her birth-parents? How do you think you would feel in that situation?
5. As an adoptive parent, how willing are you to be involved in the search process?

CHAPTER FOURTEEN

CREATING A NURTURING FAMILY
Giving Our Children What They Need

Adoptive families differ only from other families because of the circumstances that brought them together. The needs of adopted children are just like those of children who enter the family by birth. We all need to belong.

— Family Ties

Bruce and Annie Schaffer beamed with pride as their daughter Alissa walked to the platform to receive her high school diploma. Alissa had come to them at just three weeks old. The years had flown by for this loving family. As they reflected over the many, many joys of raising Alissa and their other two adopted children, they were thankful for the direction life had taken them.

Home life at the Schaffers had not been without its challenges. At moments of crisis, just like every parent will do, Bruce and Annie questioned their parenting skill. Yet at heart, the Schaffers knew that they had, to the best of their ability, created a positive, nurturing environment where each child could grow to fulfill her inborn potential.

From the beginning of their relationship with these beautiful daughters and because of the special circumstances of their lives, the Schaffers had asked themselves a simple but significant question: "What do these children need?" From that intentional consideration came a worthwhile parenting philosophy that continues to guide them as parents today.

WHAT DO THESE CHILDREN NEED?

TO BELONG

Stepping out of the car, Alissa turned to her parents. "My graduation day has been so special to me," she said. "You both have done so very much for me. Just recently I have had some real questions about what I am going to do with my life and where am I really going from here. One thing I know—whatever I do, wherever I go, I do know to whom I truly belong."

In *The Gift of Honor*, psychologist Dr. John Trent described the sense of belonging as the "need each person has to feel a special, needed and important part of the family. . . . Children who grow up with a strong sense of belonging gain ground on those who don't. Seeds of acceptance sown in children give them the ability to give and receive love and acceptance later on in life."[1]

Children removed from their families of origin are already a step or more behind in that needed emotional foundation. The task for adoptive parents is to create a family environment where their children gain a sense of belonging, of being wanted and loved. There are six building blocks of belonging through which this can be accomplished.

Block 1

Developing in the adopted child a sense of belonging in the family begins with teaching the fundamental principle that he or she was meant to be in this family, that God makes families through adoption as well as through procreation, and that there is a reason for everything, including joining a permanent family through adoption instead of by birth. Even adoptive parents who are not religious believe their child is right where he or she is supposed to be.

Block 2

Names are significant in developing a sense of belonging in a child. For an infant, the family has the privilege of giving the child his or her chosen name. For an older child whose identity is already attached to his or her name, adding a middle name of family significance promotes belonging.

Block 3

Belonging comes through being the recipient of legitimate praise and affirmation. This affirmation comes in all sizes and shapes:

- Warm hugs and physical closeness
- Time spent with a child reading the same book for the fifth time
- Verbal affirmation of a job well done
- Small gestures, such as a note in a lunch box or the preparation of a special dinner or dessert

Block 4

Belonging comes through active listening. This statement may seem obvious, but it is more often neglected than done. Dr. Trent pointed out that "the healthiest families are those who score high in the area of listening. Most of us are better lecturers than we are listeners. Even when we listen, it often is just a pause between bursts of what's really important—what we have to say."[2]

Block 5

We build a sense of belonging into the hearts of our children through a well-defined purpose for the family. So often families live, eat, and sleep under the same roof yet enjoy very little depth in their relationships.

A well-defined purpose for the family can include working toward goals together. Goals cement relationships. Activities might include planning special holiday celebrations, learning a new skill or hobby together, visiting a nursing home together, or getting involved in a community project that requires giving of oneself.

Just like adults, children need to be needed. Being dedicated to a common purpose as a family can satisfy that desire.

Block 6

Children learn that they belong to a family when they feel free to express their feelings appropriately. Insecure adopted children often mask their true feelings in order to ensure acceptance. Parents who encourage children to share their feelings and learn to draw those feelings forth deepen their children's sense of belonging.

The consequences of growing up without this sense of belonging can be severe. Dr. Trent cited such problems as the inability to give and receive love, procrastination in responsibility, the inability to handle relational conflicts, and stress of any magnitude, to name just a few.

Children growing up in adoptive families not only need a sense of belonging instilled deep within them but also need to be shown that they have permission to be an individual in their own right.

TO BE AUTHENTIC

Rachel sat in her high school counselor's office as they discussed her plans for college. "I really would like to go into teaching," Rachel said, "but both Dad and Mom have their hearts set on nursing for me. All the women in our family are nurses. I've told them I don't want to do that, but they just don't seem to listen." Rachel is the daughter of Frank and Millie Fields. She was adopted into their family as an infant. After they lost two babies through miscarriage, Rachel's presence was sheer joy to them.

The Fields' plans for Rachel were full of high expectations. They counted on her achieving in school and eventually following her mother's footsteps into a nursing program. The problem was that they never truly considered what Rachel wanted. Even more important, they never considered her innate capacities and preferences. They had molded her into what they wanted, and she had complied.

"Loss of authenticity," stated David Damico, "occurs when we are shaped and molded by the expectations of others who are trying to make us into someone they want us to be rather than allowing us to become who we really are."[3] Rachel felt that in order to maintain peace in the family, she was forced to play a role that would fit the dream of the children her parents had lost. More than anything, Rachel needed permission from her parents to grow into the person she was created to be—not into a fantasy child designed to be a parental replica.

The "grafted tree" metaphor of adoption is that the adopted child is like the branch of one tree that is removed and grafted to a different tree and becomes one with the new tree. The new tree nurtures the branch and allows it to grow and become fruitful, but the fruit from the grafted branch is genetically derived from the first tree. Adoptive parents need to allow their children to reach their God-given potential as their children are led, with the genes they inherited from their birthparents. But this, too, is really no different from the appropriate attitude parents should have toward biological children.

The need to belong and the need to be authentic are two important factors in a healthy family environment. A third need of adopted children is to be given a sense of dignity.

To Have a Sense of Dignity

When David and Karen walked out of the airport carrying their beautiful daughter, Angela from China, they knew they had an exciting journey ahead. One of the tasks ahead for them, they know as well, would be safeguarding her sense of dignity.

"When Angela was little, she drew a lot of attention because of her race — and because she is so cute," remarked Karen. "People would ask if she was adopted. I usually just answered, "Yes, this is Angela from China.""

However, as Angela has matured, part of giving her a sense of dignity is to encourage her to manage her own story. "As Angela got older and understood the question, I would ask her if she wanted to share her story. If yes, I would briefly answer a question or two and then turn it over to her. If she said no, I would simply say, "She isn't ready to share her story today."[4]

Some adopted children live with the perception that their adoption means rejection or that adoption isn't a good thing. There is no greater threat to a sense of dignity and worth than the perception that adoption means second best. Uncaring, insensitive adults or peers can gnaw away at a child's sense of dignity by unkind remarks. What can adoptive parents do to maintain a sense of dignity for their child?

1. *Start with building a strong moral, ethical, and spiritual environment.* A child will stand straighter and taller and face her world with stronger confidence when her family gives her a solid biblical worldview and a deep sense of right and wrong, sets loving boundaries, and teaches her basic responses for herself and family members. A family that communicates to her that her life has meaning and purpose will build in her a sense of dignity.
2. Learn to honor the child's heritage. If the child is internationally adopted, celebrate the differences on occasions such as holidays and birthdays. Include neighbors and friends. Also be sensitive that as the child grows, the need to be like the family and not singled out may become extremely important.
3. *Support the child's efforts to achieve.* Don't humiliate a failure but rather work with the child to be as successful as he can in other areas. Joshua stayed after school each night for two weeks trying out for the basketball team. Being shorter than his competitors, Josh's

dad knew it was probably a long shot. When Joshua failed to make the team, his dad was prepared. He picked him up from practice, took him out for dinner, and validated his courageous efforts. They talked about the upcoming baseball season, a sport in which Josh excelled, and made plans to get his new baseball shoes that weekend.

To belong, to be authentic, to be given a sense of dignity—these elements are crucial in building a positive, nurturing environment. There are two more.

TO BE VALUED

A critical block to a child's ability to receive what she needs from her parents, according to Dr. Trent, is the developmental freeze point at which children are adopted. As a result of a series of abusive or neglectful life events, these children freeze in their ability to attach. They are emotionally blocked in their capacity to give or receive love because they lack any sense of personal value.

Dr. Trent commented from his experience in working with adoptive families, "In those families where the parents became experts at extending 'the family blessing' even through the roughest of waters, each individual in the home tended to do better and grow in attachment to one another. Struggles still came, but were handled in the environment of family security."[5]

As Dr. Trent defined it, the "family blessing" is the universally longed-for sense of unconditional affirmation. In the deepest part of our being, it is the sense that we are loved, respected, and valued as a person for who we are. It is not based on what we accomplish. It is, said Trent, a gift to us from our parents.

The elements of the blessing begin with *meaningful touch*. Families that do a great deal of hugging, touching, and playful wrestling are healthier families. Adoptive families may find that this step must be taken gradually for some children who have suffered abuse or neglect. For others, a lot of hugging begins the day together and ends it as well.

The components of the blessing continue with *spoken words that attach high value* to a person. The Bible says that "death and life are in the power of the tongue" (Proverbs 18:21, NKJV). Words have great power in themselves to encourage or destroy self-esteem.

Jessica, now an adult, was adopted as an infant into Carl and Rhonda's loving family. Handicapped with a disabling limp, Jessica did not play outside much but would spend hours "playing at" the piano. Her parents soon discovered her incredible talent. They encouraged her with words of enthusiasm and reminded her frequently of the wonderful gift of music she'd been given.

Jessica has rich memories of her parents' affirmations. "It is almost like they forgot my handicap. It was never an issue, merely a fact of life. What they saw was the potential they believed God had given me to play musical instruments."

The blessing is extended as parents or loved ones *picture a special future* for a child. This involves vocalizing the belief that each child is capable of success in some area of life.

The blessing is best fulfilled in an *environment of active commitment* in which parents become students of their children and work to see that they are supported in reaching their potential.[6]

As parents provide the elements of the family blessing, adopted children can have the security and self-confidence to face their particular issues in a healthier way. They are not dependent on their birthparents' approval to mold the foundation of their lives.

In addition to the needs for belonging, authenticity, dignity, and a sense of value, there is a fifth important element of the family.

To Be Loved Unconditionally

Unconditional love is a concept taught in support groups, church workshops, and parenting classes. This key concept is necessary to provide children and teens with needed security. However, there is often a catch: The concept is taught, but the components of how to live it are not.

Components of Unconditional Love[7]

1. *Unconditional love risks rejection.* Parents who involve themselves in the life of the child they adopted must understand that their best intentions may be met head-on with rejection. Children who experience the loss of their birthparents or separation from significant foster parents do not rush headlong into other close relationships. These children arrive with a great deal of catching up to do. Unconditional love wades into relationships with these children knowing that potential rejection is part of the process of learning to attach to a new family.

2. *Unconditional love permits negative feelings.* Parents of difficult teenagers

often struggle with anger, frustration, disappointment, and numerous other difficult emotions. But these feelings are rarely communicated to the offender or to the other spouse in a healthy way. If they are not repressed, they are expressed in a manner that is later regretted. Unconditional love allows those feelings to exist openly and encourages them to be expressed in a manner that will allow resolution.

3. *Unconditional love deals with reality.* Hoping to help a child avoid the pain of facing a difficult situation, parents sometimes cloud the truth with fantasy. They equate this with love. For example, if a child encounters problems at school, instead of admitting the child has a deficit and needs help, a parent may simply say the teacher can't teach. Thinking that it is easier to avoid issues from the child's past, adoptive parents often run around questions, refusing to address them directly. Unconditional love thrives in an environment where each family member honestly faces the problems of life with a determination to overcome obstacles.

4. *Unconditional love isn't manipulative and pushy.* Desiring to shape an adopted child to fit the portrait of a "dream child" leads parents into pushing a child into activities that are of no interest to him. They manipulate circumstances that benefit only "the dream." This message comes through loud and clear to the child, who not only hears it but also feels it: "You do not accept me for who I am and what I can do. You do not allow me to be genuine." Unconditional love knows that it must put the dream aside and step in to help a child discover his own innate talents and abilities.

5. *Unconditional love allows consequences to occur.* By nature, most of us learn through experiences. It often takes the painful consequences of an action to make the lesson hit home. A parent who desires to demonstrate acceptance of a child in a profound way may be required to step back and allow painful consequences to happen to the child. Unconditional love, quietly and often while hurting, stays in the shadows while circumstances develop growth in our children.

6. *Unconditional love is always there.* Children's bad choices, such as an unintended pregnancy or drug-related problem, can erode even the best of family situations. Unconditional love, as it encompasses all the components already discussed, can withstand any situation that endangers a family's commitment to one another.

Unconditional love enables families to risk rejection, express feelings, squarely face reality, allow for authenticity, and remain bound together in the vows of the adoption promise.

THE ULTIMATE DIRECTION FOR A POSITIVE, NURTURING ENVIRONMENT

Love is patient, love is kind and is not jealous; love does not brag and is not arrogant, does not act unbecomingly; it does not seek its own, is not provoked, does not take into account a wrong suffered, does not rejoice in unrighteousness, but rejoices with the truth; bears all things, believes all things, hopes all things, endures all things. Love never fails. (1 Corinthians 13:4-8, NASB).

SUMMARY

Creating a positive, nurturing family environment requires a knowledge of what all people, not just adopted children, need. When the following needs are met, a child can grow and mature into a healthy adult:

- To belong
- To be authentic
- To have a sense of dignity
- To be valued
- To be loved unconditionally

QUESTIONS FOR SMALL GROUPS

1. In what other ways can a sense of belonging be built into a child?
2. Why is establishing a sense of dignity so important for children adopted in older childhood?
3. In what other ways can a sense of dignity be established?
4. Discuss the concept of unconditional love. Do you agree or disagree with the components listed?

ATTACHMENT THEORIES

Theories of attachment have been the focus of much attention lately; however, the concepts that underlie contemporary theories have been evolving over the past one hundred years. Sigmund Freud was the first modern thinker to theorize about the role childhood experiences play in the development of personality.[1] One of his followers, Eric Erickson, defined the psychosocial stages of development, particularly the first two stages, "Trust Versus Distrust" and "Autonomy Versus Shame." According to Erickson, an infant requires reliable and responsive care in order to establish a base of trust; inadequate and rejecting care leads to mistrust and hopelessness. A toddler's main job is to explore his world and develop autonomy and will; if not properly parented, the toddler may develop a base of shame and self-doubt.[2]

Descendants of Freud, particularly followers of the Object-Relations movement,[3] recognized the importance of early childhood experiences, but it was not until the 1950s that the study of attachment came onto the scientific scene as a way to understand the mystery of human development. John Bowlby, recognized by many as the most influential attachment theorist, was inspired by zoologist Konrad Lorrenz, who observed baby geese instinctually "imprinted" to him as a surrogate parent during a "critical period" of the orphaned goslings' development.[4] Bowlby theorized that seeking interpersonal attachment is the primary goal of development. Attachment behaviors are designed to elicit a caregiver response. Crying is designed to elicit a parental response, for example feeding.[5] Mary Ainsworth applied the concepts of Bowlby in groundbreaking research and defined the categories of attachment: secure or avoidant/anxious.[6]

Jean Piaget focused on cognitive development, including the processes of knowing, perceiving, and learning.[7] Like Bowlby and Ainsworth, Piaget viewed babies not as passive creatures who are formed by their environments but as active explorers of their worlds, striving to learn and control. Harry Harlow's research with baby monkeys amplified the crucial role tactile comfort, touch, and nourishment from the caregiver plays in survival and health.[8]

Stanley Greenspan defined the concept of developmental attachment patterns as a way to describe the enduring effects of early infant-caregiver interactions.[9] Daniel Siegel, Bruce Perry, and Allan Schore have brought neurobiological perspectives to the study of emotional development and have helped shed light on how attachment experiences affect brain development. Daniel Stern's work on the infant-caregiver relationship has revealed the crucial role of emotional attunement in the neurological, physical, emotional, behavioral, cognitive, and social development.[10]

This brief overview is a thin swipe at a glacial-size field of study. Readers are urged to build a foundation of knowledge based on the accumulated work in the field of human development, particularly attachment.

TOOLS AND RESOURCES FOR TALKING TO CHILDREN ABOUT ADOPTION

THE LIFE MAP

This tool is primarily for children who have experienced the foster care system prior to adoptive placement or, in the case of international adoption, children who have memories of life in an orphanage or foster home. It is helpful for children from four years through adolescence.

The Life Map is a technique that is helpful in reconstructing the child's placement history. The Life Map can communicate a number of important life events for a child who feels lost after experiencing a number of moves. These life events include:

- Where the child has lived
- How long he lived there
- The people, pets, and places that were important to him
- Why he had to move
- How he felt about the moves

The child should be an active participant in the drawing of his map. He should be encouraged to draw it in any manner he chooses. The key purpose of the Life Map is to generate open discussion about the child's history, to give the parents the opportunity to talk about and clarify any of the child's misconceptions, to provide support for painful feelings, and to provide reassurance about his new parents.[1]

THE FAMILY TREE

The Family Tree, a modification of the more commonly known family tree, has a unique purpose. The Family Tree can help children organize all the people who have been an important part of their lives. The biological family can be identified as the roots of the tree. These roots cannot be seen, but they anchor the tree, just as the biological family provided the child with a genetic heritage and will always be part of her. The child's foster or kinship families can be represented on the trunk of the tree since they have helped the child grow. The adoptive family may be represented on the upper trunk, branches, leaves, fruit, and flowers. Through this activity, the child learns that she can relate to both her family and her birthfamily, and she can come to understand how each family played an important role in her growth and development.[2]

TOOLS OF INTERACTIVE COMMUNICATION FOR CHILDREN (AGES FOUR TO TEN) AND PARENTS

LET'S TELL A STORY/LET'S WRITE A STORY

Another creative technique in guiding children to communicate their thoughts and feelings about their life experience is what Dr. Vera Fahlberg calls joint storytelling.

The child is asked to choose a favorite animal and name him. Then the adult starts telling a story about the animal that reflects the child's history. After several sentences, the adult asks the child to continue the story. In this way, the child has the opportunity to share emotional reactions to life events as well as his perceptions and desires for the future.[3]

Why is storytelling helpful? According to Kathryn Brohl in her book *Working with Traumatized Children*, storytelling is "an effective way to address traumatic memories, [monitor] responses and to teach problem solving. Storytelling also bypasses resistance by speaking to, as well as offering solutions to, overcoming a trauma without directly discussing the trauma."[4]

An example of using Let's Tell a Story is as follows:[5] Benjamin, age four, had been living in interim care for close to a year after being severely physically

abused by his mother's boyfriend. He had developed a close, loving relationship with his foster parents. Benjie had weekly visits with his teenage birthmother, who was no longer with the same boyfriend. The plan was for him to be
returned to his mother's care shortly. His caseworker, Mrs. Shields, wanted to
know more about how Benjamin viewed the past abuse and whether or not he
perceived his mom as now able to provide adequate physical safety. She decided
to use joint storytelling to facilitate her communications with Benjie. She knew
that with younger children it is frequently necessary for the adult to ask some
leading questions during the storytelling.

> **Mrs. S.:** Once upon a time there was a bunny named Ben. When he
> was just a baby, Bunny Ben lived with his mommy and his grandma.
> How do you think things went for Bunny Ben when he was a baby?
> **Ben:** Bunny Ben was happy with his mommy and grandmother.
> **Mrs. S.:** Then what do you think happened?
> **Ben:** Then they moved.
> **Mrs. S.:** One day Bunny Ben's mommy and grandma had an
> argument, and Ben and his mommy moved. They moved in with some
> friends of Bunny Ben's mother. How do you think things went for
> Bunny Ben then?
> **Ben:** Sad.
> **Mrs. S.:** Was Ben sad a lot? Was he missing someone?
> **Ben:** He was *very* sad for his grandma. There was a mean man.
> **Mrs. S.:** When Bunny Ben was very sad, he cried a lot. Mommy's
> friends did not like to hear crying. One of them would get so frustrated
> that he would spank Bunny Ben so hard that it really hurt him. It is
> not okay for adults to hurt children. One day some neighbors heard
> Bunny Ben crying very hard. They called some adults who help bunny
> families who are having problems. One of the adults came to visit
> Bunny Ben's family. Bunny Ben had lots of bruises on his bottom. The
> man who had spanked him was very angry at everyone. Bunny Ben
> needed to be in a safe place where he wouldn't be hurt. How do you
> think Bunny Ben felt when he moved to a new place?

By continuing the story, Mrs. Shields encouraged Benjie to talk about his
feelings in interim care and about his thoughts and feelings about the upcoming
move back to his mother's care. She learned that he missed his mom and wanted

to spend more time with her. She also learned that he was less worried about physical harm in the future than sad about anticipating the separation from his foster family. Like most children his age, the story solution he chose was for Mommy Bunny to move in with Bunny Ben and his foster family.

Mrs. Shields then modified the ending to the story, acknowledging that Bunny Ben would like one ending but that none of the adults thought it would work out for them. Instead, they decided that he should go live with Mommy Bunny but frequently visit his foster family so he wouldn't miss them so much.

This same type of story can be used to help a child verbalize his feelings regarding his adoption experience.

CAN YOU TELL ME WHAT THEY THINK?: DOLL AND PUPPET PLAY

This "play" technique is quite helpful in communicating about adoption with preschool or young school-age children, ages three to seven. There are several purposes of this activity:

1. To teach or clearly illustrate the facts of the child's history
2. To elicit feelings and perceptions from very young children
3. To correct fantasies or misconceptions (often related to "magical" thinking of children in this age range)
4. To express the feelings, wishes, or dreams of the "characters" involved in the child's past or present

The parent can use small Fisher-Price figures, other small dolls, or puppets to represent important figures in the child's past and present. Explain to the child that you are going to "play out" a story. Identify the characters, using the real names of the child, birthparent, adoptive parent, siblings, and others, or using fictitious names but actual circumstances of the child's adoption. Allow the child to control and speak for the "child" doll to elicit her perceptions and feelings. Parents should never correct feelings, but they can correct the actual events in the story by saying, "Let's play the story this way—I think this is the way the story might have happened." This play technique allows learning through a visual, experiential activity that can be repeated many times over (the child will thoroughly enjoy the attention and the activity, as well as the ability to add more details and figures as he matures). A child who has difficulty understanding language will especially benefit from seeing a reenactment of her life. This play therapy technique may provide a safe opportunity, for both the parent and the child, to express fears, anger, sadness, and good wishes for the future held naturally by all members of the adoption triad. Expression of these feelings occurs through a character, thereby creating an emotional comfort zone for all involved.

The number of figures/puppets used should be adjusted based on the child's age and developmental capacity to keep track of different "characters" in the story. A reasonable rule of thumb is to allow only as many characters as the child's age, plus one. For example, a four-year-old can accommodate a story with five characters.

Parents should not feel compelled to illustrate every detail in excruciating accuracy during the first play session. Initially, it is important only to understand the child's perception, where she is in beginning to make sense of her adoption story. As the parent and child continue to "play the story" during subsequent sessions, the parent should help the child to accomplish the following tasks, one aspect at a time:

- Understand the placements that have occurred in her life.
- Get answers to questions about siblings, birthparents, and other attachment figures.
- Understand the reasons for her separation from the birthfamily.
- Explore her feelings about her separation from the birthfamily.
- Understand other separations that have occurred in her history (orphanages, kinship families, foster families, previous adoptive placements).
- Explore her feelings about her separation from these placements.
- Understand the reasons behind the adoption plan made by agencies and courts or by her birthparents.
- Understand why her adoptive parents wanted her.
- Understand her future with her adoptive family.
- Explore her wishes and dreams for the future in relation to siblings, birthparents, and other kinship or foster families with whom she has connections.

- Understand that her birthparents want her to be happy and successful in her new family; they want her to make them proud of her.
- Understand that she can love and be loyal to many people and families at the same time.

NOTES

INTRODUCTION: A RELATIONSHIP OF PROMISE

1. House Subcommittee on Human Resources, Congressional Research Service Report, prepared by Karen Spar, specialist in Social Legislation Education and Public Welfare Division, January 15, 1997. Contact: Child Welfare League of America, 440 First Street, NW, Suite 310, Washington, DC 20001-2085.
2. U.S. Department of State, "Immigrant Visas Issued to Orphans Coming to the U.S.," http://travel.state.gov/family/adoption/stats/stats_451.html.
3. Dr. Paul Placek, *Adoption Fact Book IV*, National Council for Adoption, 2007, 5.

CHAPTER ONE: MAKING ROOM IN THE FAMILY

1. H. David Kirk, *Shared Fate: A Theory and Method of Adoptive Relationships*, rev. ed. (Port Angles, WA: Ben Simon Publications, 1983), 2.
2. Kirk, 3.
3. David M. Brodzinsky and Marshall D. Schechter, *The Psychology of Adoption* (New York: Oxford University Press, 1990), 26.
4. Kirk, 6.

CHAPTER TWO: CREATING A FAMILY

1. Child Welfare Information Gateway, "The Adoption Home Study Process: Factsheet for Families," 2004, http://www.childwelfare.gov/pubs/f_homstu.cfm.
2. David M. Brodzinsky, "Reconceptualizing Openness in Adoption: Implications for Theory, Research, and Practice," in *Psychological Issues in Adoption: Research and Practice*, ed. David M. Brodzinsky and Jesús Palacios (Westport, CT: Praeger Publishers, 2005), 149–152.
3. Harold D. Grotevant, Yvette V. Perry, and Ruth G. McRoy, "Openness in Adoption: Outcomes for Adolescents Within Their Adoptive Kinship

Networks," in Brodzinsky and Palacios, 181.

4. National Council For Adoption, "Adoption Agency Questions," 2007, https://www.adoptioncouncil.org/resources/AgencyQuestion.html.

5. National Council For Adoption, "State Adoption Specialists," 2007, https://www.adoptioncouncil.org/resources/NCFA_Help .html#stateadopt.

CHAPTER THREE: NAVIGATING INTERCOUNTRY ADOPTION

1. U.S. Department of State, "Frequently Asked Questions: Ongoing Efforts to Implement the Hague Adoption Convention," http://travel .state.gov/family/adoption/convention/convention_3026.html.

2. Dr. Dana Johnson, "Adopting an Institutionalized Child: What Are the Risks?" Better Care Network, http://www.crin.org/ben/details_news .asp?ID=12820&topicID=1014 (March 15, 2007).

CHAPTER FOUR: TRANSCULTURAL ADOPTION

1. A. L. Burrow and G. E. Finley, "Transracial, Same-Race Adoptions and the Need for Multiple Measures of Adolescent Adjustment," *Journal of Orthopsychiatry* (2004): 577–583.

2. Peter L. Benson, Anu R. Sharma, and Eugene C. Roehlkepartain, *Growing Up Adopted: A Portrait of Adolescents and Their Families* (Minneapolis: Search Institute, June 1994), 7–8, 34.

3. Rita J. Simon, Howard Alstein, and Marygold S. Melli, *The Case for Transracial Adoption* (Washington, D.C.: The American University Press, 1994), chapters 4 and 5.

4. Benson, Sharma, and Roehlkepartain, 100.

5. Richard M. Lee et al., "Cultural Socialization in Families with Internationally Adopted Children," *Journal of Family Psychology* 20, no. 4 (2006): 571–580.

CHAPTER FIVE: WHAT BUILDS HEALTHY ADOPTIVE FAMILIES?

1. These motivations were among a long list of reasons for fostering found at Casey Family Programs, *Casey Foster Family Assessments*, 2007, www .fosterfamilyassessments.org.

2. Karen J. Foli, PhD, and John R. Thompson, MD, *The Post-Adoption Blues: Overcoming the Unforeseen Challenges of Adoption* (New York: Rodale Publishers, 2004), 197.

3. Foli and Thompson, 198.

4. Foli and Thompson, 20.

5. Judith S. Rycus and Ronald C. Hughes, *Field Guide to Child Welfare, Volume IV* (Washington, D.C.: CWLA Press, 1998), 894.

6. Jerry M. Lewis, *How's Your Family? A Guide to Identifying Your Family's Strengths and Weaknesses* (New York: Brunner/Mazel, 1989), 13. The characteristics described are adapted from this resource.

7. Lewis, 48.

8. Rycus and Hughes, 894.

9. Rycus and Hughes, 895.

10. David M. Brodzinsky, "Reconceptualizing Openness in Adoption: Implications for Theory, Research, and Practice," in *Psychological Issues in Adoption: Research and Practice*, ed. David M. Brodzinsky and Jesús Palacios (Westport, CT: Praeger Publishers, 2005), 149–150.

11. Ibid.

12. Ibid.

13. Adapted from Jayne E. Schooler and Betsie L. Norris, *Journeys After Adoption: Understanding Lifelong Issues* (Westport, CT: Bergin & Garvey, 2002), 18.

14. Schooler and Norris, 18.

15. Adoption researcher Dr. Deborah Fravel, in her doctoral research, introduced the issue of the psychological presence into the adoption experience. Deborah Fravel, "Boundary Ambiguity: The Psychological Presence of the Birth Mother" (conference presentation, International Conference of Adoption Researchers, Minneapolis, MN, August 6, 1999).

16. Jayne E. Schooler and Betsy Keefer Smalley, "Post Finalization Issues and Services," *Ohio Child Welfare Training Program Curriculum* (Columbus, Ohio: Institute for Human Services, 2004).

17. Deborah N. Silverstein and Sharon Kaplan, "Lifelong Issues in Adoption," *Silveroze*, 1982, http://www.adopting.org/silveroze/html/lifelong_issues_in_adoption.html.

18. George Barna, *The Frog in the Kettle* (Ventura, CA: Regal, 1990), 35.

19. Barna, 35.

20. Susan Edelstein, quoted in Richard Lacayo, "Nobody's Children," *Time*, October 9, 1989, 95.

CHAPTER SIX: DEVELOPING A SUPPORTIVE ADOPTION ENVIRONMENT

1. Foster Cline and Jim Fay, *Parenting with Love & Logic: Teaching Children Responsibility* (Colorado Springs, CO: Piñon, 2006). Love and Logic Institute, Inc. (2007). www.loveandlogic.com. Link to quote: www.love-andlogic.com/faz.html.

2. Thomas W. Phelan, PhD, *1-2-3 Magic: Effective Discipline for Children 2–12* (Glen Ellyn, IL: Child Management Inc, 1993). See also http://www.parentmagic.com/.

3. R. P. Barth and J. M. Miller, "Building Effective Post-Adoption Services: What Is the Empirical Foundation?" *Family Relations* 49, no. 4 (October 2000): 447–456.

4. E. S. Mullin and L. Johnson, "The Role of Birth/Previously Adopted Children in Families Choosing to Adopt Children with Special Needs" *Child Welfare Journal* 78, no. 5 (September/October 1999).

5. Laura Ellman, "Talking About Adoption Within Your Family," *Adopt-A-Child, Inc.* newsletter, Summer 2001, http://www.adopt-a-child.org/nl_s_2001.html#nl_s_2001_3.

6. North American Council on Adoptable Children, "Glossary of Terms," http://www.nacac.org/howtoadopt/glossary.html.

7. National Dissemination Center for Children with Disabilities (2003) "Parenting a Child with Special Needs." *News Digest* 20 (ND20). Available from www.nichey.org/pubs/newsdig/nd20.pdf.

8. Donald Meyer, founder. See "Sibling Support Project," http://www.sib-lingsupport.org/.

9. Adele Faber and Elaine Mazlish, *Siblings Without Rivalry: How to Help Your Children Live Together So You Can Live Too* (New York: HarperCollins, 1987).

10. David Kirk, *Shared Fate*, rev. ed. (Port Angeles, WA: Ben-Simon Publications, 1984), 19.

11. Kirk, 21.

12. Accurate vs. Less Accurate Language is taken from NFCA's Consider the Possibilities IAATP Training Curriculum, 2007.

13. Lois Melina, "Guidelines for Explaining Adoption to Children Outside the Family" *Adopted Child*, vol. 10, no. 12, December, 1991, 1.

14. Cited in Lois Melina in "Teachers Need to Be More Sensitive to Adoption Issues," *Adopted Child*, August, 1990.

CHAPTER SEVEN: BARRIERS TO ADJUSTMENT

1. Betsy Keefer and Jayne E. Schooler, *Telling the Truth to Your Adopted or Foster Child: Making Sense of the Past* (Westport, CT: Bergin & Garvey, 2000).
2. Claudia Jewett Jarratt, *Helping Children Cope with Separation and Loss* (Boston: Harvard Common Press, 1982), 34.
3. The elements of the searching and bargaining stage are adapted from Jarratt, 36.
4. Jarratt, 36.
5. Jayne Schooler, "Keys to Easing Adjustment," *Adoptive Families*, 2000, http://www.theadoptionguide.com/advice/articles/keys-to-easing-adjustment.
6. These suggestions come from several sources, including Lois Ruskai Melina, *Raising Adopted Children: Practical, Reassuring Advice for Every Adoptive Parent* (New York: Harper & Row, 1998).

CHAPTER EIGHT: ATTACHMENT, DEVELOPMENT, AND THE IMPACT OF TRAUMA

1. See appendix 1 for a brief overview of attachment theories.
2. Harry W. Gardiner and Corinne Kosmitzki, *Lives Across Cultures: Cross-Cultural Human Development* (Needham Heights, MA: Allyn and Bacon, 1998), 164.
3. Daniel J. Siegel, *The Developing Mind: How Relationships and the Brain Interact to Shape Who We Are* (New York, NY: Guilford Press, 1999), 18.
4. Siegel, 19.
5. B. D. Perry et al., "Childhood Trauma, the Neurobiology of Adaptation and 'Use Dependent' Development of the Brain: How 'States' Become Traits,'" *Infant Mental Health Journal* 16, no. 4 (1995): 272.
6. Siegel, 13.
7. Allan N. Schore, *Affect Regulation and the Origin of the Self: The Neurobiology of Emotional Development* (Hillsdale, NJ: Lawrence Erlbaum, 1994), 305.
8. Allan N. Schore, *Affect Dysregulation and Disorders of the Self* (New York, NY: Norton, 2003), 44.
9. Schore, *Affect Dysregulation and Disorders of the Self*, 35.
10. Schore, *Affect Dysregulation and Disorders of the Self*, 38.
11. Schore, *Affect Regulation and the Origin of the Self*, 31–33.
12. Schore, *Affect Dysregulation and Disorders of the Self*, 38.

13. Robert V. Kail and John C. Cavanaugh, *Human Development: A Life-Span View* (Belmont, CA: Wadsworth/Thomson, 2004), 175.

14. Daniel A. Hughes, *Facilitating Developmental Attachment: The Road to Emotional Recovery and Behavioral Change in Foster and Adopted Children* (Northvale, NJ: Jason Aronson, 1997), 28.

15. Schore, *Affect Regulation and the Origin of the Self*, 80–91.

16. Schore, *Affect Dysregulation and Disorders of the Self*, 328, 383.

17. Arthur Becker-Weidman and Deborah Shell, eds., *Creating Capacity for Attachment: Dyadic Developmental Psychotherapy in the Treatment of Trauma-Attachment Disorders* (Oklahoma City, OK: Wood 'N' Barnes, 2005), 13.

18. Schore, *Affect Regulation and the Origin of the Self*, 31.

19. Schore, *Affect Regulation and the Origin of the Self*, 360–364.

20. D. Stern, *Interpersonal World of the Infant* (New York, NY: Basic Books, 1985), 70.

21. Siegel, 150.

22. Schore, *Affect Regulation and the Origin of the Self*, 479–482.

23. Siegel, 193.

24. Mark Chaffin et al., "Report of the APSAC Task Force on Attachment Therapy, Reactive Attachment Disorder, and Attachment Problems," *Child Maltreatment* 11, no. 1 (2006): 81.

25. American Psychiatric Association, *Diagnostic and Statistical Manual of Mental Disorders*, 4th ed. text revision (Washington, D.C.: American Psychiatric Association, 2000), 463–468.

26. Bessel A. van der Kolk and Christine A. Courtois, "Editorial Comments: Complex Developmental Trauma," *Journal of Traumatic Stress* 18, no. 5 (October 2005): 385–388.

27. Judith Herman, MD, *Trauma and Recovery: The Aftermath of Violence—from Domestic Abuse to Political Terror* (New York: Basic Books, 1992), 119–120.

28. Alexandra Cook, PhD, et al., eds., "Complex Trauma in Children and Adolescents," *The National Child Traumatic Stress Network*, 2003, 8, http://www.nctsnet.org/nctsn_assets/pdfs/edu_materials/ComplexTrauma_All.pdf.

29. Cook, PhD, et al., 8.

30. U.S. Department of Health and Human Services, Administration on Children, Youth, and Families, *Child Maltreatment 2005* (Washington,

D.C.: U.S. Government Printing Office, 2007), 26.

31. Cook, PhD, et al., 7.

32. A. Cook, J. Spinazzola, J. Ford, et. al. "Complex Trauma in Children and Adolescents," *Psychiatric Annals* 35, no. 5 (May 2005).

33. Marie Kanne Poulsen, PhD, "Defining Early Childhood/Family Mental Health," *CWTAC Updates: Series on Infant and Early Childhood/Family Mental Health*, 5, no. 3 (July/August 2002): 4–5, http://www.cimh.org/downloads/CWTACJuly-Aug02.pdf.

34. Herman, 116–119.

35. B. D. Perry et al., 275.

CHAPTER NINE: LIVING WITH CHILDREN WITH ATTACHMENT TRAUMA

1. Daniel A. Hughes, *Facilitating Developmental Attachment: The Road to Emotional Recovery and Behavioral Change in Foster and Adopted Children* (Northvale, NJ: Jason Aronson, 1997), 1–2.

2. Mark Chaffin et al., "Report of the APSAC Task Force on Attachment Therapy, Reactive Attachment Disorder, and Attachment Problems," *Child Maltreatment* 11, no. 1 (2006): 76.

3. American Psychiatric Association, *Diagnostic and Statistical Manual of Mental Disorders*, 4th ed. text revision (Washington, D.C.: American Psychiatric Association, 2000), 128.

4. American Psychiatric Association, 127–130.

5. Chaffin et al., 82.

6. U. M. Walter and C. Petr, "Reactive Attachment Disorder: Concepts, Treatment and Research," *State of Kansas Department of Social and Rehabilitation Services—Best Practices in Children's Mental Health*, 2004, Report #11, 3.

7. T. G. O' Connor and C. H. Zeanah, "Attachment Disorders: Assessment Strategies and Treatment Approaches," *Attachment and Human Development* 5, no. 3 (2003): 223–244.

8. Hughes, 30–31.

9. Arthur Becker-Weidman and Deborah Shell, eds., *Creating Capacity for Attachment: Dyadic Developmental Psychotherapy in the Treatment of Trauma-Attachment Disorders* (Oklahoma City, OK: Wood 'N' Barnes, 2005), 15–16.

10. U.S. Department of Health and Human Services, Administration on

Children, Youth, and Families, *Child Maltreatment 2005* (Washington, D.C.: U.S. Government Printing Office, 2007), 26.

11. American Psychiatric Association, 129.

12. Chaffin et al., 81.

13. Richard P. Barth et al., "Beyond Attachment Theory and Therapy: Towards Sensitive and Evidence-Based Interventions with Foster and Adoptive Families in Distress," *Child & Family Social Work* 10, no. 4 (November 2005): 260.

14. Walter and Petr, 6.

15. Chaffin et al., 81.

16. Chaffin et al., 83.

17. Chaffin et al., 77.

18. Chaffin et al., 86–87.

19. Chaffin et al., 87.

20. Chaffin et al., 87.

21. Chaffin et al., 86–87.

22. Hughes, 193–214.

23. Becker-Weidman and Shell, 221–224.

24. Jayne Schooler, *Embracing a Love Like No Other: Understanding the Impact of Parenting Traumatized Children on Adoptive Parents*, a training curriculum, 2007.

CHAPTER TEN: HOW DO WE FEEL ABOUT ADOPTION?

1. Betsy Keefer and Jayne E. Schooler, *Telling the Truth to Your Adopted or Foster Child: Making Sense of the Past* (Westport, CT: Bergin & Garvey, 2000), 55.

2. David M. Brodzinsky and Marshall D. Schechter, *The Psychology of Adoption* (New York: Oxford University Press, 1990), 13.

3. Keefer and Schooler, *Telling the Truth to Your Adopted or Foster Child*, 58.

4. Betsy Keefer Smalley and Jayne Schooler, "Post Finalization Services Curriculum," *Ohio Child Welfare Training Program Curriculum* (Columbus, Ohio: Institute for Human Services, 2003).

5. Child Welfare Information Gateway, "Adoption and the Stages of Development: Factsheet for Families," 1990, http://www.childwelfare.gov/pubs/f_stages/f_stagesc.cfm.

6. Keefer and Schooler, *Telling the Truth to Your Adopted or Foster Child*, 61.

7. Keefer and Schooler, *Telling the Truth to Your Adopted or Foster Child*, 62.

8. Brodzinsky and Schechter, 23.

9. David Brodzinsky, personal interview, June 1992.

CHAPTER ELEVEN: TALKING TO CHILDREN ABOUT ADOPTION

1. Betsy Keefer and Jayne E. Schooler, *Telling the Truth to Your Adopted or Foster Child: Making Sense of the Past* (Westport, CT: Bergin & Garvey, 2000), 16.

2. Keefer and Schooler, 18.

3. Keefer and Schooler, 94.

4. John and Jean Pardeck, "Bibliotherapy for Children in Foster Care and Adoption," *Child Welfare Journal* 66, no. 3 (May/June 1987).

5. Vera Fahlberg, phone interview, July 13, 1999.

6. Keefer and Schooler, 126.

7. David Brodzinsky and Marshall Schechter, *The Psychology of Adoption* (New York, NY: Oxford University Press, 1990), 19.

8. Betse Hilary and Rebecca Richardson, "Developing a Life Story Book Program for Foster Children," *Child Welfare Journal* 60, no. 8 (September/October 1981).

9. Personal interview with Marian Parker, June 1991.

10. Marian Parker, "Making a Child's Lifebook," a workshop presented through the Ohio Child Welfare Program, 1998.

11. Parker.

12. Deborah Joy, personal interview.

CHAPTER TWELVE: WHAT'S INSIDE AN ADOPTED ADOLESCENT?

1. Peter L. Benson, Anu R. Sharma, and Eugene C. Roehlkepartain, *Growing Up Adopted: A Portrait of Adolescents and Their Families* (Minneapolis: Search Institute, June 1994), 3–4.

2. Benson, Sharma, and Roehlkepartain, 24.

3. Benson, Sharma, and Roehlkepartain, 4.

4. Debbie Riley, MS, *Beneath the Mask: Understanding Adopted Teens* (Burtonsville, MD: C.A.S.E. Publications, 2007), 9.

5. Catherine Mathelin, "What I Hear, I Can't Write," *Journal of Infant, Child, and Adolescent Psychotherapy* 3, no. 3 (July 15, 2004): 369–383.

6. Riley, 9.

7. The common issues discussed in this chapter are adapted from the Parenthesis Post Adoption Project of Columbus, Ohio.

8. Dr. Alan Dupre-Clark, "Identify Main Adoption Issues," *The Adoption Network Newsletter* 6, no.1 (January 1992).

9. Riley, 63.

10. Riley, 63.

11. Betsy Keefer Smalley, personal interview, May 16, 2007.

12. David M. Brodzinsky, PhD, Marshall D. Schechter, MD, and Robin Marantz Henig, *Being Adopted: The Lifelong Search for Self* (New York: Doubleday, 1992), 107.

13. Brodzinsky, Schechter, and Henig, 22.

CHAPTER 13: SEARCHING FOR A PAST

1. Peter L. Benson, Anu R. Sharma, and Eugene C. Roehlkepartain, *Growing Up Adopted: A Portrait of Adolescents and Their Families* (Minneapolis: Search Institute, June 1994), 22.

2. Benson, Sharma, and Roehlkepartain, 26–27.

3. Benson, Sharma, and Roehlkepartain, 26.

4. Benson, Sharma, and Roehlkepartain, 26.

5. David M. Brodzinsky and Marshall D. Schechter, *The Psychology of Adoption* (New York: Oxford University Press, 1990), 69.

6. Robin Henig, "Chosen and Given," *New York Sunday Supplement,* November 11, 1988.

7. Brodzinsky and Schechter, 70.

8. Randolph W. Severson, *Adoption: Charms and Rituals for Healing* (Dallas: House of Tomorrow Productions, 1991), 101.

9. Carol L. Demuth, *Courageous Blessing: Adoptive Parents and the Search* (Garland, TX: Aries Center, 1993), 3.

10. Jayne E. Schooler and Betsie L. Norris, *Journeys After Adoption: Understanding Lifelong Issues* (Westport, CT: Bergin & Garvey, 2002), 104.

11. Lois Ruskai Melina, *Raising Adopted Children: Practical, Reassuring Advice for Every Adoptive Parent* (New York: Harper & Row, 1986), 163.

12. Jayne Schooler and Pam Severs, "'Mom, Dad, I'm Searching': The Impact of Search and Reunion on the Family," *Ohio Child Welfare Training Program Curriculum* (Columbus, Ohio: Institute for Human Services, 2004), 11.

CHAPTER FOURTEEN: CREATING A NURTURING FAMILY

1. Gary Smalley and John Trent, *The Gift of Honor* (New York: International Press, 1993), 363.
2. Smalley and Trent, 364.
3. David Damico, *The Faces of Rage* (Colorado Springs, CO: NavPress, 1992), 51.
4. This story is adapted from "Special Overseas Delivery" by Jayne Schooler, *Focus on the Family Magazine*, November, 2007.
5. John Trent, personal interview, Cincinnati, Ohio, November 1990.
6. Gary Smalley and John Trent, *The Gift of the Blessing: The Gift of Honor* (New York, NY Inspirational Press, 1998), 106.
7. Material in this section is adapted from a message given by Dr. David Schooler, delivered to the West Carrollton Ohio, Church of the Nazarene, May 1992.

APPENDIX ONE: ATTACHMENT THEORIES

1. Robert V. Kail and John C. Cavanaugh, *Human Development: A Life-Span View* (Belmont, CA: Wadsworth/Thomson, 2004), 175.
2. Kail and Cavanaugh, 174–183.
3. Barbara Engler, *Personality Theories* (Boston, MA: Houghton Mifflin, 2006), 175–185.
4. Robert Karen, PhD, *Becoming Attached: First Relationships and How They Shape Our Capacity to Love* (New York, NY: Oxford University Press, 1994), 70.
5. Engler, 131.
6. Kail and Cavanaugh, 177.
7. Kail and Cavanaugh, 130.
8. Engler, 131.
9. Daniel A. Hughes, *Facilitating Developmental Attachment: The Road to Emotional Recovery and Behavioral Change in Foster and Adopted Children* (Northvale, NJ: Jason Aronson, 1997), 15.
10. Hughes, 11–12.

APPENDIX TWO: TOOLS AND RESOURCES FOR TALKING TO CHILDREN ABOUT ADOPTION

1. Judith S. Rycus and Ronald C. Hughes, *Field Guide to Child Welfare, Volume IV* (Washington, D.C.: CWLA Press, 1998), 977.
2. Rycus and Hughes, 978.
3. Adapted with permission from the author Vera Fahlberg, *A Child's Journey Through Placement* (Indianapolis, IN: Perspectives Press, 1991), 341–342.
4. Kathryn Brohl, *Working with Traumatized Children: A Handbook for Healing* (Washington, D.C.: CWLA Press, 1996).
5. Vera I. Fahlberg, 341–342.

ABOUT THE AUTHORS

JAYNE E. SCHOOLER has over twenty years of experience in working with and speaking to families and professionals concerned with child welfare, first as a foster parent and then as an adoptive parent, adoption professional, and educator. Jayne is a keynote speaker and workshop presenter at the national level on issues related to foster and adoptive parenting and family life. An enthusiastic supporter of families formed by adoption or foster care, Jayne currently serves as a trainer, consultant, and curriculum writer with the Institute for Human Services in Columbus, Ohio. She has made guest appearances on over three dozen radio talk shows across the country, speaking on adoption and family life issues. She was the 2006 Trainer of the Year for the Ohio Child Welfare training program and also awarded the 2006 Distinguished Service in Training award by the National Staff Development and Training Association.

In addition to her training and writing responsibilities in this country, Jayne and her husband, Dr. David Schooler, serve overseas with the International Leadership and Development Center in Kiev, Ukraine. The organization also serves in Kyrgyzstan. They offer training and support to pastors and child welfare workers. Both the Schoolers are faculty members at Master's International School of Divinity in Evansville, Indiana. They are the parents of two adult children, Ray, age forty-one, who joined their family by adoption at age sixteen, and Kristy, age thirty-one, and they are the grandparents of three.

THOMAS ATWOOD, an adoptive parent himself, serves as president and chief executive officer of the National Council For Adoption (NCFA), a non-profit adoption research, education, and advocacy organization whose mission is to promote the well-being of children, birthparents, and adoptive families by advocating for the positive option of adoption. As NCFA's chief spokesperson, Tom leads the organization's ongoing efforts to ensure sound, ethical adoption policies and practices. He frequently testifies on adoption, foster care, and child welfare issues before Congress and state legislatures.

With a bachelor's degree in psychology and master's degrees in public policy and business administration, Tom has directed national research, education, and advocacy nonprofits for twenty years as chief executive, director of government and media relations, research director, editor, publisher, coalition builder, fundraiser, and strategic planner. During his eleven-year tenure at The Heritage Foundation, he served as director of coalition relations and executive editor of *Policy Review*. He was vice president of policy and programs for Family Research Council. He is the founding president of the board of directors of the National Safe Haven Alliance.

TIMOTHY J. CALLAHAN, PsyD, is a clinical psychologist who received his doctorate from Wright State University in Dayton, Ohio. Dr. Callahan has twenty years of experience working with children and families, as well as adults and teens, in a variety of settings, including community mental health centers, private practices, hospitals, schools, and correctional facilities. He is the Director of Mental Health Services for Greene County Educational Service Center in Yellow Springs, Ohio. Dr. Callahan previously served as the chief of psychology for Ohio's adult prison system and clinical director of a large youth-serving mental health agency.

Dr. Callahan has accumulated a wealth of knowledge about human development and the impact early experiences have on our capacity to thrive. He has worked extensively with adopted and foster children and their families and continues to be amazed by human resiliency and adaptability. He is committed to helping shed light on the mysteries of human development and is an advocate for an educated, compassionate, and artful approach to parenting and treatment. Dr. Callahan lives in Yellow Springs, Ohio, with his wife and daughter.

ELIZABETH A. TRACY, MSW, LCSW, LICSW, is an expert on the impact of the foster care experience on biological and adoptive children of foster parents. Her expertise comes from three main sources: (1) Her parents were foster parents for over thirty years; (2) She was a foster parent for over a decade; and

(3) Ms. Tracy has focused her academic and professional career on researching and interviewing biological and adopted children of foster parents.

Ms. Tracy is a licensed clinical social worker, national trainer, and consultant specializing in the areas of foster care, adoption, behavioral health, crisis response communications, leadership, and team development. She has presented at national, regional, and state conferences around the country.

To contact Ms. Tracy, write to 380 Lafayette Rd #11-312, Seabrook, NH, 03874 or e-mail info@ElizabethTracy.com.

Check out these other great titles from NavPress!

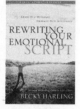